Modern Trends in Jewish Education

Modern Trends
in Jewish Education

By Z. E. KURZWEIL

New York • THOMAS YOSELOFF • London

Thomas Yoseloff, *Publisher*
8 East 36th Street
New York 16, N. Y.

Thomas Yoseloff Ltd
18 Charing Cross Road
London W. C. 2, England

Acknowledgments

Thanks are due to the editors of the following publications for permission to republish essays, some of which appear here in their original form, and others which have been revised and elaborated before inclusion in this book.

"Buber on Education" appeared in the Winter 1962 issue of "Judaism."

"Rabbi Israel Salanter and the Mussar Movement" is an elaboration of an article which appeared in the Spring 1959 issue of "Judaism," and a Hebrew version of this essay was published in "Sinai" (Vol. 47) in 1960.

The article on "A. D. Gordon" appeared in "Jewish Education," in the Spring 1961 issue (No. 3, Vol. 31).

The essay "S. R. Hirsch, Educationist and Thinker" is an English rendering of an article which appeared in "Sinai" (Vol. 45) in Ellul 1959, and subsequently in "Tradition," issue No. 2 of Spring, 1960.

The chapters on N. H. Weisel and Rabbi Kook are elaborations of articles which appeared in "Hachinuch" in the Nissan 1960 issue (Nos. 2-3) and the 1961 issue (No. 1) respectively.

Part of the article on Rosenzweig appeared in the January 13th, 1961 issue of the Jewish Chronicle, while the second part appeared in a subsequent issue.

Part of the chapter "the Revival of Hebrew" appeared in "Sifrut" Contemporary Hebrew Literature," published in Oxford (Ed. Ch. Rabin), issue of July 1956.

A shortened version of the chapter on Korczak appeared in "Hachinuch" in the Shevat 1961 issue (No. 2).

In memory of my parents,
Rabbi Abraham A. Kurzweil
and Rachel L. Kurzweil, née Eckfeld.

Preface

This book includes essays written over a number of years. Some have appeared in Hebrew and English periodicals; others, such as the essays on "The Revival of Hebrew," "Kibbutz Education," "Sarah Schenirer," and "How Jewish are Israel's General Schools?" appear here for the first time. Those already published have been revised and expanded.

While not claiming that this book represents a complete survey of Jewish educational thought of the post-Emancipation period, I feel that it is more than a collection of essays on Jewish education casually strung together. It does, I believe, present an exposition and critical evaluation of the more important schools of thought in modern Jewish education. The postscript at the end endeavors to survey the educational scene as a whole; its purpose is to link the essays and to channel the various trends in Jewish education which are described in the book.

My thanks are due in the first place to Mrs. Rachelle Kushner for her help and to Professor S. H. Bergmann of the Hebrew University, who has read the typescript and offered valuable comments and suggestions. Thanks are also due to Mr. H. Sopher and Mrs. Ruth Shalif of the Technion, Department of General Studies; and finally, to Mesdames Sarah Vatikai and Naomi Navot for typing out the manuscript.

7

In the absence of an adequate central library in Haifa, I have had recourse in the first place to the magnificent private library of the late Mr. Tuvia Miller, Hebrew scholar and doyen of Haifa bibliophiles; Dr. J. Bin-Nun also lent me books from his private library, for which I am duly grateful.

Haifa, Technion, Israel Institute of Technology, 1963.

Z. E. Kurzweil

Contents

Contents

Modern Trends in Jewish Education

1

N. H. Weisel's Place in Jewish Education

Naphtali Herz Weisel was born in Hamburg in 1724. One of his ancestors, Joseph Reis, fled from Podolia in 1648 after the Chmielnitzky pogrom, in which his whole family had perished. Reis's survival was considered miraculous, and after many wanderings through Poland, Silesia, and Central Europe, Joseph Reis came to Amsterdam. Here he settled, and in the course of time acquired great wealth.

In his old age, he and his son Moses moved to the town of Wësel, which was then part of the Electorate of Brandenburg and from which the family took its name. Naphtali Herz's father was Issachar Ber Weisel. He is described by his son as an enlightened and honored man who had free access to court circles.

Naphtali Herz spent his childhood in Copenhagen, where his father was arms purveyor to the king. He received a traditional Jewish education in *Heder* and *Yeshiva*. His training in Judaism and Rabbinical scholarship he owed to the famous Rabbi Jonathan Eybeschütz, who was Rabbi of the communities of Hamburg, Altona, and Wandsbeck. As far as secular education was concerned, Weisel was self-taught and acquired proficiency in German, French, Dutch, and Danish. Unlike Mendelssohn, however, he was a mere amateur in the various branches of secular culture, and his main interest throughout life remained in the field of Judaism and its allied subjects.

He became a representative of the Jewish bank of Feitel, as well as a merchant in his own right, and led the life of a man of position. Later, when in Berlin, he lost his fortune and lived mainly on the proceeds of his prolific writing and teaching. His first Hebrew publication, *Lebanon* (1765/66), is a philological investigation into Hebrew synonyms and roots. Among his many publications are: A commentary on Leviticus, included in Mendelssohn's edition of the Bible with German translation; a translation into Hebrew of the "Wisdom of Solomon," which he erroneously believed to be an authentic work of King Solomon; and a book of Hebrew poetry which he called *Shirei Tiferet (Songs of Glory)*. His most important work is the *Divrei Shalom ve'Emet (Words of Peace and Truth)*, addressed in letter form to the Jewish communities living under the sovereignty of the Emperor Joseph II, in which he proposed far-reaching changes in the existing system of Jewish education. This book was translated into several European languages. Weisel died in Hamburg on February 28, 1805.

I

Naphtali Herz Weisel was one of the leading harbingers of the era of Jewish enlightenment (*Haskalah*) of the eighteenth and nineteenth centuries. There are historians of Hebrew literature who view his poetry as marking the beginning of modern Hebrew literature.

Weisel also occupies a prominent position in the history

of Jewish education, and his book *Divrei Shalom ve'Emet* paved the way for the modern system of Hebrew education. This book proved a source of inspiration for a number of leading educationists, who continued his activities in this field.

It is difficult to agree with the opinion of the Jewish historian Graetz that Weisel was merely one of Mendelssohn's arms bearers, carrying out the tasks allotted to him by the great master.[1] In Graetz's time Mendelssohn was regarded as a spiritual giant who predominated in all branches of culture, general and Jewish, and whose colleagues and intimates merely carried out plans drawn up by him. Thus, in Graetz's opinion, Mendelssohn appointed his friend Weisel to reform the system of education in the Jewish communities within the territories under the jurisdiction of the Emperor Joseph II, just as he had delegated to the Christian liberal, Dohm, the duty of fighting for Jewish civil equality.

Mendelssohn's well-known reluctance to enter the arena of Jewish education himself may have been due to his uncertainty concerning the content and character of the new type of Jewish education that changing historical circumstances called for. He hoped that with the publication of the Edict of Tolerance of Joseph II the gates of the ghettos would gradually open and the life of European Jewry would undergo a revolutionary change. This in turn would call for a change in the general setup of Jewish education. However, in contrast to Weisel, Mendelssohn was far more conservative and cautious, and he had a more keenly developed historical perception. He believed that enlighten-

[1] H. Graetz, *Geschichte der Juden* (Leipzig: Verl. Oskar Lerner, 1900), 11, 83.

ment, if it were not to prove harmful, must proceed slowly and gradually. ("Those who spread enlightenment, if they do not wish to act recklessly and cause great harm, must take into careful account the prevailing circumstances of the period, and lift the curtain only so far as the light will prove beneficial to the patient.") [2]

Needless to say, Mendelssohn regarded the position of the Jews in the ghettos as unhealthy and abnormal (the metaphor of the "patient" indicates that clearly), and would have welcomed the emancipation of the Jews but for the fact that he suspected an ulterior motive behind the Emperor's Edict of Tolerance. He did not share the hopes that Weisel placed in it. "He who was so wise and moderate suspected the Emperor Joseph either of designs for financial gain, or of an attempt to assimilate the Jews to Christianity, a process which was at that time encouraged as a step toward the 'Unification of Religious Faiths.' This suspicion was not entirely without foundation." [3]

Nor was he greatly impressed by the educational activities of the Philanthropists, and their new schools, which opened their gates both to Christian and Jewish children. Mendelssohn opposed radical changes in the Jewish educational system as long as the Jews did not enjoy full civil equality. It is noteworthy that Mendelssohn did not even send his children to the schools which were later established through Weisel's influence, but preferred to have them educated partly by himself and partly by private tutors, though without great success.

When, in the year 1768, Johann Bernhard Basedow

[2] Letter to Hennings in Kaiserling's *Moses Mendelssohn, sein Leben und seine Werke* (Leipzig: 1862), p. 536.

[3] Klausner, *Hasifruth ha' Ivrit ha' chadasha* (Jerusalem: Hebrew University Press, 1930), I, 106.

(1724-1790), who was the moving spirit in the Philanthropist Movement, approached Mendelssohn with a request that he collect Jewish subscriptions for the book *Elementarwerk* which Basedow was then preparing for publication, Mendelssohn retorted: "Tell me, for God's sake, if you succeed in fully carrying out your aims, what will you have achieved? You will have educated enlightened people, conscious of the rights of human beings, who have the desire and ability to serve the country where they live; and that is just what the Jew cannot, and is forbidden to do. . . . Why should he learn about the rights of humanity? If he does not wish to be altogether wretched in his state as an oppressed citizen, it would be better if he knew nothing at all about these rights. Why should he love truth and the freedom that springs from knowledge, only to become disillusioned when he realizes that the civil government only aims at depriving him of both? Will he be trained to serve the state? The only service that the state accepts from the Jew is his money." [4]

Rabbi Pinchas Hurwitz of Frankfurt on Main (1730-1805) argued similarly against giving a general education to Jewish children as long as they suffered from civil disabilities. When the supporters of the enlightened Berlin type of education wished to open a school which would supplement the Hebrew instruction given in the *Cheder* and *Talmud Torah* with lessons in general school subjects such as German, French, arithmetic, etc., Rabbi Hurwitz said to them, "What benefit can general education and philosophy bring to the Jews of Frankfurt—desirable

[4] A. E. Simon, *Haphilanthropism Hapedagogi Vehachinuch haYehudi, The Jubilee Book in Honour of M. M. Kaplan* (New York: Jewish Theological Seminary, 1952), pp. 158-59.

though they be? What good will these refinements do to the Jew? . . . Will they not add to his present misfortunes? . . . Will he not despair and curse his fate . . . instead of accepting his burden with humility and self-effacement as is fitting for a Jew of simple faith . . . ?" [5]

A similar reply was given by the Jews of Minsk in 1842, when Dr. Lilienthal (a German educationist of the "enlightened" type who was invited by the Russian government to reform the system of Jewish education) acquainted them with the program drawn up by the Russian education Minister, Ubarov. "As long as the state does not grant us full rights as citizens, education will only bring us disaster. As long as he [the Jew] is an ignoramus with regard to secular knowledge, he does not despise the livelihood he earns as a peddler or petty merchant, etc.; he finds his joy and consolation in his religion, relies on God, and he and his large family are content with the meager results of his hard work. But if he is educated and enlightened, and nevertheless debarred from the least service he can render the state, his feelings of resentment will lead him to conversion, and no pious Jewish father will educate his sons in a way that may lead to such a fate." [6]

The fact that Mendelssohn did not openly hasten to defend Weisel when the latter's book *Divrei Shalom ve'Emet* aroused such a storm in the Jewish world also proves that Weisel did not act merely as the executor of Mendelssohn's plans. The bitter dispute grieved Weisel greatly, and Mendelssohn, in a letter to his friend Wolf, explained his inability to intervene more effectively in

[5] S. Adler's article in the *Jubilee Book* issued on the occasion of the 75th anniversary of the founding of the Samson Raphael Hirsch School, Frankfurt A. M.

[6] Simon, *op. cit.,* p. 159.

Weisel's favor: "I know very well what little influence I have on the masses. My sphere of activity embraces a few friends only; and since I have assumed the task of educating my children, this circle has become smaller still. Outside this circle I neither have nor seek any influence. I emphasize the limits set upon my powers, and I have therefore to refrain from further involvement in controversy." [7]

II

Professor Klausner's biography of Weisel, included in the former's *History of Modern Hebrew Literature,* is written with great thoroughness and is supported by rich historical evidence. Nevertheless, it may be worth-while pausing to reconsider the historical and psychological factors which led Weisel to write his important *Divrei Shalom ve'Emet.* First and foremost we must take into account the fact that Weisel was the scion of a wealthy and cultured family, had lived in the large cities of Western Europe, and moved very freely from town to town. This brought him into contact with many people and enriched his knowledge and understanding of worldly affairs. He saw the life of the Jews in various ghettos as an outsider, and felt keenly the disabilities they suffered. He learned to appreciate the value of a general education and possibly exaggerated its importance as a means to the attainment of full civil equality. It is important to remember that in Copenhagen he was influenced decisively by the learned grammarian Rabbi Shlomo Zalman Hena (Hanau), author of *Tzohar Hateva,* by whom he was tutored in his father's home. Rabbi Hanau aroused in

[7] Moses Mendelssohn, *Zeugnisse, Briefe, Gespräche von Bertha Strauss* (Berlin: Welt Verlag, 1929).

the young man a profound love of the Hebrew language, Holy Writ, and Biblical commentaries based on grammatical and philological principles. This love never left him. Weisel's knowledge of secular matters was not extensive and his command of the German language was somewhat imperfect. During his stay in Amsterdam and Copenhagen he came very close to the Sephardic Jewish community, which possessed a cultural tradition differing widely from that of the *Ashkenazi Jews*. He adopted the *Sephardic* pronunciation of the Hebrew language and although his parents were *Ashkenazi Jews,* he regarded himself as belonging to those Jews who continued the tradition of Spanish Jewry and who, unlike their brethren in the German-speaking countries, tended to combine Judaism with secular knowledge. Indeed, he never correctly evaluated the distinction between the *Ashkenazi* (German and East European) tradition, on the one hand, and *Sephardic* (Spanish) culture on the other.

In describing Weisel's educational activities, we must also note the important changes in education which were then taking place in other countries, and which doubtless influenced him. As already mentioned, in his time the Philanthropist Movement in European education reached its peak. J. B. Basedow sought to make the process of learning as easy as possible and to base elementary instruction on play. Basedow's theories included ideas borrowed from Rousseau, which no doubt exerted an influence upon Weisel. Basedow called for the grading of pupils according to their standard of knowledge and worked for the establishment of a wide educational network for the common people, side by side with special schools for children of the wealthier classes. He fought for the freeing of the schools from the domination of the church and the abolition of all religious sectarian instruction.

The stress on moral education combined with vocational training, which characterizes the educational system of the Philanthropists, is found in Weisel's writings also. He was fully aware of the fact that contemporary Jewish educators blandly ignored the developments and changes taking place in non-Jewish schools. He saw many faults in the Jewish system of education: its atmosphere of stagnation, lack of organization, and failure to adapt itself to the historical changes, which were then beginning to make themselves felt. He felt keenly for the Jewish pupil in the *Cheder* who never tasted the joys of carefree childhood or indulged in games and other childish pleasures. Weisel, who had been taught in the traditional Jewish *Cheder,* sympathized with the Jewish pupil who was obliged to tackle subject matter that was quite beyond the grasp of his childish and immature mind. In his biographical essay on Weisel, Kalman Schulman writes: "When he was nine years old and had not yet mastered the reading of Hebrew sufficiently to understand Holy Writ he was thrown into the great sea of the Talmud, there to swim and flounder in its depths." [8] Weisel's desire to reduce the Jewish pupils' hours of study is revealed in the contents of his second letter in *Divrei Shalom ve'Emet,* where he writes: "Three to five hours of daily learning of Bible and Talmud are enough for a boy, and will not make his lessons a burdensome task to him. The child must be treated gently, he must learn gladly, and

[8] Kalman Schulman's introduction to Weisel's *Divrei Shalom ve'Emet* (Warsaw: 1886), p. 4.

hear words of love and joy from his teacher. The boys must also have a few hours of recreation and play, and the enlightened teacher should supervise this recreation period and take part in the boys' amusements, for they can learn moral values from their teachers even in ordinary conversation." [9]

Weisel was opposed to corporal punishment. He writes: "When the Rabbi uses faulty language to his pupil and explains the lessons without pedagogical insight the child does not understand what he says, and the Rabbi becomes very angry and beats him in his rage. The child's heart contracts within him for fear of his teacher; he detests him and his teaching, and his only longing is to run away from school. The results of these incidents are such as cannot here be dealt with at length." [10]

Although Weisel does not write at length on the defects of traditional Jewish education, we have evidence of these shortcomings from several of his contemporaries. I refer in particular to the remarks of Rabbi Shaul Lewin, the President of the *Beth Din* (Rabbinical Court) of Frankfurt an der Oder, the son of the learned Rabbi Zvi Lewin, of Berlin. His comments are found in *Mekoroth le'Toldoth ha'Chinuch be'Israel* (*Sources of the History of Jewish education*), by Professor Simcha Assaf, pp. 242ff. Shaul Lewin's pamphlet, called satirically *Ktav Yosher* (*Letter of Sincerity*), is a biting satire on traditional Jewish education. The author pretends that he is also attacking the innovations suggested by Weisel, but in reality pours all his contempt on Weisel's opponents. Lewin mentions three outstanding faults in traditional Jewish schools:

[9] Weisel, *Divrei Shalom ve'Emet,* p. 68.
[10] *Ibid.,* p. 69.

1. *The children are taught incorrect Hebrew, and to read and write ungrammatically.*

Lewin writes with biting sarcasm: "The study of grammar is the first step on the road to apostasy, for that is the way the evil spirit works. Today, it will tell the boy to learn grammar and when he has mastered it, it will urge him to write polished phrases and perhaps even poetry and when he is in complete command of Hebrew he will not accept far-fetched interpretations or commentaries on the Scriptures but adhere to the simple meaning inherent in the words. He will reject angrily all the explanations, additions, and commentaries traditionally linked with the text of the Scriptures and all the infinite number of books written in this field. Thus, transgression will lead to transgression and eventually he will reject the prayers and our wonderful holy liturgy dismissing them as being ungrammatical."

2. *Corporal punishment in the Heder.*

"Look here, sir," he answers the hypothetical questioner who points out that there are boys who prolong their studies in the Heder up to thirteen or fourteen years of age and make no headway, "you are asking what benefit these boys derive from wasting so many years on nothing useful and practical, and what is their reward for sitting over their books for so long? These boys who sit for seven or eight years at school and do not even learn one word, nevertheless succeed immeasurably. The boys' obdurate heart gives in to the beatings and scoldings of the teacher which are meant to force him to learn something frightening and incomprehensible, and the great submission of the boys becomes deeply engraved in their hearts and minds, fixing therein forever the exaltedness of the Talmud and the greatness of its commentaries.

"There is yet a further benefit derived from corporal punishment, for it enables the teachers to reap a reward, a means of livelihood, seeing that a teacher who punishes frequently is thought extremely capable and is therefore suitably rewarded. Another good point about corporal punishment is that children who are beaten for being backward at school seek the favor of their teachers and bring them presents, thereby winning their good graces; and when the festival season comes round the children beg their parents to give them gifts for the teacher, which are to serve as ransom. Thus, from early childhood they become accustomed to giving charity to learned men who earn their daily bread in hardship and misery. This disposition becomes so pronounced in their character that sometimes they will take something without their parents' knowledge and bring it to their teachers, and this in turn is also considered a good deed by the Almighty and a multiplication of such good deeds will hasten the coming of the Messiah."

3. *The teachers are unsuitable for their task.*

Like Weisel, Rabbi Shaul Lewin complains about the teachers who taught in Jewish schools in his time, many of whom spoke unintelligibly, with a faulty and confusing *Ashkenazi* pronunciation. He ridicules the complete ignorance of some of them on secular matters, the superstitious beliefs that they spread among their pupils, and the various "side lines" they engaged in to supplement their earnings. The fictitious author of *K'tav Yosher* introduces himself as follows: "Praise be to God, I am a ritual slaughterer, a butchers' inspector and I hold certificates from all the important people in the country. In addition, I am a religious scribe, a reader in the synagogue; I blow the *shofar*, circumcise, visit the sick and also act as a gravedigger. I possess a store of medical knowledge, acquisition of which is permitted by the Torah; and I hope, sir, you will not think I gained this knowledge from the gentile schools and churches, as many of our renegades did. Far be it from me to do likewise! Do we not possess our own Jewish medical books, full of profound wisdom, of which the gentiles haven't the faintest idea, books that are full of supernatural wisdom. I can also dispel the evil eye by incantation, cure fever, pour lead on sufferers from shock, and stem hemorrhage by means of spells, etc. . . ."

III

The Emperor Joseph II's Edict of Tolerance of 1781 provided Weisel with a good opportunity to call for widespread educational reform. This edict brought much relief to the Jews, albeit within certain limitations. The point that touches our subject is "the King's decree that Jews were entitled to educate their children in the 'normal' [primary] schools and the general '*Realschulen*,' as well as the higher institutes of learning. In addition, they were accorded the right to open their own 'normal' schools." [11] We have already mentioned that Weisel regarded this decree as an important turning point in the attitude of the authorities toward the Jews, and therefore he heaped praise upon Joseph II. "We have heard in this royal decree words of peace and truth directed to all his people and tempered

[11] Klausner, *op. cit.*, p. 106.

by wisdom whose source is the love of mankind. In his magnanimous deeds, he did not forget a poor people [the Jews] and his kind and consoling words have reached our hearts also, as the words of a father to his sons and a guide and teacher to his pupils. . . . He also recognized our shortcomings . . . that very few of us speak the German language adequately and therefore understand neither the books on history and world events nor those dealing with *'nimusiot'* [i.e., correct speech, polite manners, moral principles], *'tiviot'* [i.e., arithmetic, the natural sciences—astronomy, biology, and botany], *'limudiot'* [i.e., history, geography, and other humanistic subjects]. Nor are they able to converse freely with the country's inhabitants and its ministers . . . and therefore they are required to establish schools where their children will be taught the spoken and written German tongue. . . ." [12]

Although the Emperor decreed, *inter alia,* that Jews should teach their children German and that merchants, artisans, and manufacturers should keep their books in pure German and not in Judeo-German, the clause about instruction in *nimusiot, tiviot,* and *limudiot* has its source in Weisel's own interpretation only.

In his first letter Weisel divides education into two separate spheres, "The Law of God" and "The Law of Man." "The Law of God" obviously includes the specific content of the Jewish religion. "The Law of Man" is identical with *nimusiot, tiviot,* and *limudiot* and is sometimes referred to by Weisel as *Derech Eretz* (literally, way of the land; in this context, however, it means secular studies).

Of *Derech Eretz* he says that "it is of benefit to society in that it teaches man how to fare in worldly matters and to

[12] Weisel, *op. cit.,* p. 16.

enjoy everything under the sun. It brings success to a man's undertakings and helps him to be of assistance to his fellow men in all their actions and daily affairs." [13]

As for the relative importance of "The Law of God" and "The Law of Man," Weisel says that "although the sages of Israel may not enjoy the light of wisdom of a man who transgresses against the 'Law of God,' yet observes the 'Law of Man,' nevertheless the rest of mankind will derive benefit from him [i.e., he will be acceptable to the rest of mankind]. On the other hand, a person offending against the 'Law of Man' [i.e., possessing no secular culture], though observing the 'Law of God' will bring joy neither to the sages of Israel nor to the rest of mankind." [14]

This passage shows clearly that in Weisel's opinion the "Law of Man" is more important than the "Law of God," not only because it takes precedence over it in point of time, as is conveyed by the Rabbinical saying, *"Derech Eretz* preceded the Torah," but also because of the many practical benefits it confers upon men. In other words, Weisel gives preference to the "Law of Man" as against the "Law of God" because of the former's usefulness to society.

Similarly, Weisel interprets the saying of the Rabbis, "A carcass is preferable to a man learned in the Torah, who yet has no *'Deah.'* " Weisel interprets *Deah* as synonymous with *Derech Eretz,* i.e., refinements and knowledge of general culture. He says: "Every man learned in the Torah who has no knowledge of secular matters benefits neither the wise men of Israel nor those of other nations, for he degrades his knowledge and is despised by other human beings, whereas a carcass is nothing despicable in itself;

[13] *Ibid.,* p. 5.
[14] *Ibid.,* p. 6.

and therefore it is not forbidden to eat of its flesh, except for the Jews, to whom it is forbidden by divine commandment. Other people, however, may consume its flesh." [15]

We may then summarize and say that in Weisel's first letter "The Law of Man," that is secular studies, is given preference to the study of Torah. This, however, means a complete reversal of traditional values. Traditional education has always subordinated the study of secular subjects to the study of Torah. The Scriptural injunction, "Thou shalt meditate day and night that thou mayest observe to do according to all that is written therein," was taken very seriously.

The objections of the Rabbis to Weisel's innovations, of which more will be said later, are therefore understandable.

Weisel warmly recommends Mendelssohn's translation of the Bible, which is written in a pure and highly polished German. "When the pupils are taught the Torah by their teachers by means of this German translation, they will become accustomed from childhood to speaking perfectly the tongue of the country's inhabitants, and thus they will understand correctly what is written in the Scriptures, for up to now the teachers spoke unintelligibly due to their lack of a thorough knowledge of the German tongue, and thus were unable to explain the Hebrew passages in a way that would make their meaning clear to the pupils." [16]

It appears that Weisel recommended Mendelssohn's translation for two reasons:

a) "Because by this means the boys would become accustomed to speaking the language of the country's inhabitants perfectly"; that is to say, the German translation

[15] *Ibid.*, p. 6.
[16] *Ibid.*, pp. 24-25.

would act as an instrument for the teaching of German.

b) "By its means they will understand perfectly what is written in the Scriptures"; which means he maintained that with the aid of the easily understood German translation the pupils would grasp the Biblical text more accurately. On the basis of this textual analysis it seems difficult to accept the opinion of Klausner, who says: "If there is still room for the assertion that perhaps Mendelssohn meant by his translation to encourage the spread of the German language, in the case of Weisel there is not the slightest doubt that in his view Hebrew was the main language and German subsidiary to it." [17]

On the contrary, there is room to claim that Weisel's main purpose was to encourage the use of the German tongue by the pupils, for it is difficult to understand precisely why pure German should be the medium of learning the Scriptures most easily and accurately. Judeo-German was the pupils' mother tongue and the language they spoke most fluently. Moreover, from the children's point of view, Judeo-German was undoubtedly closer to Hebrew than pure German. The first Hebrew words that the children learned in *Cheder*—I refer to the prayer, *"Modeh ani Lefanecha, Melech chai vekayam,"* etc.—were closely bound up with the Yiddish addendum, *"Ich will folgen Tate Mame, ich will folgen alle gute frumme Leit, a Broche un Hazloche auf mein Keppel, Amen, Selah* ("I will obey father, mother, I will obey all good pious people; may success and blessing be on my head") . In the soul of the Jewish child, therefore, the Yiddish and Hebrew tongues were organically linked together, whereas pure German no doubt sounded foreign to him. If Weisel really

[17] Klausner, *op. cit.*, p. 100.

intended to facilitate the comprehension of the Hebrew text of the Bible he surely would have realized that the best medium through which this could be done was the children's mother tongue, which was Judeo-German. In other words, the second reason given by Weisel is completely invalidated, and the two reasons are actually one: He wanted to use Mendelssohn's translation as a means of teaching the pupils pure German (*Hochdeutsch*).

Moreover, Weisel proposed the compilation of methodical books of instruction in the principles of the Jewish faith—a kind of Jewish catechism—as is the custom in Christian schools. He writes: "It is worth-while compiling a book setting forth the doctrines in which every Jew should believe, written in clear and lucid language and in a method fitted to the understanding of the children, so that they may learn from childhood and by means of a uniform method the detailed principles of their creed. Each detail will be inculcated into the child by the reading of scriptural passages, which the author of the book will elucidate in detail. They will learn the truth and righteousness of the Scriptures, so that, even when they grow up and do not succeed in adding to their store of knowledge by the study of the Talmud, they will not abandon the fundamental knowledge they have previously acquired, which is essential to the life of man in both worlds." [18]

A point of great interest is Weisel's proposal to divide the school into several classes, grade the children according to their ability, and then adapt the teaching material to the level of the class. Weisel's main aim was to make the study of the Talmud a principal subject compulsory only for the most gifted children, and to direct the other children to

[18] Weisel, *op. cit.*, pp. 21-22.

practical work and the acquisition of various skills and handicrafts. "And pay special attention," says Weisel, "to the selection and grading of the boys, so that the child who learns the Hebrew language and grammar in his class should not be allowed to go up to one where he will be taught the Scriptures, religious precepts, and a little ethics before he is examined by the headmaster, who will judge whether or not he has completed the studies of the previous class satisfactorily. Similarly, the boy who has been learning Scriptures and ethics must not be allowed to go on to a class where he will be taught Talmud until he is deemed to have satisfactorily completed his previous class studies. In cases where the child is judged to be incapable of learning the Talmud it will be better for him not to attempt the more difficult studies but to learn the handicraft of his choice, and continue with the study of the Torah and ethics only." [19]

This proposal was revolutionary, and if it had been put into practice it would have led to a great reduction in the number of pupils studying the Talmud and the gradual conversion of the *Cheder* into a type of institution which is today known as a vocational school, with the addition of religious instruction.

The new system of education envisaged by Weisel called for a new type of teacher—one who had perfect command of both Hebrew and German. Weisel well knew that such teachers were almost nonexistent in the Austro-Hungarian Empire, and he demanded that they be brought in from afar. "And if you are at the moment unable to find in your own districts people who have an adequate knowledge of both languages you must seek them among all the Jewish

[19] *Ibid.*, p. 34.

communities and bring them in from afar! For in another
three years or so you will find that . . . the mainsprings
within your own community will overflow and many of
your own children will acquire a command of German and
be of assistance to their brothers, for many pupils will make
an effort to learn diligently from those teachers who will
come to you from abroad." [20] The phrase regarding the
"mainsprings within your own community," which, Weisel
foresees, will "overflow," is somewhat obscure. He probably
meant that in the course of a comparatively short time the
"enlightenment" of the Jews would proceed with great
momentum and the desire to acquire the language of the
country would become great indeed. This would increase
the eagerness of the Jewish boys to learn the German
language from their teachers as quickly as possible.

IV

From all that has been said so far it is abundantly clear
that Weisel went very far in his aspirations for a revolution
in the educational system and it is difficult to accept the
opinion of Klausner that "Weisel's proposals contain no
innovations, even from the viewpoint of his own time. His
book [*Divrei Shalom ve'Emet*] is written in an inoffensive
way; it is full of profound and sincere religious belief and
does not attack the tradition and the customs of the people.
On the contrary, the book even justifies the more alien
customs adopted by the Jews, by tracing their origin to the
persecutions and discriminatory decrees of the gentiles.
And as for the Rabbis, Weisel offended them only in his
harsh interpretation of the Talmudic saying that a carcass

[20] *Ibid.*, p. 33.

is preferable to a scholar who has no refinements and knowledge of general culture. Besides this one point, he offended neither their dignity nor their authority." [21]

The American-Jewish educationist Zvi Scharfstein takes a similar view. He writes: "We look upon Naphtali Herz Weisel not as a revolutionary in the field of education, but rather as a cautious reformer. The changes in Jewish education suggested by him are not so very different from those proposed by the exalted Rabbi Loeb of Prague and other Orthodox and God-fearing Rabbis. He only added the study of ethics and handicrafts to the traditional curriculum. I have already observed that the origin of the need for the study of ethics lay in the anti-Semitic prejudice prevailing in government circles that the Jews were corrupt, especially in their dealings with the gentiles, and therefore injurious to society. They therefore believed that this defect would be remedied by the introduction of the study of ethics into the classrooms." [22]

It is interesting to note that Scharfstein explains Weisel's call for special lessons in moral precepts in Jewish schools as the result of an attitude which took for granted that the moral behavior of the Jews was corrupt. Scharfstein's assumption that Weisel shared this attitude does not seem fully justified. Weisel's call for the teaching of moral principles in schools is well in keeping with the teaching and practice of the Philanthropists.

Professor Ernst Simon goes more deeply into the question under discussion, although his previously mentioned essay is mainly concerned with the educational activities of the Philanthropists—a fact which does not permit him to

---

[21] Klausner, *op. cit.*, p. 109.
[22] Zvi Scharfstein, *Toldoth ha'Chinuch be'Israel* (New York: 1945), I, 77.

deal with Weisel's writings at any length. His evaluation of Weisel's views, therefore, is by no means exhaustive. He comments on Weisel's concept of *"Torath ha'adam"* ("The Law of Man") as follows: "There is not much doubt that in his first letter he accorded it a place preceding that of *"Torath ha'Elohim"* ("The Law of God"), not only from the point of view of time but also from that of its essential value to the Jewish people, especially the common people, who were for the most part unlearned in the Torah." [23] It follows, therefore, that Simon also sees in Weisel the radical reformer and not the cautious and conservative critic of the existing system of education.

When the Jewish community of Trieste approached Mendelssohn with a request for proposals for the reform of its educational system he referred them to Weisel, and in his second letter in *Divrei Shalom ve'Emet* Weisel modified his stand on several points, because he had heard about the storm which his first letter had aroused in the Jewish community. He withdrew the harsh and offensive interpretation which he had given to the Rabbinical saying that "a carcass is preferable to a man learned in the Torah but lacking in *Deah*," and admitted that this saying was a mere figure of speech, an overstatement and exaggeration, and, therefore, not to be taken at its face value. He quotes similar proverbs to show that the Rabbis were wont to exaggerate in their sayings. For example, "A Rabbinical scholar who is clad in stained garments deserves death," or, "It is permitted to stab a boor to death on the Day of Atonement, even if it falls on a Sabbath, and to tear him to pieces like a fish." Weisel goes on to say, "It is clear that all these proverbs are mere figures of speech not to be taken

[23] Simon, *op. cit.*, p. 172.

literally, a fact which is obvious to anyone versed in literature and poetry." [24]

A retraction from his former attitude is also discernible in the rest of his proposals. In his second letter, addressed to the community of Trieste, he allowed greater importance to *"Torath Elohim"* than to *"Torath ha'adam."* He stated that *"Torath Elohim"* contains and includes *"Torath ha'adam,"* and does not negate the concepts of general culture and refinement. Moreover, he then attached less importance to "general culture" and a "knowledge of secular matters and the natural sciences," saying he had not intended that every child should study all these subjects. The study of secular matters was only for the chosen few, and even these need not do so with great thoroughness. For instance, he then said about the study of geography that the teacher need not teach this subject through the medium of books, "which would only prolong the lessons and confuse the children's minds," but should only point out the places on the map with his finger, and that "if the boy can draw well he will learn the essential points in a very short time.[25]

In this letter Weisel's aim of raising the dignity of the Jews in the eyes of the gentile is manifest; this was doubtless one of his motives in writing the letters. In this letter, also, Weisel most emphatically expressed his desire to adopt some of the tradition of Spanish Jewry and to remodel the educational system of the *Ashkenazi* Jewish communities on the pattern of the systems prevailing in the Dutch and Italian communities.

"I have visited the Jewish community of Amsterdam and I met there important people, as well as many Rabbinical

[24] Weisel, *op. cit.*, p. 87.
[25] *Ibid.*, p. 72.

scholars. I have also been in their school where there are graded classes. I observed that the children learn the Torah from Genesis to the end of Deuteronomy; thereafter the remaining twenty-four books of the Bible; then the *Mishnah,* and only when the child is grown up does he study the Talmud and its commentaries. And yet they grew up and prospered, and I wept on thinking why we could not do likewise in our country. May God grant that this custom spread throughout the Jewish communities in the Diaspora." [26]

In his third letter, Weisel replied to Rabbi Tewele, Head of the religious court of the Lissa Jewish community, who on the Great Sabbath (the Sabbath before Passover), 1782, had delivered a sermon attacking Weisel's first letter. The dispute between Weisel and the great Rabbis of Germany and Poland is of great historic interest, and is worth discussing here. It must be borne in mind that the unfavorable impression created by Weisel's first letter proved to be lasting, and all subsequent efforts to modify the rather revolutionary attitude he had taken up in that first letter failed to produce the desired effect. Because he was a deeply religious Jew the attacks of the Rabbis made a profound impression on him and he was deeply distressed by his inability to correct the adverse impression created by his first letter. Historically, it is his first letter, and not his later pronouncements, for which he will be remembered and with which his name will be associated.

V

Weisel's opponents were headed by three of the greatest Rabbis of that time: Rabbi David Tewele of Lissa, R.

[26] *Ibid.,* p. 64.

Yeheskel Landau of Prague, and the Gaon (exalted Rabbi) of Vilna.[27]

Rabbi Tewele based his opposition to Weisel's proposals on three main points:

1) By his undue emphasis on the study of secular subjects in the Jewish school Weisel reverses the order of preference in the traditional Jewish school curriculum. Rabbi Tewele did not object in principle to the teaching of German or to the introduction of secular subjects into Jewish schools, as long as "the secular subjects remained subsidiary to the principal subject, the study of the Torah." [28]

2) Weisel's proposal to grade the twelve- and thirteen-year-old children according to their abilities and interest in Talmud, and to direct most of them to vocational training seemed dangerous to Rabbi Tewele, because everyone is required to obey the precept; "And thou shalt meditate upon it [The Torah] by day and by night." He also adds a purely pedagogical argument: "Do not listen to the foolish and evil one [Weisel] who writes that if the boy is not capable of studying the Talmud it is better for him to abandon these studies. Beware, ye communities of *Yeshurun,* of lending a willing ear to him, for we have often witnessed instances where a boy of twelve or thirteen seems to have difficulty in learning, but when he is a few

[27] Several historians are doubtful as to whether the Rabbi Eliahu of Vilna mentioned by Rabbi Tewele in his sermon is identical with the Gaon Eliahu of Vilna. The arguments presented by Lewin and Klausner to prove that R. Eliahu Chassid may be identified as the Gaon are entirely conclusive. See Dr. L. Lewin's article *Aus dem jüdishen Kultur-Kampfe,"* in *Jahrbuch der jüd.-liter. Gesellschaft,* 13.XII, 182-194; also Klausner, *op. cit.,* pp. 111-12.

[28] Rabbi Tewele's sermon is printed in full in the previously cited *Jahrbuch.* The reference to the subsidiary nature of secular studies occurs on p. 194.

years older and works hard he will excel in the study of the Torah." [29]

In other words, it is unwise to determine the future of a child according to his studies at school and to decide at that early age whether or not he is suited for advanced study of the Oral Torah and other theoretical subjects.

3) Weisel's proposals are dangerous because he claims to speak with authority, as interpreter of the Edict of Tolerance and as one to whom the Emperor has entrusted the execution of his plans in the field of Jewish education. The Rabbis feared that his proposal might gain official approval —a highly dangerous possibility. They therefore made every effort to prove that he was not correctly interpreting the Emperor's intentions but "twisted and distorted the sovereign's advice according to his own interpretations, telling us that his exalted Majesty the Emperor himself commanded you thus." [30]

4) By his emphasis on the teaching of morality and ethics as separate subjects in addition to the teaching of traditional Jewish subjects, Weisel by implication casts aspersions on the ethical content of Judaism as well as on those Jews who have no general secular knowledge. "On which of the holy men does he dare to cast aspersion? Who among the holy band of men who learn the laws of God is not an example of the finest among men? If such a Jew is learned, righteous, and thoroughly understanding of the teaching of the Torah, even though unlearned in worldly refinements and unversed in polished phrases, will he [Weisel] call such a man lacking in the knowledge of the Law of Man? Will not the words of our sages spur him on

[29] Rabbi Tewele's sermon, published by Dr. L. Lewin, *ibid.*
[30] *Ibid.*, p. 184.

to tread a righteous path? Will not the morality inherent in the sayings of our holy Rabbis learned in the Talmud show him how to converse with his fellow men and lead him to honesty and virtue in character and inclination? Are not the injunctions of Maimonides in *Sepher ha'Madah* and other Tractates which teach men saintly ways of life sufficient for him? These also include the book *Chovot ha'Levavoth* [*The Duties of the Heart*], and all the other writings on morality which are derived from the teachings of the Prophets. . . . If against such [saintly] men he raised up his hand then may his own hand wither!" [31]

In the sermon attacking Weisel's pamphlet which Rabbi Yeheskel Landau preached on the same Great Sabbath in 1782, we find two further criticisms:

1) The teaching of German in Jewish schools would enable the children to read secular literature, which seemed to him undesirable from an educational point of view. "As soon as you become accustomed to the German language you will wish to read books which have nothing to do with improving the knowledge of the language [German] but deal with research on the subject of religion and the Torah, and thus you may, God forbid, become estranged from your faith. For all who talk and write about religion from a rational point of view cause only harm." [32] (Presumably the reference here is to "Deism," a philosophical trend which was then widespread.)

2) Rabbi Yeheskel Landau's second point is essentially didactic. If Mendelssohn's translation were introduced into the schools German would become the main subject and

[31] *Ibid.*, p. 184.

[32] *Derushei Zion le'Nefesh Hayah, derush 39;* see also Assaf, *Mekoroth le' Ioldoth ha-chinuch be'Israel,* p. 238, and Klausner, *op. cit.,* p. 109.

the Scriptures a subsidiary one. "Seeing that the language of Mendelssohn's translation is deep and difficult for the child to understand, the teacher must in the first place teach the pupil pure German. Thus the day will pass with the teacher's explaining Mendelssohn's German and the boy will miss the main points of the Torah. If the children are to be taught only by means of this translation they will have to spend their time with foreign books in order to become accustomed to German. Thus our Torah will become the handmaid serving as a means for the dissemination of the German language among the younger generation, while they remain ignorant of the meaning of the words written in the Hebrew tongue." [33]

We hear of the Gaon of Vilna's opposition to Weisel's proposals in a letter from Weisel to the Trieste Jewish community, in which Weisel mentions that his third opponent was a resident of Vilna, called Rabbi Eliahu Chassid. In his famous sermon; Rabbi David Tewele also said: "I have heard from trustworthy sources something that is of great comfort to me; that in the Jewish community of the great and holy town of Vilna a despicable book was burned in the streets, after it was first hung up on an iron chain in the synagogue yard. In my opinion, the judges carried out their sentence in a fitting manner." We have no written evidence of the opinions of the Gaon of Vilna, but we can assume from the "judgment" that they were very similar to those of Rabbi Tewele and Rabbi Yeheskel Landau of Prague.

Professor Gershom Scholem in his essay *"Mitoch Hirhurim al Chochmat Yisrael"* ("Reflections on *Wissenschaft des Judentums"*) mentions the "contradiction between the

---

[33] Yeheskel Landau's sermon, quoted by Klausner, *op. cit.*, p. 55, and also by Assaf, *op. cit.*, p. 241.

scholars' repeated declarations of its [*Wissenschaft*] pure objectivity as a science, which, as claimed by its founders, is only a branch of general science, with no other object, and the obvious fact of the political role it played with the acquiescence of public opinion. How strange is this picture of learned men whose entire work proves that they wished to create a practical instrument in the Jews' fight for civil equality, and even continually made use of this instrument in discussions; yet closed their eyes lest this principal purpose be more clearly revealed and declared that they desire nothing but the study of *Wissenschaft* itself for its own sake." [34] This comment holds good in the case of the educational writings of Naphtali Herz Weisel. He felt keenly the distress of the Jews, who were deprived of civil rights and despised by the gentiles. His main purpose in publishing his educational program was, therefore, to impart to the Jews secular knowledge by means of which they would become worthy of full civil equality. It follows, therefore, that he viewed education mainly as an instrument for carrying out a revolution in the social life of the Jews of his time and did not evaluate correctly the conservative aspect of education—the fact that it serves as a means of preserving essential values which have to be passed on from generation to generation. Moreover, even Klausner, who feels very favorably inclined toward Weisel, admits that Weisel used to publish his work with undue haste, a fact which did not permit him to take a balanced view of the extremely complex problem of Jewish education. It is a well-known fact that he published his *Divrei Shalom ve'-Emet* only a few months after Joseph II had published his

[34] Gershom Scholem, "*Mitoch Hirhurim al Chochmat Yisrael*," *Luach ha'Aretz* (Schocken, 1944.)

"*Toleranzedikt,*" and was insufficiently versed in the problems of Jewish education. Nor must we overlook the fact that Weisel interpreted the edict with undue optimism—a feeling that was shared neither by the Rabbis nor even by Mendelssohn. It is this difference that underlies the famous dispute between Weisel and the Rabbis.

It is not at all difficult to perceive that he was far removed from the actual practical work of education. He had no experience of teaching children, and of his experience with adults he himself writes: "I had only just made it known that I desired to interpret the Scriptures in public, and many people who wished to listen to my lectures gathered together every morning and filled the rooms from end to end. After several days the numbers of my audience grew less and less, until they filled only one room. Soon I was lecturing on the Sabbath only, and then I saw only one young man who came to listen to me. Then I saw only the chairs around me, and so I sat in solitude, as I had done for the previous thirty-six years." [35]

On the other hand, it cannot be denied that he had a full grasp of educational ideas and even seems to have been versed in the educational literature of his time—we have mentioned his affinity to the doctrines of the Philanthropists; but it is one thing to have a knowledge of educational theory and another to understand the basic facts of practical teaching. Nor did he grasp the fact that any radical change in the educational system was fraught with danger. Although the traditional type of education was, as we have pointed out, faulty in many respects, it could have been corrected without rocking its very foundations in the process.

[35] Klausner, *op. cit.,* p. 101.

In retrospect, most of his reforms seem sufficiently justified, and his ideas are accepted today even in the most Orthodox Jewish circles. One or two of his proposals, however, meet with disapproval even today. Jewish education has always resisted the attempt to catechize the principles of the Jewish faith. This is an approach alien to Jewish susceptibilities, as religious faith has always been accepted rather as an underlying assumption of Jewish teaching than as its main subject. Jewish education also rejects any attempt to subordinate the teaching of the Scriptures to extraneous aims. (In the case of Weisel, it was the teaching of the German language.) Nor must it be forgotten that traditional Judaism even today refuses to grant prime importance to secular studies, as advocated by Weisel in his first letter.

It is true that Weisel himself was a pious and observant Jew, and it is a tragic fact that a man who "always behaved like all other believing Jews, and even fully observed the smallest of customs which many ignore," [36] paved the way to the complete assimilation of German Jewry. He himself regretted his actions when he perceived their consequences, and he writes in one of his letters: "I grieve to say that His Majesty the Emperor's commands have been fully carried out, and the Torah of God has been abandoned." [37] This disillusionment came when he saw the trend of the "free schools" which were established according to his program and which he had at first supported. In most of these schools only four hours a week were allotted to Hebrew, and of these only two hours were devoted to the study of

[36] Schulman, *op. cit.,* p. 31.
[37] Assaf, *op. cit.,* p. 235.

religion. The direct descendant of this type of school is the present-day Jewish Sunday School in the United States.

I do not believe that the stand of Professor Klausner in the dispute between Weisel and the Rabbis, and that of those who follow him, is justified in the light of history and of a critical sifting of relevant sources. Klausner himself was cradled in the tradition of *Haskalah,* that movement so dear to him because it gave a powerful impetus to the creation of modern Hebrew literature. This fact may account for his harsh censure of the Rabbis and the part they played in the bitter controversy that followed the publication of Weisel's book *Divrei Shalom ve'Emet.* It is true enough that the Rabbis conducted the controversy with Weisel too acrimoniously, but, as Lewin points out in *Die Jüdische Monatsschrift,* the language of contention was generally harsh at a time when the laws of libel and slander were not nearly so stringent as they are today—in point of fact they barely existed at all. In Klausner's view, Rabbi Tewele's sermon is a mere "encyclopedia of curses"; that very sermon, however, contains, as I have shown, a number of extremely valid objections of a purely educational nature. If in fact the problem under discussion is viewed dispassionately and objectively the impression gained is that the dispute between Weisel and the Rabbis was conducted with the utmost seriousness on both sides and it is indeed one of the great historical disputes of Jewish thought in the field of education.

The Rabbis were sceptical of Weisel's integrity and thought him a hypocrite, a man "who covers with honeyed words the rage of crocodiles and the poison of vipers." [38] Their scepticism was, I believe, unjustified. Despite Wei-

[38] Rabbi Tewele's Sermon, *op. cit.*

sel's aspiration to change the system of Jewish education, a sincere love for Judaism in all its aspects is a dominant feature of his many-sided and complex character.

His later retractions, though ineffective, must be taken into account if justice is to be done to him personally. He could not, however, turn back the wheels of history after he had set in motion the movement for the radical reform of Jewish education.

Thus the way was paved for the almost complete assimilation of Jews in German-speaking countries. That this movement should have been initiated by a man whose Jewish Orthodoxy and personal integrity were unquestionable and that he should have been aided in his activities by the Orthodox Rabbi Shaul Lewin is one of the ironies of history.

2

Samson Raphael Hirsch: Educationist and Thinker

I

Though famous, Samson Raphael Hirsch is now but little read. His personality and work are insufficiently known in Israel. In the Diaspora, the publication in London of an English edition of some of his writings[1] and the recent splendid edition of the Hirsch *Chumash* in English (translated by Hirsch's grandson, Dr. Isaac Levy, and containing a massive introduction by Rabbi I. Grunfeld) are likely to mark a turning point in English Jewry's interest in S. R. Hirsch. It is to be expected that this *magnum opus* of Hirsch will exercise an influence on the Jewish religious scene in all English-speaking countries.

In Israel the situation is different. There his influence, slight as it is, is actually on the decline, and this in spite of the fact that a fair proportion of his writings have been translated into Hebrew. True, he is appreciated for his devotion to the cause of traditional Judaism and for having propounded a philosophic basis for Orthodoxy; true, he is mentioned in textbooks of Jewish history used in all Israeli

[1] Samson Raphael Hirsch, *Judaism Eternal*, ed. Rabbi I. Grunfeld (London: Soncino Press, 1958).

46

schools, and a number of his articles in Hebrew translation
are included in anthologies of Jewish thought used in religious high schools and secondary *Yeshivot* in Israel.
Nevertheless, religious circles tend to ignore Hirsch's conception of Judaism, and, in their spiritual isolation, look
askance at the work of a thinker whose writings display a
marked "extrovert" tendency—a tendency which to them
appears suspect.

There are three reasons for the lack of interest in
Hirsch's writings. First, his involved and flowery style is
a hindrance to easy reading. Secondly, one who reads his
work in German, or, for that matter, in English or Hebrew
translation, cannot fail to be aware how much his ideas,
though fundamentally Jewish, were steeped in contemporary German thought. No wonder that some Jewish historians, notably Wiener and Elbogen, considered him a
typical nineteenth-century German-Jewish intellectual, not
altogether unlike his most outspoken Liberal opponents.
It is no easy task to extract the pure Jewish content of his
thinking from the trappings and intricate convolutions of
mid-nineteenth-century German thought in which it is
wrapped.

The third reason lies in Hirsch's apparent lack of nationalistic feeling. He believed in the universal mission of
the religion of Israel and in its fulfillment through the dispersal of the people of Israel. He believed that the Jewish
people, by living an exemplary life, could bring the nations
of the world to realize the truth of the Jewish faith and
long to attain it. This belief in the universal mission of the
Jewish people in the Diaspora and in the passive hope of
bringing the Redeemer through righteous conduct (rather
than by active participation in the attainment of political

independence of the nation) is expressed in the sixteenth of his *Nineteen Letters*.[2] There he says: "Land and soil were never Israel's bond of union, but only the common task of the Torah; therefore [Israel] still forms a united body, though separated from a national soil; nor does this unity lose its reality, though Israel accepts everywhere the citizenship of the nations among which it is dispersed. This coherence of sympathy, this spiritual union, which may be designated by the Hebrew terms *'am'* and *'goy,'* but not by the expression 'nation'—unless we are able to separate from the term the concept of common territory and political power—is the only communal bond we possess, or ever expect to possess, until the great day shall arrive when the Almighty shall see fit, in His inscrutable wisdom, to unite again His scattered servants in one land, and the Torah shall be the guiding principle of a state, an exemplar of the meaning of Divine revelation and the mission of humanity.

"For this future, which is promised us in the glorious predictions of the inspired prophets, whom God raised up for our ancestors, we hope and pray; but actively to accelerate its coming is a sin, and is prohibited to us, while the entire purpose of the Messianic age is that we may, in prosperity, exhibit to mankind a better example of 'Israel' than did our ancestors the first time, while, hand in hand with us, mankind will be joined in universal brotherhood through the recognition of God, the ALL-ONE."

Undoubtedly Hirsch cannot be numbered among the supporters of the national ideal in its politico-secular meaning, or among the *Chovevei Zion,* whose ideas were nur-

[2] Hirsch, *The Nineteen Letters of Ben Uziel,* trans. Dr. B. Drachman, 1899.

tured in the spiritual climate of Eastern European Jewry. His idealism was a religious and not a nationalistic one. Hirsch exalted the Jewish faith above other faiths, thought of it as the "religion of religions," and, like the author of the *Kuzari,* considered the people of Israel as endowed with a religious capacity fundamentally different from that of other peoples. This point is clearly brought out in Rabbi Y. Y. Weinberg's article on Hirsch, in which he says: "Rabbi Hirsch, whose essential thought was to regard the Jewish people as the axis around which all world history revolves, must be deemed as an extreme nationalist in heart and spirit, a religio-ethical rather than a secular nationalist." [3]

II

Hirsch's thought has many facets, reflected in a literary production that is vast and many-sided. He excelled as an original commentator on the Pentateuch, the Psalms, and the Prayer Book. He added greatly to our understanding of the meaning of the Biblical commandments. His observations on symbolism in Judaism are embodied in two substantial essays as well as in his commentary to the Pentateuch (but have not yet received their rightful evaluation and appreciation). Moreover, he was also a man of action, and while he was Rabbi of Nikolsburg, Moravia, from 1848 to 1851, he helped to further the cause of equality of rights for the Jews. He worked for the unification of all Jewish communities of Moravia and the creation of a single organization to which they were to belong. Later, when he was Rabbi in Frankfurt, he fought successfully for an inde-

[3] *"Deoth," The Journal of Religious Academic Youth,* No. 40, 1959.

pendent organization of the Orthodox Jewish communities in Germany. But his greatest contribution was in the field of education. He was a noted educational philosopher as well as a practicing pedagogue, acting as headmaster of what was then a unique school. It was there that his influence was most felt, and that influence has, to some extent, continued until the present.

The greatest problem he had to face was how to integrate Jewish and European culture, how to effect a relationship between sacred and secular studies in the school. This problem can be seen clearly only when the historical position of post-Emancipation European Jewry is known.

This Emancipation came suddenly and found Jewry unprepared. Whereas in Christian society the process of secularization had been a long one and the change from a religious to a secular culture had taken hundreds of years, the Jews had to adapt themselves to the change in a very few years. When the gates of the ghetto were opened they found it difficult to accustom themselves to the cultural, social, free-thinking life of the countries in which they lived. They failed to grasp the character of such a culture, for it was alien to them, and acclimatization to the new way of life was an arduous process. How was the continued existence of Judaism to be ensured in this new environment? The greatest stumbling block to integration with the strange community was the Jewish religion itself, which "ordained a different speech, a different dress, different food, different ways of rejoicing and mourning, and different mode of thought. The Jew was far more Jewish than the Christian was Christian." [4]

[4] Wiener, *Die Juedische Religion im Zeitalter der Emanzipation* (Berlin: Philo Verlag, 1933), p. 7.

Judaism as practiced in the ghettos was no longer viable, and so there arose the question of how to adapt it, if it was to continue to exist at all, to the changed conditions. Reform circles tried to establish what they thought to be the essence of Judaism, and chose the historical method as a means of distinguishing between what they called the "spiritual content" of Judaism and what had been grafted on Judaism by accident of historical circumstance. They regarded as a disturbing element not only the dress and language of the Jews but also those positive statutes which became difficult of fulfillment in an alien environment and whose very right to existence seemed to them dubious. From such sources sprang their opposition to Jewish laws dealing with man's relationship to God, and their antagonism to the Talmud and the Rabbinic interpretation of Judaism.

Hirsch chose a completely different solution. Like Rabbi Yehuda Halevi, he accepted the Torah as a fact as "real as heaven and earth," a creation analogous to nature itself. This analogy of Torah and nature was developed in the eighteenth of his *Letters*: "A word here concerning the true method of Torah-investigation. Two revelations are open before us, Nature and Torah. In Nature all phenomena stand before us as indisputable facts, and we can only endeavor *a posteriori* to ascertain the law of each and the connection of all. Abstract demonstration of the truth or, rather, the probability of theoretic explanations of the facts of Nature, is an unnatural proceeding. The right method is to verify our assumptions by the known facts, and the highest attainable degree of certainty is to say, 'The facts agree with our assumption'—that is, all observed phenomena can be explained according to our theory. A single contradictory phenomenon will make our theory untenable. We must, therefore, acquire all possible knowledge concerning the object of our investigation, and know it, if possible, in its totality. If, however, all efforts should fail in disclosing the inner law and connection of phenomena revealed to us as facts of Nature, the facts remain nevertheless undeniable and cannot be reasoned away. The same principles must be applied to the investigation of the Torah. In the Torah, as in Nature, God is the ultimate cause; in the Torah, as in Nature, no fact may be denied, even though the reason and the connection may not be comprehended; as in Nature, so in the Torah the traces of Divine wisdom must ever be sought for. Its ordinances must be accepted in their entirety as undeniable phenomena, and must be studied in accordance with their connection with each other and the subject to which they relate. Our conjectures must be tested by their precepts, and our highest certainty here also can only be that everything stands in harmony with our theory. But, as in Nature, the phenomena are recognized as facts, though their cause and relation to each other may not be understood, are independent of our investigation, and, rather, seem to be contrary to our understanding; in the same way the ordinances of the Torah must be law for us, even if we do not comprehend the reason and the purpose of a single one. Our fulfillment of the commandments must not depend upon our investigations."

To this analogy of nature and Torah must be added a second point essential to our understanding of the fundamentals of Hirsch's outlook—the relationship between Judaism and history. We have mentioned that the Reformists of his time, such as Geiger, Frankel, and Holdheim, used the historical criterion as a means of adapting the Jewish faith to the post-Emancipation conditions of life. Hirsch opposed this historical approach to Judaism because he rejected the view that Judaism was subject to the historical process. Nathan Rottenstreich explains this position in the following way: "Hirsch thought it possible to save the [Judaic] legal order, which is innately static and not easily altered, from the corrosive action of the historical process. The legal sphere is one where permanent features are more prominent than transient ones, where the enduring has sway over the mutable. The preference for law over doctrine and faith reflects a certain conception of the essence of Judaism. . . . Preference for Jewish Law reflects a tendency to withdraw the true essence of Judaism from the historical process, posing it incontrovertibly as divinely revealed and an eternal statute." [5]

In his critical survey of Samson Raphael Hirsch's *Nineteen Letters,* Geiger vehemently rejects the analogy of Torah and nature. "Hirsch surely cannot seriously believe," writes Geiger, "that his apodictic statement that Torah is as factually real as heaven and earth expresses an alternative theory to the historical proof. In this way, all religions could attribute absolute authority to the books on which they base their ideas, such as the Koran and the Gospels. How can one compare Torah to Nature when the latter is a lofty and incomprehensible creation which cannot be examined exhaustively, whose beginning and end are difficult to grasp, and which stands above the powers of man? On the other hand, Torah is a book intended solely for us and is subject to the historical process; its age

[5] Nathan Rottenstreich, *Ha'Machshavah Ha'Yehudit B'eit Ha'Chadashah,* (Tel Aviv: 1945) I, *"Am Oved,"* 115.

can be estimated accurately." Geiger concludes this paragraph of criticism with the words: "For goodness sake, what an error have we here! May God save Israel from such a spirit!"

In view of such a profound difference of opinion over so basic a matter, any further discussion between Hirsch and Geiger would have been fruitless and a compromise between the two views unlikely. In Hirsch's opinion, it was impossible to adjust Judaism to the spirit of the times; he believed that the Torah was a criterion by which we should assess the ideas of the times and reject that which failed to measure up to the Torah's lofty Divine spirit.

In order to develop more clearly his religious attitude and give it a firm theological basis, Hirsch considered it necessary to evaluate critically Mendelssohn's philosophy of Judaism. This was essential, since Mendelssohn's philosophy, accepted by many Western European Jews, appeared dangerous to Hirsch, and this danger became greater as Mendelssohn's ideas passed to his pupils and to those who continued his work. Hirsch's criticism of Mendelssohn was expressed in the eighteenth of his *Letters* in these words: "This commanding individual—who had not drawn his mental development from Judaism, who was great chiefly in philosophical disciplines, in metaphysics, and esthetics, who treated the Bible only philologically and esthetically, and did not build up Judaism as a science from itself but merely defended it against political stupidity and pietistic Christian audacity, and who was personally an observant Jew—accomplished this much, that he showed the world and his brethren that it was possible to be a strictly religious Jew and yet to shine distinguished as the German Plato.

"This 'and yet' was decisive. His followers contented themselves with developing Bible study in the philologic-esthetic sense, with studying the *Guide,* and with pursuing and spreading humanistic letters; but Judaism, Bible, and Talmud, as Jewish science, were neglected. Even the most zealous study of the Bible was of no avail for the comprehension of Judaism, because it was not treated as the authoritative source of doctrine and instruction but only as a beautiful poetic storehouse from which to draw rich supplies for the fancy and the imagination. The Talmud thus neglected, practical Judaism thus completely uncomprehended, it was but natural that the former symbolizing and abstract interpretation of Judaism, which had for a time been interrupted, again became prevalent and was carried to an extreme which threatened to destroy all Judaism." [6]

Four things, then, are clear: 1) Hirsch found fault with Mendelssohn's main preoccupation with the general philosophies and his neglect of specific Jewish thought; 2) according to Hirsch, Mendelssohn developed Judaism not in an immanent spirit, but from without—that is, from the viewpoint of the general rationalist philosophies; 3) what really angered Hirsch was Mendelssohn's excessive desire to excel as an eminent German philosopher while remaining a practicing Jew; 4) the Talmud was neglected by Mendelssohn, and his followers no longer saw in it an authoritative source of Jewish doctrine.

Mendelssohn was one of the last philosophers to believe that it was possible to prove theological and metaphysical truths as rationally as mathematical ones. Mendelssohn admitted that metaphysical truth is more complicated and harder to grasp than the laws and theorems of mathematics,

[6] Hirsch, *The Nineteen Letters of Ben Uziel,* pp. 190-91.

but he believed that metaphysical truth is equally universal and immutable. Mendelssohn, therefore, denied that there is a specific faith for the Jewish people, confirmed, as it were, by Divine revelation, because faith, according to Mendelssohn, is based on reason, and reason is universal and common to all men. Hirsch's criticism of Mendelssohn for considering Judaism not from a Jewish but from a universal standpoint, is, I think, understandable and justified.

Whereas Mendelssohn preserved, as a historical legacy of Sinai, the validity of the practical commandments, which he regarded as the essence of Judaism, we cannot deny that by his insistence on the commandments alone and by his neglect of the peculiar faith that inspired them he narrowed the concept of Judaism. This caused a dichotomy in his Jewish outlook, a split which became a danger for those who followed him. He was a Jew in that he complied with the commandments of the Torah, but as a philosopher he belonged to the thinkers of the "Enlightenment" (*Haskalah*).

When speaking of Hirsch's attitude to the relationship of the Torah to universal culture and of the contradictions that such a comparison reveals, mention must be made of Hirsch's biting criticism of Maimonides' attitude to this same problem as expressed in Letter Eighteen: "This great man, to whom and to whom alone we owe the preservation of practical Judaism to our time, is responsible—because he sought to reconcile Judaism with the difficulties which confronted it from without, instead of developing it creatively from within—for all the good and the evil which bless and afflict the heritage of the father. His peculiar mental tendency was Arabic-Greek, and his conception of the purpose of life the same. He entered Judaism from without, bringing with him opinions of whose truth he had convinced himself from extraneous sources and which he reconciled. For him, too, self-perfection through the knowledge of truth was the highest aim; the practical he deemed subordinate. For him knowledge of God was the end, not the means; hence he devoted his intellectual powers to speculations upon the essence of Deity and sought to bind Judaism to the results of his speculative investigations as to postulates of science or faith. The *Mitzvot* became for him merely ladders, necessary only to conduct to knowledge or to protect against error, this latter often only the temporary and limited error of polytheism. *Mishpatim* became only rules of prudence, *Mitzvot* as well; *Chukkim* rules of health, teaching right feeling, defending against the transitory errors of the time; *Edot* ordinances, designed to promote philosophical or other concepts; all this having no foundation in the eternal essence of things, not resulting from their eternal demand on me, or from my eternal purpose and task, no eternal symbolizing of an unchangeable idea, and not inclusive enough to form a basis for the totality of the commandments." [7]

Two points in this criticism of Maimonides' *"Guide"* need special attention. The first is the argument that Maimonides in the *Guide* did not creatively develop Judaism from its intrinsic qualities but rather entered it from without and imposed upon it alien attitudes—in this case, the Aristotelian ideal of a contemplative life and the perfection of man through meditation upon the concept of an abstract God-head. The second point springs from the first: if the contemplative life expresses the highest value it is clear that the positive, practical side of Judaism—

[7] *Ibid.*, p. 182-3.

that is, fulfilling the commandments—is of secondary and subordinate importance. In other words, in Hirsch's opinion, there appears in the *"Guide to the Perplexed"* a kind of relativization of the commandments, whereas in Hirsch's view they have a supreme value and validity which is eternal. This is the source of Hirsch's constant demand for developing Judaism immanently, from within itself (*sich selbst begreifendes Judentum*).

Hirsch, himself an admirer of the secular intellectual environment of his time, did not object to Maimonides' and Mendelssohn's interest in non-Jewish philosophies but in the way they used them. Synthesis cannot be imposed from without, but, like a flower opening to the sun, can only be reached from within.

III

But was Orthodox European Jewry ready, in the middle of the nineteenth century, to consider the possibility of a synthesis of any kind?

Heinemann, in his introduction to the *Nineteen Letters,* sums up the antagonistic attitude of traditional Jewry to European culture in the pithy and pointed Talmudic proverb, "I want neither your sting nor your honey." This saying epitomizes the Rabbinical viewpoint from the Middle Ages down to the time of S. R. Hirsch. The following are two typical facts that exemplify this approach: 1) In the last years of Rabbi Pinhas Hurwitz, author of *Hafla'ah* (died 1805), a group of *Maskilim* in Frankfurt began to draw up a scheme for a school of secular studies which would complement the traditional education provided at *Cheder* and Talmud Torah. The children would have lessons in German, arithmetic, and French; in all, two or three hours a day. Hurwitz and his followers were bitterly opposed to this scheme, and to prevent its realization placed a ban (excommunication) on the school. The local authorities intervened on behalf of the school and declared the ban of excommunication illegal, hoping thereby to force Rabbi Hurwitz into annulling it. The Rabbi fought against this decision, and not only did he refuse to submit but complained to higher authorities about the interference of the Frankfurt Senate in internal Jewish affairs.[8]

2) Abraham Geiger relates an interesting episode from his childhood. On his becoming *Bar Mitzvah* in 1823, he delivered a discourse of a general ethical nature. The speech was delivered in German but he had to preface his address with an introduction in Yiddish, and when he began to speak German many of the people present covered their faces in shame.[9]

This was the trend when Hirsch began his activities as a Rabbi and writer. However, during the following decades the process of assimilation among German Jewry developed rapidly until, by 1851, when Hirsch came to Frankfurt, only a small remnant of the old Orthodoxy still existed. None the less, Hirsch, in spite of his zeal for European culture and his hope of attaining a synthesis of Jewish and European education in the spirit of *Torah im Derech Eretz,* did not regard this ideal as a concession to the new liberalism. He advanced his ideas as an integral part of his general outlook on Judaism. His views on this point may be summarized as follows:

[8] *The Seventy-Fifth Anniversary Book of the Hirsch School (Festschrift zum 75 jährigen Bestehen der Realschule mit Lyzeum der isr. Religionsgesellschaft* (Frankfurt a. Main: Herman Verlag, 1928), pp. 160 ff.

[9] Ludwig Geiger, *Abraham Geiger, Leben und Lebenswerk* (Berlin: Verl. Georg Reiner, 1910), p. 12.

Unlike other religions, Judaism does not only aim at raising man's spirit and directing it toward God at certain times and on set occasions. Judaism is a way of life that permeates every aspect of a man's life, deeds, and thought. In the new reality of the post-Emancipation era Jews could isolate or dissociate themselves from the prevailing intellectual climate but had nevertheless to recognize the new spiritual environment and evaluate it by the standards of the Torah. To make this evaluation demanded a profound understanding of intellectual trends in the world around them.

It is for this reason that Hirsch insisted that Jews take part in the intellectual life of the gentiles and assess every attainment by the eternal criterion of the Torah. Moreover, divinity is revealed not only in the Torah but also in nature and in history. It therefore becomes essential to study nature and, through nature, learn to worship God, since "the heavens declare the glory of God and the firmament showeth His handiwork." The influence of God in the historical process is manifested in Divine Providence revealed both in the phenomena of nature and in the history of mankind. Divinity reveals itself, too, in the spirit of man, in great works of art and literature, and in every creative activity of man. This idea lies at the root of Hirsch's *Torah im Derech Eretz* conception. Hence his reverence for cultural phenomena, his readiness to study the arts and sciences, and to be impressed by them. Thus Hirsch introduced a fresh note into the *Ashkenazi* (German-Jewish) intellectual climate of his time.

Still, we must admit that Hirsch occasionally weakened his position by explaining, as he does, that his principle of *Torah im Derech Eretz* requires the sciences to be taught at school only as aids to a clearer understanding of the Torah and *Halachah* (*Hilfswissenschaft*). For example, in his commentary on the verse in Chapter 18 of Leviticus ("Mine ordinances shall ye do, and My statutes shall ye keep, to walk therein, I am the Lord your God"), Hirsch, citing *Torat Kohanim,* states that the seemingly superfluous words "to walk therein" point to a special emphasis— " 'to walk therein': to make them the main aim and not the subordinate one; *to absorb oneself wholly in them and not mix other things with them;* that you do not say, 'I have learned the wisdom of Israel, now I shall learn the wisdom of the world.' Therefore, it says 'to walk therein'—you are not permitted to release yourself from them at all." It seems as if this statement completely negates the study of the sciences and, if so, would refute Hirsch's attitude. But his ingenious exegesis to eliminate the apparent contradiction itself emphasizes Hirsch's perspective: if it says "that to do them is the main and not the subordinate aim," it follows that it was not the studying of foreign wisdom that was forbidden but absorbing oneself in it to the exclusion of all else. Thus, Hirsch finds a logical basis for regarding sciences as subsidiary—that is, as an aid to a profounder understanding of the Torah.

This passage represents a rather narrow conception of the relationship between Torah and world culture—a conception that hardly appears representative of the man when we study the rest of his writings on this subject. Looking at his work as a whole, one can hardly doubt that it reflects a new emphasis on general culture as a vital complement to Judaism. His articles on this subject reveal an enthusiasm for Western literature and culture that is not to be found in other traditional Jewish thinkers. Many examples of this enthusiasm can be found in his writings. One especially impressive one is his speech given at the Hirsch School on the occasion of the fiftieth anniversary of Schiller's birth.

Schiller's poetry, said Hirsch, is permeated with true idealism. His belief in liberty, fraternity, and the rule of justice springs from a definitely religious outlook. Hirsch wondered greatly at this, and blessed Schiller in the traditional formula, "Blessed be He who allows other men to partake of His wisdom." He saw an echo of the Hebrew prophets in Schiller's poetic work and rejoiced at this. It is very possible that his optimistic attitude toward contemporary German idealism sprang from his appreciation of the post-Emancipation era, which he regarded as the "Beginning of Redemption" not only for Israel but also for all the people of the world.

Some interpreters of Hirsch look upon him as a thinker whose main achievement was the rehabilitation of ancient Judaism rather than a novel and revolutionary interpretation of it. It all depends whether he is viewed against the background of medieval or premedieval Judaism. Rabbi Grunfeld says on this point: "If anything had been forced on the Jew, it was not his adherence to, but his exclusion from, general culture and education. When at the beginning of the nineteenth century the Jews again found their way into the world of science and general education they came in reality back to their own. For the estrangement was not organic but superimposed. It had by no means arisen from the essential character of Judaism. Just the contrary was true, as the golden eras of Jewish history in Babylonia and Spain had shown. In those eras the highest Talmudic and general scientific efficiency were combined.

Apart from the enormous support which the study of Torah, *Mishnah,* and Talmud receives from secular knowledge, the whole task of the Jew as a servant of God in this world depends on his insight into the natural historical and social conditions around him." [10]

This same point is made by Rabbi Weinberg in the article mentioned previously. In his opinion, at the time of the *Tannaim,* the *Amoraim,* the *Gaonim* of Babylon, and the Golden Age of Spain, Judaism embraced every facet of intellectual and spiritual life. The change came at the time of the Crusades. Only as a result of persecution, atrocities, and the restriction of liberty of movement did there appear spiritual isolation and segregation. So that Weinberg, too, does not regard Hirsch as a revolutionary innovator but as one who continued the tradition of premedieval Judaism.

IV

He also worked in the field of practical education, founding the archetype of the Modern Orthodox Jewish school. The founding of a Jewish school in Frankfurt was, for him, so important a task that he even postponed the building of a central synagogue until this school was built. The school was built in 1853, and was destroyed by the Nazis before the Second World War. It was of the *Realschule* type, with preparatory classes and a high school for girls. Statistics of the years 1903-1925 show little variation in the number of pupils, which ran from five to six hundred.

Hirsch at first found it a heartbreaking task to persuade parents to send their children to him, and the problem of

[10] Hirsch, *Judaism Eternal,* ed. Rabbi I. Grunfeld, I, 26-27.

the upkeep of the school worried him as much as the search for pupils. The aim of the school was to integrate Jewish religious studies with the normal curriculum of "realistic" high schools in Germany. Many people mistrusted this aim and had no faith in its success. The old-type Orthodox Jews looked askance at the secular studies, whereas the assimilated Jews feared that the emphasis on religious studies would detract from the secular subjects. Hirsch had literally to go from house to house and beg the parents to send their children to him. In the first year only the less talented children were sent, for the parents did not want to experiment with their more able children. In 1881 the school moved into the fine building donated by Karl von Rothschild. This building did not fall below the standard of other high schools of that time, and its furniture and equipment were of a high standard. Hebrew studies occupied two to three hours and the rest of the time was devoted to secular studies. The secular studies were also imbued with a Jewish spirit in the sense that they were taught from a Jewish point of view. For instance, in German lessons, literature with Biblical associations was chosen for study. Lessing's dramas reflecting his tolerant and broad outlook on matters of religion were read. The integration of national consciousness and humanism in the works of Herder was especially valued. In non-German literature, too, preference was given to those works which portrayed Jewish characters; and their historical and social background was clearly demonstrated. The question of what was "the attitude of the Torah" toward various literary problems was frequently discussed. The esthetic value of this approach might be doubtful, but its educational value was great, for it was as Jews that the students read and evaluated the literary masterpieces of Christian culture. History and science were taught from a religious point of view and divergences between science and the Orthodox Jewish attitude to the world were considered and discussed. The aim was not to teach the Jewish and secular subjects separately but to demonstrate their relationship. Thus the teacher tried to foster in his pupils a fine Jewish outlook based on a profound grasp of Judaism. This explains the fact that so many pupils remained Orthodox after leaving the school.

Articles by pupils, appearing in various publications commemorating the Jubilees of the school, give personal accounts of Hirsch's work as headmaster. His lessons on Jewish subjects greatly impressed his pupils. They listened to his lessons on Torah with intense concentration and even awe. He was not content with explaining the written word of the Bible but chose passages to illustrate the development of the spiritual world of Judaism. One of his pupils writes that for a whole term Hirsch taught no more than Chapter 12 of Exodus. The emphasis lay on quality and not quantity. The article of another pupil throws light on Hirsch's relations to his students. The pupil tells of an interview with the headmaster. As the representative of his class he had come on rather a daring venture—to request an afternoon off so that the class could go skating. Permission was most unexpectedly granted and in order not to favor one class above another Hirsch gave the whole school a half holiday! In summer when the pupils went swimming in the river Main they would call on him at his home beside the river for a friendly chat. Stories such as these illustrate the friendly nature of his relations with his pupils.

The teaching of Hebrew as a literary, as opposed to a

spoken language, held an honored place in Hirsch's plans. He believed that Hebrew as a language had an innate value that was not to be found in other languages. Whereas the words of other languages are results of accidental connotations, Hebrew words, being derived from a relatively limited number of roots, reveal logical relations and reasoned analogies, and thus display the creative spirit in which Hebrew apprehends the objects. Hebrew etymology, in his opinion, is the essence of ideas on man and nature. He held that Hebrew words are not the result of the accidental or biased impressions of the senses but bear the stamp of lucid and logical relations. Every Hebrew word, he believed, conveys an explicit idea or conception. He regarded the Hebrew language as a means of developing intelligence and preciseness of thought. Its educational value was therefore greater than that of any other language. He gives many examples of Hebrew words whose common root or similarity of sound indicate some inner relations (*Lautverwandtschaft*).

I have doubts as to whether this evaluation of the superiority of the Hebrew language as a means for thought expression can stand up to criticism. There is no contemporary Jewish educationist who would claim that the study of Hebrew as a language has educational and intellectual values not to be obtained from the study of other languages. It is more reasonable to suppose that Hirsch attributed to the Hebrew language a mystical quality such as our sages believed in; that is, that "the Hebrew letters enlighten and give wisdom." This is only additional proof of Rabbi Weinberg's estimation of Hirsch as an extreme religious nationalist.

At Hirsch's school Talmud was studied in the original,

without abridgments or omissions; *Gemara* and Rashi were taught without *Tosafot.* The simplicity of the teaching and the avoidance of any forced interpretations undoubtedly sprang from the attitude of the founder, who himself had taught in that fashion. Under Hirsch's guidance the Bible was studied with all the modern paraphernalia of dictionaries and Concordance, which did not please the old-fashioned students of Torah in Nikolsburg. They said that before Hirsch came Jews studied *Gemara* and recited Psalms, but that since his arrival they recited *Gemara* and studied Psalms.

Hirsch valued general studies as much as Jewish studies, and gave them both equal attention. Later on, secular studies took by far the larger part, but that was because the school was recognized by the government and had, therefore, to show the same number of hours for general studies as any other *Realschule* in the country.

V

The influence of Hirsch's school on Orthodox education throughout the Diaspora is very considerable and was felt outside German Jewry. Twenty-five years ago, Rabbi Avigdor Shonfeld founded the first Jewish Day School in London based on Hirsch's principles. This school has been very successful and has gradually become a nucleus of a wide network of Jewish schools that constitute a strong Jewish factor in the pattern of Anglo-Jewry. Anglo-Jewry has a long tradition of Jewish Day Schools, of which the first was founded as long ago as 1780, but the schools founded by Rabbi Shonfeld are entirely different from the old type. The Anglo-Jewish school in the eighteenth and nineteenth centuries emphasized mainly secular studies and Jewish studies were given only very restricted attention. The aim was to Anglicize the children of immigrants from Eastern Europe, whereas the Shonfeld schools aimed at Jewish religious education in accordance with Hirsch's principle of *Torah im Derech Eretz.*

Education based on the principles of Samson Raphael Hirsch proved itself a potent means of preserving Judaism in an alien environment and an important instrument for waging war on Jewish assimilation. It is fitting to note in this connection that German Jewry drew the strength for its continued existence from within itself, without encouragement, spur, or aid emanating from the rest of world Jewry.

Hirsch's influence is easily recognized in religious schools in Israel, many of which were founded according to Hirsch's theories.

Two main influences are noticeable in religious education in the State of Israel. One is the influence deriving from Hirsch; the other from the Hebrew schools founded by Mizrachi in Eastern Europe—the *"Yavneh* schools," which were the religious counterparts of the Hebrew *"Tarbut* schools"; these religious schools were based on religio-national principles, with the addition of "general humanistic features." The term "general humanistic features" was defined by the founders of these schools as "elementary practical subjects which afford some kind of preparation for life." It is clear that this aim differs from that of Hirsch, who laid the foundations for an education equally divided between Jewish religious and general humanistic principles. The *Yavneh* schools, unlike Hirsch, regarded the "general humanistic" element as merely an additional or supplementary factor in the basic religio-national education, which was their major aim. Moreover, in the programmatic declaration of the founders of *Yavneh* the general humanistic element acquires a vocational bias. In other words, the founders made secular education compulsory only so far as it could be used for "preparation for life," and not, as Hirsch envisioned it, as a pure educational principle and matter of educational policy. This trend has strengthened its hold on religious schools in Israel and this is reflected in the decline of the religious high school and expansion of secondary Yeshivot, which are altogether inclined to minimize the importance of secular teaching, leaving it to the afternoon or evening hours and restricting its scope to the bare minimum demanded by the matriculation syllabus of the "Torah trend." This fact reveals a departure from Hirsch's outlook and reflects the present isolationist tendency of religious Jewry.

One of the greatest *Halachists* of our time expressed the reason for this turning away from Hirsch's teachings in the following words: "Germany in its decline cannot be compared with Israel in her upbuilding and rebirth." [11] This terse statement clearly indicates the attitude of a certain section of Israel's Orthodoxy to the educational policy of S. R. Hirsch. They regard *Torah im Derech Eretz* as historically justified as an emergency measure which had to be taken in view of the complete disruption of the Orthodox Jewish communities following the post-Emancipation era. Present-day Israel, however, is a different matter. There the fitting educational ideal is Torah only, without

[11] Rabbi Chaim Ozer Grodzenski, in a private letter to Rabbi Yaakov Yechiel Weinberg at the time of the discussions on the proposed moving of the Seminary for Orthodox Rabbis from Berlin to Israel.

the addition of general culture. This at least is the view of many present day representative Rabbinical scholars of Israel, whose attitude, though not unchallenged even within the Orthodox fold, carries a great deal of influence.

The importance of Hirsch lies exactly in the fact that he believed in the possibility of a fusion of Torah and general culture, not as a compromise and emergency measure but as an integral part of the Jewish *Weltanschauung*. His conception of Judaism has as great a future in Israel as in the Diaspora.

We need not expect that in Israel the isolationist trend in religious education will remain as strong as it is at present. There are definite signs that religious educators are becoming readier than ever before to accept Hirschian ideas. The existence of a religious University in Ramat Gan proves the vitality of the Hirschian conception even in the sphere of higher education. The younger generation of Orthodox Jews in Israel are desirous of taking their rightful place in all walks of life, including the free professions. This desire can only be fulfilled if their education aims at a synthesis between Jewish culture and secular learning. Hirsch's religious and educational philosophy affords the best vehicle for the complete integration of religious Jewry in the modern state of Israel.

3

Rabbi Israel Salanter and the Mussar Movement

I

The *Mussar* (ethical self-perfection) movement, which originated in Lithuania in the middle of the nineteenth century, is associated with the name of Rabbi Israel Lipkin-Salanter, though it would not be true to history to regard him as its sole initiator. Many of its ideas had already been conceived by the *Gaon* of Vilna, and its ideals were embodied in the life of Rabbi Israel's teacher, the saintly Rabbi Zundel of Salant. In a wider sense, Rabbi Israel was preceded by a long line of Jewish moralists of medieval and modern times, the best known of whom are Bachya ibn Pakuda, author of *Chovoth ha'Levavoth* (*The Duties of the Heart*), Gabirol, who wrote *Tikun Midat ha'Nefesh* (*Reform of Human Qualities*), Rabbi Jonah of Gerondi, author of *Sha'arei Tshuvah* (*Gates of Repentance*), and, in the middle of the eighteenth century, Rabbi Moshe Hayim Luzzato, whose *Mesilat Yesharim* (*Path of the Upright*) has been translated into English by Mordecai M. Kaplan.

When comparing Rabbi Salanter and his work with the earlier Jewish moralists three striking differences are immediately discernible. Firstly, the earlier moralists, despite the influence they exercised, never became the heads of

71

what may be termed a movement of *Mussar*. Secondly, whereas the earlier Jewish moralists are known mainly from their books, which have become the sole instruments for the dissemination of their ideas, it is the inspiring personality and living example of Rabbi Israel Salanter which impressed itself upon his disciples and those who came under his influence. The posthumous publication by his disciples of some of their notes on homilies and other talks on *Mussar* delivered by him, as well as private letters addressed to themselves, helped to create a new *Mussar* literature which sustained the movement and spread its ideas. Thirdly, whereas the earlier moralists had presented their writings in a more or less systematic way, Rabbi Israel Salanter's *Mussar* teachings have an incidental character, and are often interspersed with homilies and exegetical interpretations of various Biblical passages and Rabbinical sayings. This fact makes it difficult for the modern reader who is used to a systematic presentation of subject matter to follow the thread of his thought. On the other hand, Rabbi Israel Salanter's incidental presentation of *Mussar* goes back to an older tradition of Jewish teachers who linked organically all reflections on philosophy and world outlook with the classical sources of Judaism. We discern in Salanter's writings a wonderful unity of thought which is characterized by his unwillingness to detach himself from Holy Writ and its *Halachic* and *Agadic* interpretation. His "*Mussar* talks" are an incidental fruit of his preoccupation with Torah.

The emergence of a movement which emphasized the ethical content of Judaism was favored by two historical factors. The first was the rise of *Chassidism*, which swept through most of the Jewish communities of Eastern Europe, without, however, being accepted by Lithuanian Jewry. There are historians who tend to attribute this fact to the resistance of the *Gaon* of Vilna, the chief opponent of the *Chassidic* movement. This however, is only a partial explanation of this peculiar phenomenon. The powerful movement of *Chassidism* could not have been halted by the influence of one man alone, however towering his personality, unless Lithuanian Jewry itself had displayed certain characteristics from which the opposition to *Chassidism* could emanate. Rabbi J. Weinberg, in an essay published in the former German monthly *Yeshurun* gives a very full account of these characteristics. He points to the sober rationalism of Lithuanian Jewry, their obstinate clinging to the simple *Halachic* interpretation of Jewish teaching, and their opposition to mystical speculation. They looked askance at the powerful upsurge of feeling and enthusiasm which the *Chassidic* movement had engendered, its indulgence in ecstatic outbursts of emotion which sometimes brought them into conflict with the minute day-to-day regulations of *Halacha*. Nor did they approve of the peculiar relationship between the Chassidic rabbis and their followers, whose devotion to them very often bordered on hero worship. Finally, the Lithuanian Jew was essentially an individualist, and did not relish the idea of seeing his ego submerged in the collective personality of a group.

On the other hand, the emergence of *Chassidism* as a religious movement, aiming at a renewal of Judaism, acted as a challenge to Lithuanian Jewry and led to a reappraisal of their traditional way of life. In a way, the emergence of the *Mussar* movement was the result of such a critical reappraisal, as will be shown later.

At the same time, the Jewish *Haskalah* movement,

emanating from Berlin with Mendelssohn and Weisel at its head, spread throughout the Eastern Europe communities and received support from the Russian authorities, who were interested in assimilating the Jews with a view to their eventual conversion to Christianity. The *Haskalah* movement acted as a further challenge, calling for a critical re-examination of traditional Judaism and its essential values. By its very nature, it led the Jew out into the world, endeavored to diminish his specifically Jewish traits, and transform him into a citizen of the world. This trend was countered by Rabbi Israel Salanter, who led the Jew back to Judaism and made him aware of its profound ethical content.

The teaching of Rabbi Israel Salanter does not demand the submission of the individual to the authority of a leader. On the contrary, by its rigorous demand for the individual's self-perfection through his own intellectual and spiritual efforts, it has, unlike *Chassidism,* made the individual self-reliant and enhanced his dignity and worth. Salanter's followers, far from submerging their individuality in the collective personality of the group, were most anxious to preserve and cultivate it.

Viewed against the background of his time, Rabbi Israel Salanter strikes a new note by accentuating the importance of *Mussar* without which, in his view, no Jew can ever acquire a full measure of "fear of Heaven" nor attain the spirituality that preoccupation with *Mussar* alone can give. His urgent insistence on the study of *Mussar* as the prerequisite of higher Jewish education implies a twofold criticism of current notions concerning Judaism. First, it expresses his belief in the insufficiency of Talmud as the sole and all-inclusive medium of Jewish education. More important still, his urgent insistence on the study of *Mussar* stems from his deep conviction that the undue accentuation of the Commandments concerning our relation to God and the neglect of that sphere of Judaism which deals with the relation between man and man has led to an impoverishment and a distortion of Judaism. Rabbi Israel Salanter says expressly: "In our country—Lithuania—the average Jew has trained himself in the observance of the dietary laws to such an extent, that without any effort he not only abstains from the use of prohibited food, but even abhors it. On the other hand, dishonesty in commercial relations is a frequent occurrence. Many do not trouble themselves to find out whether their dealings with their fellow-men are always honest, and not a few will even attempt to cover up their dishonest actions when they are found out. Now when we ask, how does it happen that the ceremonial law is automatically observed at great sacrifice of comfort and money, while the ethical law is often disregarded—a sin for which according to the Rabbis, neither the Day of Atonement nor death can atone—we can give only this answer. The long training of the Jew, theoretically and practically, in the observance of the dietary laws has had the result that in following his own nature, he feels an abhorrence for everything ritually unclean, while the ethical teachings of the Torah theoretically never formed such an important part of the body of Jewish studies as the dietary laws, and practically did not offer themselves as an exercise in virtue but as something convenient and useful. This, however, is to be greatly regretted; the ethical teachings of the Torah are a most important part thereof, and in practical life we must train ourselves so that we may no longer obey the dicta of morality reluctantly as a severe rule, but that we may follow them with the natural bent of our desires." [1]

This passage is important because it shows that it was Rabbi Israel Salanter's ardent desire that the ethical precepts of Judaism penetrate the soul of the Jew so deeply that their fulfillment becomes almost instinctual.

It is interesting to note that the activities of Rabbi Israel Salanter in the field of Jewish education were the result of a "call" that came to him by his saintly teacher, Rabbi Zundel. Rabbi Israel had followed Rabbi Zundel one day as the latter was walking in the woods, seeking solitude. When Rabbi Zundel became aware of his pupil's presence he turned round and called to him; "Israel, study *Mussar*, and you will become a God-fearing man." This experience made a deep impression upon the soul of Rabbi Israel Salanter, and he later related that when he had heard the voice of his teacher it "entered like a flash of lightning into the innermost depths of his heart."

This incident is interesting because it bears the mark of a sudden conversion and awareness of a mission. Such a phenomenon is essentially a disturbance of the psychic equilibrium, as a result of which the soul ascends to higher levels of consciousness. An experience of this kind is characteristic of the mystic. Later we shall return to this point and present further evidence of a strong mystical strain in the character and teaching of Rabbi Israel Salanter.

This "call" constituted a turning point in Rabbi Israel Salanter's life, which was subsequently renowned for its saintliness. Three well-known stories that follow illustrate Rabbi Israel's saintly character. The first one tells of the

[1] Salanter, *Even Israel* (Jerusalem: 1954), pp. 58-59. The quotation from *Even Israel* appears here in the very free paraphrasing of Louis Ginzberg, in his *Students, Scholars and Saints* (Philadelphia: Jewish Publication Society), pp. 176-77.

Rabbi, on his way to the *Kol Nidrei* service on the eve of
Yom Kippur (The Day of Atonement), passing by a house
from which there issued the bitter crying of a child. Rabbi
Israel went inside, and found that the baby's little sister,
who had been left to watch it, had fallen asleep. He thereupon soothed the baby and stayed with it until the parents
returned from the synagogue, thus voluntarily absenting
himself from the most solemn and important religious
service of the whole year. On another occasion, when Rabbi
Israel was a guest at a meal, it was noticed that he used only
an extremely small amount of water for the traditional
netilat yadaim (washing the hands before a meal). When
questioned by his host, Rabbi Israel explained that he had
observed the maid carrying the water from a great distance
and felt that a person's meticulous observance of a *mitzvah*
(commandment) should not be allowed to impose hardship
on a fellow human being. On yet another occasion, during
the preparation of *Matzah Shmurah*, the special *matzoth*
which are baked under strict supervision, to ensure that
there is no fermentation during any part of the preparation, he enjoined his followers not to harass the poor
widow who was kneading the dough but to let her work in
peace.

In the practical pursuit of his aim to make the ethical
teaching of Judaism a pervasive force in everyday life Rabbi
Israel Salanter introduced into *Yeshiva* (Talmudical College) education two new features which at first glance do
not appear revolutionary at all. Firstly, he demanded from
his disciples that they devote one hour daily to the study
of the classics of *Mussar* literature, as he believed that our
moral sensitiveness becomes sharpened by the daily study
of ethical writings. Secondly, he suggested that his disciples

study the *Hoshen Mishpat,* for preoccupation with civil
law which is concerned with the rights and duties of man to
man would develop their sense of justice and make them
more scrupulous in their dealings with their fellow-men.

II

Mussar presupposes introspection and contemplation and
aims at developing the human faculty for critical self-analysis. It is permeated by a deep concern for the mind and the
soul, whose welfare is accorded the same importance as the
health of the body. Characteristic in this respect is an autobiographical remark in his *Igeret ha'Mussar* (*Letter of
Mussar*), where Rabbi Israel Salanter speaks of his opposition to *Pilpul* (casuistry) in the study of the Talmud. As a
youth he had decided to give up *Pilpul* and concentrate
only on the plain, straightforward interpretation of Talmudic texts. But then he realized that his desire to show
the strength of his intellect had become too strong and
threatened to ". . . sweep away the fence of truth. And so
I said to myself, it is better for me to indulge in *Pilpul* and
thus free myself from the shackles of the *Yetzer* [evil in-
clinations]." [2] This indicates that he accepted what, according to Jung, is the "shadow" of a man's personality, and
endeavored to appease it in a harmless way, in order to free
himself from the bondage of an evil inclination.

The writings of Rabbi Israel Salanter show a peculiar
tendency to analyze the springs of human conduct and
probe into the nature of sin. When the author of *Hafetz
Hayim* had brought out his famous book on *Lashon Harah*
(malicious gossip), Rabbi Salanter warmly welcomed its

[2] *Ibid.,* p. 61.

publication and expressed the view that such books should be written on each one of man's sinful inclinations, because "every human quality represents a complete field of study and without such study we remain ignorant of the true motives of human behavior."

It goes without saying that Rabbi Israel Salanter's accentuation of the ethical teachings of Judaism does not imply a critical attitude to the dogmatic basis of *Halachah*, as was wrongly supposed by the spokesmen of the *Haskalah* movement of his time, who saw in him a "progressive" man who might be won over for their ideas. They went so far as to offer him the post of principal of a Jewish theological seminary which was to be opened in Vilna with the support of the Russian government and run on progressive lines. As Rabbi Israel Salanter had no desire to accept this offer and was embarrassed by the pressure brought to bear upon him to accept it, he decided to leave Vilna and settled in Kovno.

On principle, he does not seem to have opposed the study of secular sciences. There is evidence in his writings of his own reading in the philosophical and psychological literature of his time. Apart from his distrust of the true intentions of Czar Nicholas I, his main objection to the establishment of a modern Rabbinical seminary in Vilna was based on his conviction that a Rabbi could not be expected to master the entire body of Jewish tradition unless he concentrated all his efforts on the study of Talmud and Codes. In a letter to the "enlightened" communal leader, Dr. Trachtenberg, in which he justifies his opposition to the establishment of the Vilna seminary, he says: "In order that a Rabbi may be able to solve properly any difficult [*Halachic*] problem which in the case of poor people may be questions impinging upon their daily lives, he must have a wide and fundamental knowledge of all the branches of Torah. He must also be inspired by deep faith and 'fear of Heaven.' I do not believe that the students of such an institution would fulfill all these requirements." [3]

In *Halachic* matters he continued in the tradition of Lithuanian scholars who were renowned for erudition, intellectual acumen, and the courage to differ, whenever they felt it was justified, from the rulings of earlier authorities. These qualities enabled Rabbi Israel Salanter to make lenient judicial decisions whenever he thought that circumstances justified it. His biographers quote many examples of his leniency in *Halachic* matters, proving his great wisdom as well as his flexibility in the application of *Halachic* principles to complex human situations.

A considerable part of Rabbi Israel Salanter's writings is devoted to the question of the efficacy of *Mussar,* i.e., its psychological influence on man. In order to clarify this point we have to summarize his doctrine of sin, which is the basis of his educational philosophy of *Mussar.*

The sinfulness of man springs from his *yetzer ha-ra* (evil inclination), which Jewish moralists have interpreted in two different ways. Some say that the *yetzer ha-ra* is the *koach ha-tum'ah* (impure spirit) which enters into man and causes him to act sinfully. Others identify it with the *koach ta'avat ha-adam* (sensual desire in man) that often makes him mistake momentary pleasure for the true good which he ought to pursue. Rabbi Israel Salanter accepts both interpretations and considers them complementary; for, he argues, *koach ta'avat ha-adam* does not account for

[3] Salanter, quoted by Rabbi Dov Katz, *Tenuath Ha'mussar* (Tel Aviv: Bitan Hasepher, 1952), I, 164.

all of man's wrongdoings, as there are some (greed, ambition, spite, etc.) which do not necessarily stem from man's sensuality. On the other hand, if the *yetzer ha-ra* were merely *koach ha-tum'ah*, why does it not affect all human beings equally?"

Louis Ginzberg in his essay on Rabbi Israel Salanter interprets the "impure spirit" as an immanent force, characterizing it as "the decay of man's spiritual energy, with the result that he becomes a slave to his evil habits, committing at the slightest incentive the most depraved actions." [4] However, this interpretation does not seem acceptable. First, the very term *koach ha-tum'ah* seems to suggest a transcendent force, like the power of the Tempter or Satan, and not a force inherent in man. Moreover, Rabbi Israel Salanter's question—why the *yetzer ha-ra* does not affect all human beings in equal measure if it is to be understood as the "spirit of impurity"—is only understandable if the "impure spirit" is conceived of as an external entity, such as Temptation personified, and not as the decay of man's spiritual energy, which of course may vary from person to person. The clarification of this point is necessary because it helps to detect a mystical strain in the thought of Rabbi Israel Salanter.

Rabbi Israel Salanter's acceptance of both theories of sin as equally right and essentially complementary is important in view of the educational measures he recommends in order to combat man's sinfulness. Education must take into account both man's sensuality and the existence of the "impure spirit." The enhancement of man's holiness through the study of the Torah and the performance of its commandments is the sure panacea for the "spirit of im-

---

[4] Louis Ginzberg, *Students, Saints and Scholars*, p. 170.

purity." But man must also learn to control his sensuality, and this self-control is enhanced by the study of *Mussar,* by deep reflection upon the nature of man, frequent meditation on the sayings of our Sages and the *dicta* of our moralists. The study of *Mussar* is therefore an essential complement of the study of *Halachah.* A *Yeshiva* curriculum which does not include *Mussar* fails to provide the student with a means for self-education in moral perfection.

At first, Rabbi Israel Salanter's introduction of a daily hour of *Mussar* study did not arouse any opposition. However, when one of his disciples endeavored to accord it a place almost equal in importance to the study of Rabbinics, the Rabbis protested strongly. It is therefore understandable that the introduction of *Mussar* into the *Yeshiva* curriculum was not universally accepted.

III

But how does the study of *Mussar* impress itself upon the soul of man? How does it conduce to the curbing of *koach ta'avat ha-adam?* In his attempt to answer these questions, Rabbi Israel Salanter makes psychological observations which have to be summarized and critically appraised.

Rabbi Israel Salanter distinguishes between two different psychic forces in man, one of which he calls "clear" and, alternatively, "outward," and the other "dark" or "inward." It is the "dark" impulses which in his view are the strongest and which exercise a dominating influence upon man. Rabbi Katz in his book *Tenuath Ha'mussar (The Mussar Movement)* related the "dark forces" to the subconscious mind, and thus sees in Rabbi Israel Salanter's theory an anticipation of Freud's psychology of the subconscious.[5] However, as will be shown later, this view seems unjustified on a closer reading of the relevant texts in Rabbi Israel Salanter's writings.

Knowledge, rational insight, and any influences acting through our rational faculties merely touch the "outward" forces of the soul. Since *Mussar* has to impress itself upon man's sensuality, which is the essence of our *yetzer ha-ra,* it has to penetrate the deeper layers of our consciousness and affect what Salanter calls the "dark forces" of the human soul. Now what are those "dark forces"? Rabbi Israel Salanter gives the following illustrations, which help to elucidate the meaning he attached to this concept.

1) "As the psychologists probed into the soul of man they found two kinds of forces in it, outward and inward ones. For example, when we begin to learn the *Aleph Beth* or study a foreign language, we have to learn the letters, then join them with the aid of vowels into words, then into whole sentences. But later on, when we become more proficient in the use of the language, we can with one glance read whole sentences and the organs of speech produce the sounds of the words without our knowing how this is done. For in the inwardness of the soul there exists an association formed of many words and sentences which helps us to read without knowing how we do it. Those 'associations' exist within us as it were in a state of dimness, and through the least stimulus they come forth and become clear and bright." [6]

2) A *Midrash* commenting on the binding of Isaac says

[5] Rabbi Katz, *Tenuath Ha'mussar,* p. 250.
[6] Salanter, *Or Yisrael;* also Hayim Isaac Lipkin (grandson of Rabbi Israel Salanter) *Rabbi Israel Salant* (Bnei Brek, 1959), pp. 30-31.

that when Abraham went to sacrifice his son tears fell from his eyes until his whole frame was covered with tears. But there is another *Midrash* which declares that the Holy One, blessed be His Name, saw Abraham bind Isaac "with his whole heart." The contradiction between these two *Midrashim* is resolved by Rabbi Israel Salanter in the following way: "Here we can see clearly that even in the case of our father Abraham, to whom none can compare in faith and righteousness, the inner forces of his soul were so strong as to cause him to weep, though he performed his deed with great perfection and with his whole heart." [7]

The second example seems to indicate that Rabbi Israel Salanter uses the term "dark forces" (*kochot kehim*) as synonymous with human instincts—in the above-quoted example the parental instinct, which, according to Mc-Dougall, "becomes more powerful than any other and can override any other, even fear itself; for it works directly in the service of the species while the other instincts work primarily in the service of the individual life for which Nature cares little."

More difficult to interpret is the example referring to the psychology of reading. What Rabbi Israel Salanter calls here the "inner forces of the soul" are obviously associations of the mind—in the case under discussion, our ability to supply mentally by suggestion or interpretation the meaning of words and sentences when we glance at the visual symbols which are exposed to the eye.

It is not easy to find a common denominator for the two examples quoted above. However this may be, there is not sufficient justification for the identification of what Salanter meant by *kochot kehim* with the subconscious mind in the

[7] Lipkin, *op. cit.*, p. 31.

Freudian sense. Moreover, it follows from what has been said so far that it is the aim of *Mussar* to train our instincts, facilitate the formation of desirable habits, and improve character to such an extent that virtue becomes instinctive in us. This is called by Rabbi Israel Salanter *tikkun hamidot* (improvement of character).

Louis Ginzberg summarizes Salanter's doctrine of *tikkun hamidot* in the following words: "Moral effort, or, to use his own term, the suppression of the evil *yetzer,* important as it may be, is, however, only the prelude to *tikkun hamidot,* the improvement of character, by which he meant the reduction of virtue to second nature. Moral effort is the negative part of self-education, which must finally lead to the positive, viz., the entire change of our impulses and inclinations, our passions and desires. We draw nearer to the ideal by always thinking of it, by examining everything in its light. The continuous effort, however, is fatiguing, and therefore when swept by great passions we are unable to withstand them, though we thought we had gained control over our will. Accordingly, our only safeguard lies in moral knowledge, which must be sufficiently clear to lay hold on us and carry us away; this knowledge must become a passion with us so that we act automatically under its imperious injunction." [8]

Salanter's doctrine of *tikkun hamidot* is vague, and so is Ginzberg's presentation of it. No doubt it is difficult at first sight to interpret this doctrine in terms of valid psychological principles. However, it contains two salient points which call for appraisal and comment.

Salanter insists on the frequent repetition of scriptural verses, particularly from the Psalms, or the moral *dicta* of

[8] Ginzberg, *op. cit.,* p. 175.

our Sages, believing that the cumulative effect of such repetition leaves a permanent mark on the soul. According to Rabbi Katz, this belief is somewhat akin to Émile Coué's doctrine of autosuggestion.

However, it would appear that the term "autosuggestion" does not fully characterize those spiritual exercises practiced by the disciples of Rabbi Israel Salanter. From their written records describing these spiritual exercises it would appear that they were similar in character to those ecstatic states described by writers on mysticism and mystical education (such as Evelyn Underhill in her book *Mysticism* or Aldous Huxley in *The Perennial Philosophy*). What really happened during that half-hour of contemplation in which the followers of the *Mussar* movement indulged was as follows: After silent meditation upon some text chosen from Jewish moralist literature, which generally did not last longer than half an hour, the leader or elder, who was one of the initiated, would recite some verses from the Psalms or Ethics of the Fathers, which contained in a succinct form a description of the supreme aim of human life, the ultimate destiny of man, or the desire for a change of heart. Next the disciples would repeat the verses after him and recite them several times with ever-increasing intensity of feeling, until they had induced a mental state bordering on ecstasy. Then, after a short silence, there followed the usual evening prayer which was recited with great emotion and fervor.

Evelyn Underhill describes this state of contemplation or concentration on one idea as "mono-ideism." It is brought about first of all by the withdrawal of the conscious mind from the world surrounding it, followed by a deliberate attempt at concentration on one object. In the spiritual exercises practiced by Rabbi Israel Salanter's disciples, the object is a scriptural verse touching upon the possibility of a change of heart and purification of character. It is the supreme aim of mystical education to bring about that fixity of attention in which the outer world is completely forgotten, and, as it were, nonexistent. For the disciples of Rabbi Israel Salanter this kind of spiritual exercise is completely subservient to the aim of modification or improvement of character. Each time the scriptural verse upon which attention is fixed is repeated it is done with heightened intensity, until it has penetrated their hearts and imprinted itself upon their souls. In this way the "dark forces of the soul" are affected and the major objective of character modification is achieved.

Rabbi Israel Salanter warns his disciples not to expect immediate results from these spiritual exercises, and he exhorts them not to lose heart when they feel that their occupation with *Mussar* does not bear immediate fruit. He likens the influence of the study of *Mussar* on the human soul to the action of the constant dripping of water on a stone, which is thus slowly but surely worn away. To prove his point, he relates the well-known legend concerning Rabbi Akiva, who, on observing a stone hollowed out by the corroding action of drops of water, realized that by constant and tireless application any man could acquire learning. This made him repent of the life of ignorance he had led and brought about his complete reformation.

We have on several occasions drawn attention to a pronounced mystical strain in the thought and teaching of Rabbi Israel Salanter and pointed to a similarity between his practice of spiritual exercises and that of non-Jewish mystics. However, we do not wish to imply that he was in any way influenced by the writings of mystical thinkers of other denominations. His teaching was wholly drawn from Jewish sources. Religious phenomena are universal in character and not peculiar to one particular race or creed; especially striking is the similarity displayed by the mystical thought of religious thinkers of various denominations. This similarity bears witness to the authenticity of man's religious experience.

There is, however, one striking difference between the spiritual exercises suggested by Rabbi Israel Salanter and those practiced by Christian and Mohammedan mystics. Whereas the latter practice introspection and contemplation in perfect solitude, the disciples of Rabbi Israel Salanter practice their spiritual exercises in communal meetings preceding the evening prayer. This specific variation of the practice of contemplation and religious exercise may be explained by the great importance which Judaism attaches to the community and the individual's place in it. According to Jewish teaching, it is the congregation that is holy, and it imparts holiness to the individual member. Judaism does not favor religious observance detached from the holy congregation of believers, and stresses in particular the importance of communal prayer, which is more acceptable to God than the prayer of the individual. It is this fact which accounts for the peculiar form of spiritual exercise practiced by Rabbi Israel Salanter and his disciples.

IV

Tikkun hamidot is impossible without consciousness of sin. According to Rabbi Israel Salanter, human sinfulness has an additional aspect which we have not previously mentioned. Rabbi Salanter characterizes sin as a symptom of a serious sickness of the soul. Like a tree that withers if sunshine is withheld from it, so does the soul sicken if it is deprived of communion with its Divine source. In his doctrine of sin the dogma of reward and punishment plays a prominent part. Almost every page of his moral writings contains exhortations reminding the reader of the Divine retribution which awaits the sinner. The following is a characteristic passage taken from his *Letter of Mussar:* "It is incumbent upon man to contemplate upon the 'fear of God' and the fear of retribution [for sins committed] until he actually hears with his ears and sees with his eyes the terrible punishment awaiting the sinner." In keeping with this thought, Rabbi Israel Salanter applies to every individual human being the rabbinical saying: "A judge should always think of himself as if he had a sword hanging over his head, and *Gehenna* gaping beneath him."

Moral insight, in order to pass from mere comprehension to profound conviction, must be accompanied by the stirring of our emotions—*sa'arat hanefesh.* Hence the importance of an appropriate atmosphere at the time of the study of *Mussar* and Salanter's insistence on a peculiar mode of studying it: "In the room where *Mussar* was studied, by oneself or together with others, preferable at twilight when the falling darkness creates a melancholy atmosphere, one can surrender oneself entirely to one's emotions, one can weep and recite in a loud voice those soul-stirring words of the Prophets, Psalmist and later moralists on the vanity of human life, or give oneself over to reflect in silence upon death which will bring one before the Heavenly Judge to give an account of one's life." [9]

[9] *Ibid.,* p. 169.

Rabbi Israel Salanter's attempt to evoke fear of retribution as an effective deterrent against sin may appear objectionable. Among the modern philosophers, Alfred North Whitehead particularly objects to the appeal to man's instinctive fear of the Divine wrath, viewing it as a distortion of true religion. He says: "This appeal to the ready instinct of brute fear is losing its force. It lacks any directness of response, because modern science and modern conditions of life have taught us to meet occasions of apprehension by a critical analysis of their causes and conditions. Religion is the reaction of human nature to its search for God. The presentation of God under the aspect of power awakens every modern instinct of critical reaction. This is fatal; for religion collapses unless its main position command immediacy of assent." [10]

Buber's retort to Whitehead is highly interesting and very much to the point, inasmuch as he presents in a most lucid way the viewpoint of Jewish theology. "An important philosopher of our day, Whitehead, asks how the Old Testament saying that the fear of God is the beginning of wisdom is to be reconciled with the New Testament saying that God is love. Whitehead has not fully grasped the meaning of the word 'beginning.' He who begins with the love of God without having previously experienced the fear of God, loves an idol which he himself has created, a god whom it is easy enough to love. He does not love the real God who is, to begin with, dreadful and incomprehensible. Consequently, if he then perceives, as Job and Ivan Karamazov perceived, that God is dreadful and incomprehensible, he is terrified. He despairs of God and the world

[10] Whitehead, "Religion and Science," *Great Essays in Science,* ed. Martin Gardner (Pocket Library), p. 217.

if God does not take pity on him, as he eventually did pity Job and make him love Him. . . . That the believing man who goes through the gate of dread is directed to the concrete situations of his existence means just this: that he endures in the face of God the reality of life, dreadful and incomprehensible though it may be. He loves life in his new-born love of God." [11]

However, Salanter's teaching is essentially educational, and though his doctrine of sin and retribution may be theologically sound from a Jewish point of view the educator will rather feel inclined to agree with Whitehead on this point. He will certainly reject the application of Salanter's doctrine to educational practice, as it is almost an axiom of modern education that any appeal to the instinct of fear is psychologically harmful. It is probably this consideration which has caused the teachers of *Mussar* in present-day Jewish religious schools not to give undue emphasis to this aspect of Salanter's teaching.

Moreover, modern teachers have realized that the excessive preoccupation with oneself and the constant attempts at self-analysis inherent in *Mussar* are not suitable to the youthful temper. Rousseau stated that education comes to us from nature, from man and from things, which presupposes an extrovert attitude, a mind wide open and receptive to the influences of the external world and not impervious to it. The mental attitude presupposed by *Mussar* is much more akin to the temper of the old than to that of the young. "Ageing people should know that their lives are not mounting and unfolding," says C. G. Jung, "but that an inexorable process forces the contrac-

[11] Martin Buber, *Eclipse of God* (New York: Harper and Brothers), pp. 36-37.

tion of life. For a young person it is almost a sin, and certainly a danger, to be too much occupied with himself; but for the ageing person it is a duty and a necessity to give serious attention to himself. After having lavished its light upon the world, the sun withdraws its rays in order to illuminate itself." [12]

It is important to note that Rabbi Israel Salanter did not originally recommend the study of *Mussar* to youngsters in their teens, but to people of maturer years. His teaching, when later introduced into *Yeshivot,* was duly modified; Yeshiva teachers endeavored to comply with the above-mentioned psychological principle without violating the Rabbi's own stated purpose.

In practice this modification expresses itself in the application of the propensity for analysis to the treatment of Biblical figures as well as characters described in *Aggadic* literature, instead of fostering this tendency in the student himself. The student is left to draw the moral conclusions from such analysis. This procedure is somewhat akin to the teaching of literature from a moral rather than esthetic angle.

Viewed from a pragmatic standpoint, there can be no doubt that the *Mussar* movement initiated by Rabbi Israel Salanter has proved itself a most valuable and potent force. It left a strong mark on the *Yeshivot* of Eastern Europe, which have served as models for some of the *Yeshivot* of Israel. *Mussar* has given the *Yeshiva* student a certain moral quality which is pervasive and lasting. While the Israeli educator is faced with a grave problem of juvenile delinquency (though not quite as serious as it is in many

[12] Jung, *Modern Man in Search of a Soul* (London: Kegan Paul, 1934), p. 125.

European countries and in America), Israeli statistics do not show a single instance of a *Yeshiva* student guilty of a criminal act which is peculiar to youngsters in their teens.

The study of *Mussar* has helped to widen the *Yeshiva* curriculum and has brought *Aggadah* and Jewish philosophy within the orbit of its scholastic pursuits. The writings of the Jewish moralists are very often linked with discourses of a philosophical nature; thus the transition from *Mussar* to philosophy of religion, as well as to Jewish thought in general, is most easy and natural. *Mussar* has also enriched the curriculum of the Israel religious secondary schools; under the influence of *Mussar* a subject called *Machshevet Israel* (Jewish thought) has been introduced into the curriculum of these schools.

In a wider sense, the *Mussar* movement has acted as a check upon that trend in Judaism which started with Mendelssohn and today is most prominent in the writings of Isaiah Leibovitz. That school of thought sees the essence of Judaism in the observance of *Halachah* divested of its doctrinal roots, viewing it as a *Gesetzesreligion* (juridical religion) in which faith and religious doctrines are of secondary importance. The study of *Mussar* has given a powerful impetus to the re-evaluation of Judaism by placing emphasis on its ethical content; thus it has helped to rescue Judaism from the shortcomings inherent in a formal legalistic interpretation of its teachings.

If we view the *Mussar* movement historically we cannot resist the impression that it bears witness to *Chassidism* triumphant. Although Lithuanian Jewry opposed *Chassidism*, it nevertheless came under its influence in the process of the conflict with it. The strong mystical strain in the teaching of *Mussar* is tangible proof of this influence. In a way, the *Mussar* movement may be regarded as the result of the impact of *Chassidism* on the Jewish way of life of the *Mitnagdim* (Objectors to Chassidism) who, while opposing *Chassidism,* nevertheless unconsciously adopted some of its peculiar features.

4

The Educational Philosophy of
A. D. Gordon

Aharon David Gordon was born in the village of Troianov, in Podolia, Ukraine, on *Shavuoth* 1856. His father, Uri Gordon, had lost four children, and Aharon David was the only child left to him. He was not sent to school, but was educated at home by private teachers. He spent one year at a *Yeshiva* after which he returned home.

The family, being related to Baron Joseph Ginsburg, was put in charge of the baron's estates, which included forests. The young Gordon thus spent the most formative years of his life in the midst of nature—an experience that was of decisive influence in his later life, for through it he formed the attachment to nature which was to become the basis of his philosophical teaching.

Unlike the Jewish writers of the *Haskalah* (Enlightenment) period, Gordon always had free access to the sources of a secular education. His father had not disapproved of this, for, although himself strictly orthodox, he had a liberal outlook in matters of education. Thus, Gordon never became a conscious rebel against traditional Judaism. In his father's house traditional Judaism was combined with general culture.

95

Under the influence of Zionism he decided to immigrate to Palestine and devote himself completely to a life of physical work on the land. In the course of time, his writings and way of life made him the spiritual leader of the Hebrew Labor Movement. His teaching was epitomized by the idea of *Dat Avodah* (Religion of Toil). Gordon died in Degania in the year 1922.

I

No attempt has yet been made to collect and assemble into one complete and coherent work the educational ideas of A. D. Gordon contained in the three volumes of his diaries, letters, and articles on various subjects. We shall attempt in this essay to gather his casual remarks on the subject and present them in a form which faithfully reflects his ideas.

Despite the seemingly unmethodical and casual nature of his comments on the subject, education nevertheless constituted the focus of his life work, and all his efforts were directed towards the re-education of the Diaspora Jew who returns to his homeland. That he himself did not attempt to develop his educational theory more systematically can be explained by the fact that he did not regard his writing on education as an end in itself. He considered action, and not theory, the main aim in education. His writings were only the means to interpret his activities in the field of education.

Gordon's friends, colleagues, and pupils have already presented a vivid picture of him as one who practiced and fully realized the educational ideas he advocated. An attempt will be made here to describe him as a thinker, as a theoretician of Jewish education, and the architect of an educational philosophy of great import and widespread influence.

For Gordon, the distinction between education and instruction is fundamental. In teaching he saw only a preliminary step leading to the actual educational process. The release of man from ignorance by instruction and the dissemination of knowledge is only a preparatory phase in his true education, which, in Gordon's view, follows later. He did not lay emphasis on the educational value of teaching and dissemination of knowledge for their own sake, and it is therefore not surprising that, unlike J. C. Brenner and other Jewish thinkers of the *Haskalah* and Revival periods, he did not devote himself to teaching. The reason for this is to be found not in his disinclination to use teaching as a means of livelihood but in the fact that he did not identify teaching with education in its broadest and fullest sense.

The reader who is acquainted with European educational thought will no doubt find many parallels—which will be discussed later—between A. D. Gordon's ideas on education and those of Rousseau, Tolstoy, Froebel, and others. But the approach to Gordon must be essentially Jewish, for, despite the similarity of his ideas to those of the writers mentioned, his philosophy is almost wholly derived from Jewish sources, and adapted to the special circumstances of the Jewish people resettling in Palestine.

Notwithstanding the revolutionary nature of his educational ideas and his advocacy of the introduction of a new type of education differing widely from the accepted traditional form of Jewish education, he does not insist on the destruction of this traditional education. The number of revolutionaries who, like Gordon, built afresh without destroying that which preceded them is small indeed. Gordon opposed the rejection of Jewish educational thought in favor of the European theories, harbored a deep love and profound respect for the Jewish religion, Jewish spirit, and all that is inherent in us that does no conform to alien tastes and to the alien spirit. In his letter to Brenner he writes: "To this day I cherish the Jewish religion to the depths of my soul, although today I am neither observant nor religious in the accepted sense; and Rabbinical literature is dear to me despite all that it contains which does not conform to my taste and spirit." [1] Gordon's sympathy with the Jewish *Luftmenschen* whom Mendele Mocher Sepharim ridiculed, is touching to the extreme; yet all his activity and his whole way of life constitute the direct antithesis of what a *Luftmensch* stands for.

According to Gordon, education means essentially the education of the individual, of the single human being within the natural framework of the family. "Here we find all the natural bonds, both physical and emotional, material and spiritual, which are essential for a perfect communal life. Here are found the vital links, not only between individuals of the same generation, but also between them and generations to come. In fact, from this point the renewal of humanity should begin." [2]

The emphasis on the significance of the individual in the educational process is characteristically Jewish, for Jewish philosophy likens the single human soul to a world complete in itself. All renewal of society, nationhood, and

[1] Gordon, *Michtavim Ureshimot*, ed. S. H. Bergmann and L. Shochat (Jerusalem: *Ha-Sochnut Ha-Yehudit*, 1954), p. 89.
[2] Gordon *He'adam Vehateva*, ed. S. H. Bergmann and L. Shochat (Jerusalem: *Histadrut Ha-Zionit*, 1951), p. 202.

humanity must, according to Gordon, begin with the education of the individual, who shares in the responsibility for the whole nation and upon whom he makes his exacting demands. "Our national existence rests solely upon every single individual human being. Our national independence has no other redeemer at the present time but the 'I,' that is, each one of us." [3]

Gordon did not approve of what is today called "group education." An educational relationship in the fullest sense of the word is possible only between the educator and the individual pupil, or even more deeply in the relationship of man to himself. As part of a group, one is likely to lose one's individual identity; but Gordon preached free growth of the spirit, and opposed the subjection of the individual to the group. He stressed with great force the value of the individual, stating that "it is forbidden to sacrifice him, even on the altar of the nation." [4]

Gordon rejected all attempts to compel the pupil to accept the ideas and doctrines of his teacher. He considered this a transgression against the integrity of the human soul. In his opinion there is no teaching that is equally suitable for all. "Is there anyone," asks Gordon, "who is entitled to educate others? To impart his ideas to others? Who is the man whose ideas, tastes, world outlook, and concepts of life are absolute, decisive, and universal to such an extent that he is entitled to impose them upon others? Should not the possibility be taken into account that such an attempt may be a violation of someone else's individuality? Is there a common universal formula for education which will be

[3] *Ibid.*, p. 233.
[4] Gordon, *Haumah Vehaavodah*, ed. S. H. Bergmann and L. Shochat (Jerusalem: *Histadrut Ha-Zionit*, 1952), p. 366.

suitable for everybody? Does there exist any image of a human being, or of a people, which is fixed for generations to come, and to the likeness of which all human beings must be uniformly molded?" [5]

From this it follows that a good educator is cautious, and does not impose himself upon his pupil. Gordon ridicules the educator with a strong personality, "for the more one towers above one's fellows, the more oppressive one becomes, the more discomfort one causes, instead of creating scope for self-education." [6]

According to Gordon, the teacher brings out in his pupil's personality those characteristics with which nature has endowed him, and his task is merely to assist him to live as "himself" from childhood to his ultimate fulfillment. Every teacher who attempts to do more and to force upon his pupil that which is not stamped upon his soul by nature is not an educator, but a "hypnotist." Gordon labels as "hypnotism" every type of education which oversteps its legitimate bounds and attempts to be more than an aid to self-education. This "hypnotism," which is one of Gordon's basic concepts and which he frequently mentions in all his writings, has, in his view, its roots in the modern way of life.

The Industrial Revolution brought in its wake the desire for mass organization of people, mass movements, which fundamentally changed the spiritual make-up of the individual. Under the influence of mass movements, the individual has become as if "hypnotized" by thinkers, reformers, and doctrinaires; or, to make use of Kierkegaard's expression, "Man has become a mere part of horse power."

[5] *Ibid.*, p. 274.
[6] *Ibid.*, p. 275.

"This hypnosis engendered by mass movements," says Gordon, "turns people's actions into a blind force, which, though facilitating unity, makes the people's actions automatic, like those of the legendary Golem. Wherever such blind forces are found, there also is found someone to exploit them, whether with good or deliberately evil designs. In such cases there is always enslavement—conscious or unconscious—and an obliteration of personality." [7]

Gordon's insistence on the preservation of individuality has assumed even greater importance in our time, when the mass media of propaganda of the press, radio, television, and cinema are influencing the mind of humanity to an extent which can hardly be exaggerated. Those influences destroy individuality and engender a stereotyped outlook on life. There can be no doubt that Gordon's fundamental distinction between education and hypnosis touches upon the most serious and widespread *malaise* of modern man.[8]

The only means of rescuing man from this mass hypnosis and of developing the independence of his spirit to the fullest extent is, according to Gordon, self-education; and the main task of the educator is to guide his pupil along the road that leads to it.

Professor S. H. Bergmann of the Hebrew University sees the essence of A. D. Gordon's greatness as a teacher in his stress upon self-education. In Bergmann's opinion, that

[7] *He'adam Vehateva*, p. 197.

[8] In a very interesting recent book by Hans Müller-Eckhard, *Weltbewaeltigung (Mastery of the World)* (Stuttgart: Ernst Klett Verlag), p. 197, we find the following passage: "In what an uncritical, dull, and entirely passive fashion do we accept the opinions of others! We lack the means—some organ of perception—of grasping the absurdity inherent in the basing of our opinions about man and the world on one single newspaper or on one single radio station. How ghostly and uncanny is the idea that millions of people listen in at the same time to the same things, accept them and assimilate them."

which characterizes the teacher is the fact that he rouses his pupil, stirs him to action, trains him to choose and decide for himself, without imposing his own will upon the pupil or using compulsion in any form. This is in direct contrast to the role played by the "Leader," who relieves the people of the onus of making their own decisions and acting for themselves, by deciding everything for them. "I recognize that the greatness of A. D. Gordon lies in his fight against the hypnotic influence of the 'Leader.' If we open his books at random we invariably find him preaching against 'Lack of independence,' as he calls it simply— Kant would have called it the 'moral autonomy of the personality.' Think for yourself, decide for yourself, give expression to your inner thought—that is his call to us from every line of his writings. Gordon is the great exposer of the danger of 'hypnosis' in every sphere of our public life." [9]

In his diary, in which he writes about his wanderings up and down the country, Gordon gives a vivid example of what he calls "mass hypnosis." He meets many young people who have just disembarked, approaches them, and engages them in conversation. He is shocked by the fact that these young people repeat the banal clichés and stock phrases with which they have been indoctrinated, instead of talking of themselves, of what is in their hearts, of their life and outlook on life. "Is it desirable," asks Gordon, "that those who come to build the country with their own strength, and to revive it with their spirit, should act under the influence of some party or other, or some individual,

[9] S. H. Bergmann, "A. D. Gordon Hamoreh," *Hapoel Hatzair*, Nos. 22-23.

and according to someone else's ideas? Is it not an inviolable principle that those who come to renew themselves in their work of building a new life should first and foremost learn to renew themselves from an inner source?" [10]

The main task of the educator is to guide the pupil along the road to self-education, which, according to Gordon, is attained through a life of work close to nature.

II

A. D. Gordon's attitude toward nature is rather involved. Three different approaches to nature and its educational influence on man are distinguishable in his writings. One approach is rational and completely comprehensible, and is shared by educators of other nations. They, like Gordon, stress the simplicity and rootedness that characterize the life of a man living in the heart of nature; hence their preference for village to urban life. Life amid nature endows man with self-confidence and a feeling of stability, which result from the very fact of the unchanging cycle of natural phenomena—day and night, light and darkness, the change of seasons, organic growth and decay—which have a decisive influence on the life of rural man. These manifestations give to man an inner calm, a certain harmony of the soul, which directs his actions and makes him feel a part of creation.

There are, however, many passages in Gordon's writings which reveal a mystic attitude to nature, a feeling founded on personal experiences, in which man wholly identifies himself with nature, merges with it; or, to use Gordon's

[10] *Haumah Vehaavodah*, p. 565.

own words, "Man has to be completely absorbed by nature with all the fibers of his being.[11] Gordon also speaks of nature as the stream of universal existence; by contact with it man draws fresh strength and renewed life.

His third approach—and it seems to me the most important one—is his conception of nature as a "sphere of work," the framework within which man works and thereby breaks down the barrier that exists between nature and himself. Nature and physical labor, therefore, are not two separate factors in the educational process of man but are combined into one factor only, work in the midst of nature.

Gordon could not envisage any educational activity which was not bound up with manual labor. Man, and especially the Jew, must first of all free himself from being what Gordon rather harshly calls a "parasite"; in other words, from exploiting the labor of others. The misfortune of the Jewish people in the Diaspora lies in their complete alienation from nature and its detachment from a life of manual work. "A people which has become accustomed to every kind of life but that of manual labor, engaged in on its own initiative and for its own benefit, cannot become again a normal working people unless it makes a supreme effort of will. We lack the main thing—work; not compulsory work, but work to which man is bound by a natural organic bond, and through which the people is bound to its land, and thereby to its culture, which springs from the soil and man's work upon it." [12] (Gordon's remarks about the complete estrangement of the Jewish people in the Diaspora from manual labor is not established on fact; any sociological study of the Jews in Europe will

[11] *He'adam Vehateva*, p. 154.
[12] *Hauma Veha'avoda*, p. 134.

prove that his contention, if not altogether false, is somewhat exaggerated.)

The points of interest here are the connection between man's culture and physical work and Gordon's conception of culture as springing from man's work upon his own land. Gordon did not identify culture exclusively with its higher manifestations such as poetry, religion, and science, but included in it man's civilizing activities which embrace all spheres of life. "Culture embraces all that life offers for the benefit of the living. Work on the land, construction of houses and every kind of building, paving of roads, etc. All forms of labor and craftsmanship may be called 'culture.' That is the basis of culture, the stuff of which it is made." [13]

The life of the Jewish people in the Diaspora was characterized by the fact that this basic foundation of culture was laid by others, and Jewish culture was divorced from the land and nature. Hence the return to nature and to work in the midst of nature constitutes the main educational factor in the shaping of the new Jew and the new Jewish Nation.

Gordon does not regard education as something that can be imparted to man through the medium of books. He does not attach special importance to the intellectual side of a person's education. Education, therefore, is first and foremost self-education, and the educator's task is to bring about, by personal example, the pupil's return to nature and to work.

Gordon's attitude to the Jewish religion is in keeping with his views on nature. Although a full interpretation of his attitude to religion would require a separate article,

[13] *Ha'adam Vehateva*, p. 148.

it is impossible not to touch briefly upon this important subject. Gordon mentions the subject of religion in his writings on education, and most noteworthy is his article on The Day of Atonement, under the heading "Our Attitude to Religion," which remained unfinished. This fact seems to me characteristic, and not accidental. In his essays on religion we sense a continual struggle to present clearly defined opinions. There is also a certain vagueness in his thought, a fact which indicates the absence of a clearly defined stand on the subject, a groping for a new path which had not yet matured in his mind. Although he sympathized with traditional Judaism and felt that it had molded every fiber of his being, he nevertheless gradually detached himself from it. It can be said that Gordon set religious feeling above the observance of religious practices, and he made a basic distinction between the outward forms of religion and its commandments, on the one hand, and its spiritual and emotional content, on the other. He defined religious feeling as "The feeling of absolute unity of the human 'I' with the entire cosmos, an emotional state which precedes intellectual perception. This is the only religious principle which will exist universally and to all eternity, and there are no other religious laws save those which spring directly from this higher feeling, and which renew themselves with the renewal of this feeling." [14] The absolute unity of the human "I" with the cosmos is brought to fulfillment by the very act of work on the land, and hence the passage quoted confirms the opinion of Professor Yeheskel Kaufmann of the Hebrew University that all the precepts of Judaism are reduced by Godron to one supreme commandment—"Man shall live by his toil"; or, according

[14] *Ha'adam Vehateva*, p. 148.

to Professor S. H. Bergmann, "The return of the Jew to his furrow, and his wielding of the hoe, constitute his praying. For Gordon, the spade becomes the prayer shawl and phylacteries. In tilling his soil, the Jew becomes immersed in the holiness that lies hidden in the Holy Land." [15]

Those are rather extreme conclusions drawn—with some justification—from Gordon's teaching. However, it may appear doubtful whether Gordon himself was fully aware of the revolutionary implications inherent in his ideas. He was a moderate by nature and may not have been fully conscious of having condensed the whole body of Judaism to one supreme postulate.

However, there is another point in Gordon's conception of Judaism that has to be mentioned. Gordon regarded the forms of religion as being unduly rigid and unbending as a result of the detachment of man from nature. Upon his return to nature Gordon looked forward to a reform of religion resulting from man's unity with nature, which was the essence of life and the source of man's religious creativeness. He seems to have visualized a renewal of Judaism stemming from the fresh contact of the Jewish people with its native soil, without advocating a total abrogation of traditional Jewish precepts.

III

It may be worth-while to comment upon one of Professor Kaufmann's principal arguments against the teaching of A. D. Gordon. I refer to Gordon's idealization of nature and his expectation of the renewal of the Jew's moral character as a result of a return to nature. This whole concept

[15] S. H. Bergmann, *Mavo Le'Ha'adam Vehateva*, p. 30.

it categorically rejected by Kaufmann. "The culture of a
nation," says Professor Kaufmann, "has at all times and
everywhere reached its peak in towns, far from the heart of
nature. The language of the peasant is poor and inadequate, and his cultural level low. The town is the place
where a nation's creativeness is at its highest, both in language and literature, art, and science." [16] In the same chapter Kaufmann says: "What advantage does the return to
village life offer? Throughout history, agricultural nations
have fought each other in no less measure than town dwell-
ers. What makes us believe in the redeeming force of
nature? Nature had never taught man kindness, morality,
or mercy. Who more than the genuine Bedouin dwells in
the heart of nature? And yet his whole life is one of robbery
and violence. And if man becomes a partner in creation
with nature itself, will that bring about a change of heart?
Is not nature itself a terrible battleground? In order to
learn morality from nature, one must first long for nature
with the inner ecstasy of a mystic and look upon it from a
'cosmic' angle. But what about the ordinary man?" [17]

Kaufmann's criticism is serious in that it touches upon
the very source of Gordon's teaching. Nevertheless, it seems
to me that what is here expressed by Kaufmann is only a
part of the truth. Gordon's ideas on nature are a belated
echo of the Romantic period, that era which culturally was
so fruitful precisely because a most intimate relationship
existed between man and nature. Romantic literature
shows that man's moral sense is aroused by that very nature
which Kaufmann calls a terrible battleground. The poetry

[16] Kaufmann, *Benetivoth—Prakim Becheker Hamachshavah Haleumit,*
published by the Reali School, Haifa, 1952, p. 191.
[17] *Ibid.,* p. 191.

of Wordsworth bears witness to this when he clearly states
that when observing nature, he is overcome by feelings:

> . . . such perhaps
> As have no slight trivial influence
> On that best portion of a good man's life,
> His little, nameless, unremembered acts
> Of kindness and of love. . . .

Nor can it be denied that nature exerts a healthy influence
upon us all. It teaches stability, simplicity, modesty, devotion to work. It is also wrong to state that the cultural
standard of the villager must necessarily be below that of
the town dweller and his powers of expression poorer.
Wordsworth, in his Preface to his *Lyrical Ballads,* states
that the opposite is true.

> . . . The language, too, of these men has been adopted (puri-
> fied indeed from what appear to be its real defects, from all
> lasting and rational causes of dislike or disgust) because such
> men hourly communicate with the best objects from which the
> best part of language is originally derived; and because, from
> their rank in society and the sameness and narrow circle of
> their intercourse, being less under the influence of social vanity,
> they convey their feelings and notions in simple and unela-
> borated expressions. Accordingly, such a language, arising out
> of repeated experience and regular feelings, is a more perma-
> nent, and a far more philosophical language, than that which is
> frequently substituted for it by poets. . . .[18]

Moreover, even if Yeheskel Kaufmann were right in his
views on village life, one should take into account the fact
that all educational philosophy should be evaluated not
only by the criterion of its objective inner truth but also

[18] William Wordsworth, *The Prelude, Selected Poems and Sonnets,*
(Rinehart Editions), pp. 4-5.

by its functional value at a specific period. Here it must be noted that the influence exerted by Gordon's teaching was both necessary and beneficial, even if its intrinsic truth be debatable. Yeheskel Kaufmann cannot deny that there was, and still is, a pressing need to redeem the soul of the Jew from his one-sided preoccupation with commerce and the intellectual professions, and to guide him back to the land and the cultivation of the soil. No nation can be called healthy unless a fair proportion of its people live on land and engage in agricultural work. From a pragmatic point of view, Gordon has been proved right.

However, it has to be pointed out that Gordon's call of "back to the land" has proved right only within a limited period of the country's resettlement. It would now appear that the limits of agricultural development will soon be reached and that the future development of Israel is bound up with its industrial expansion. This does not detract from the pragmatic truth of Gordon's teaching, but merely qualifies it.

The educational philosophy of A. D. Gordon has many parallels in European thought, and it may be worth mentioning them in this context. His rejection of all forms of compulsion in the educational process and his profound respect for every single individual are reminiscent of the ethics of Kant, which stress the moral autonomy of man.

The definition of education as self-education and the emphasis laid upon the individual in the educational relationship first appear in the teachings of Socrates, who defines the teacher as a person who, by means of leading questions, draws out the truth hidden within the pupil's mind. He likens the function of the teacher to that of a midwife. The teacher merely liberates and develops the mind of his pupil without adding anything of his own.

IV

There are many parallels in the teaching of Gordon and that of Rousseau. Rousseau was of the opinion that education does not consist in imparting ideas but in fostering the natural growth and inner development of the human soul, and that the teacher's main task is to watch over this development, removing from it any negative and harmful influences. Though Gordon and Rousseau both advocated a "natural life," their attitudes to nature differed. To Rousseau, nature was a kind of haven, a refuge from the life of the town, whereas Gordon could not conceive of life in nature except combined with work.

The mystic experience of the merging of the soul of man with the soul of nature found its expression in the nature poetry of Wordsworth, which may be regarded as the poetic counterpart of Rousseau's *Emile*.

Gordon reminds us of Tolstoy in many of his educational ideas, and the similarity is not accidental; one can actually feel the latter's influence on Gordon. Both believed in a new type of education as a means leading to the creation of a new human being and the reform of society. It is known that Tolstoy founded a school in Yasnaya Poliana, where he himself taught the village children according to methods drawn mainly from the ideas of Rousseau. Gordon and Tolstoy both condemned the town and preached the return of man to a life of rustic simplicity. Gordon, however, did not agree with Tolstoy's negative attitude to culture; he merely rejected the type of culture which was detached from work and nature.

The many similarities in the life of Gordon to that of the American Thoreau have already been pointed out by Buber in his article "Gordon *Hamagshim*" ("Gordon, The Man Who Practiced What He Preached.") Thoreau's aspirations toward a return to a full and simple life were expressed by his decision to leave the town and live in the forest of Walden, where he built himself a hut with his own hands and lived the life of a recluse. His purpose was to avoid all "dissipation of life" inherent in town life, to avoid haste, and to earn his livelihood by manual labor. It must be stressed, however, that this experiment of Thoreau's was merely a passing episode in his life; he stayed in the forest for only two years, whereas Gordon remained on the land to the day of his death.

There is no doubt that Gordon's influence on Jewish education was great indeed, and still continues. However, his teaching has not been completely accepted and some of its basic theories are indeed unacceptable. There is some doubt as to whether Gordon was right in saying that no human being is entitled to influence others, as there is no *Weltanschauung* so absolute and unanimously accepted that it may be "taught" to others. On the one hand, he contradicts himself, for he himself made every effort and used his unusual abilities in order to advocate a particular world outlook and a certain way of life. On the other hand, the teacher who takes Gordon's opinion seriously, merely exercises restraint and allows his pupil to develop in his own way, and thereby allows all sorts of mass slogans and other harmful influences free access to his pupil's mind. Thus a situation is created which Gordon labored so hard to prevent; the way is left wide open for what he called "hypnosis." If the genuine educator, out of spiritual fastidiousness and an exaggerated sense of responsibility, refrains from influencing his pupil, the vacuum thus created in his pupil's mind will be filled by those extraneous influences against which Gordon fought so zealously.

Israeli education was most influenced by Gordon's belief that education must not be detached from a life of work, and in this respect the *kibbutz* schools followed in his footsteps. The teaching of Gordon, which raises education above mere teaching and dissemination of knowledge, was fulfilled by the development of the "Childrens Society" and the establishment of strong individual relationships between the educator and his pupils. But the Israeli urban school is far removed from the educational concepts of Gordon, since it emphasizes instruction and knowledge. But even the Israeli city child is not entirely cut off from agricultural work, as he often goes off to workcamps and to help in *kibbutzim,* which is not customary in urban schools in Europe.

Israeli secular schools are not imbued with Gordon's religious spirit. Gordon saw in religion the "source of all higher emotions in the soul of man, the basis of all his being and the renewal of his existence." In the present attempts to introduce "Jewish Consciousness" into the general schools we can observe the first *rapprochement* to Gordon's concept of religion and the central role he attaches to it in education.

A. D. Gordon's educational theory is unique in Jewish educational thought. It has no connection with the educational ideas of the era of *Haskalah,* neither is it in any sense "traditional." To some extent it may be explained as the fruit of the Zionist impact on modern Jewish history, but it bears the mark of Gordon's highly individual personality and character. Indeed, the truth must be told that in some of its aspects it is bound to remain mere theory. Gordon's call for self-education, with only a limited recognition of the value of organized education, is altogether impracticable. Moreover, Gordon's educational solution, with its stress on self-education, is only valid for a small intellectual élite, which is susceptible to, and therefore easily moved by, ideological considerations. It does not hold good for society as a whole. Nevertheless, his teaching will always provide a source of inspiration for many educators, who will see in him a singular personality possessing a spiritual quality of his own and exceptional intellectual independence. First and foremost, he will be remembered as one who practiced what he taught, and his life, which is the fulfillment of his teaching, is no less important than his writings.

5

The Revival of Hebrew and the Foundation of the Tarbut Schools (Brenner in London—Hebrew versus Yiddish)

I

Brenner's fame is not based on any single one of his literary works, nor on all of them combined. It is his personality, his capacity for friendship and love that "verge on the angelic," his sufferings and tragic death in 1921—he was murdered by an Arab in one of the first Arab riots in Palestine—which have stirred the deepest emotions of the Jewish people and which caused him to be remembered not only as a pioneer of modern Hebrew but also as a martyr and saint.

Brenner's early writings, containing as they do most faithful reflections of his gradual estrangement from, and later revolt against, the Jewish traditional way of life as it existed in Eastern Europe toward the close of the last century, are well known, as is also the genesis of his national Hebrew consciousness, whose outstanding manifestation is Brenner's attempt to make Hebrew the dominating literary medium of expression in Jewish literature. His writings of the London period, however, and his contacts with and reactions to the way of life of Western Jewry are less widely known. And yet it is Brenner's London phase which exercised a profound influence on his spiritual development. Brenner's Hebrew nationalism and his extreme Palestino-centric orientation became only possible after he had come into contact with the Western alternative of Jewish Diaspora life and, by reason of a series of fateful circumstances, as well as certain deeply rooted peculiarities of his character, had totally rejected it. Only a full comprehension of the circumstances which led to his rejection of both the Eastern and Western way of Jewish Diaspora life makes intelligible Brenner's final fixation on Palestine as the only remaining hope of the Jewish people.

He came to London in the spring of 1904 at the age of twenty-five, after having served in the Russian army, where he suffered incredible hardships and humiliations. At the outbreak of the Russo-Japanese war he deserted from the army, was caught by the police, and sent back with a train of convicts to his home town for identification. On the way, he was rescued by two members of the Jewish socialist organization "The Bund," who risked their lives in the process.

Though known as a publicist and editor of the Bundist Yiddish Periodical *The Struggle,* and later as a Hebrew writer and poet of note, a contributor to such Hebrew magazines as *Hashiloach,* the author of several Hebrew stories, and at least one autobiographical novel of unquestioned literary merit, he chose to remain incognito during the first months of his stay in the East End of London. He took on work as a librarian of the East End Russian Library at a salary of two pounds a month. His lodgings at 48 Mile End Road were drab and primitively furnished. After a few months he gave up his post as librarian, learned typesetting, and took up a post as compositor in the printing establishment of a Yiddish daily paper.

The Jewish quarter of the East End of London had from the very first day of his arrival made an extremely bad impression on him. All his writings of his London period are permeated by a violent revulsion against the ugliness of this overcrowded district and the utter misery of the newly arrived refugees residing there. His sense of human dignity revolted against their degrading mode of life, and his tortuous imagination painted a somewhat exaggerated picture of the uprooted existence which the Diaspora of London had forced upon them. Profoundly influenced by socialist economic theories, he saw in those East End peddlers, newly arrived *émigrés* and other *Luftmenschen*[1] an essentially unproductive element, and in his outbursts he goes so far as to call them gypsies, parasites, and dung. Yet he never made the slightest attempt to move out of the East End of London and take up residence elsewhere. His self-imposed restriction to the ghetto of Whitechapel is somewhat reminiscent of the mentality of that East End tailor in Sydney Street, of whom D. Weizmann tells us that he never went beyond the Bank, where he would stop and say: "I never go beyond this point."

Moreover, he does not appear to have made any serious effort to acquire a full command of English and never attempted to become integrated into English society. From the day of his arrival in England until his departure four years later he must have regarded it as merely a transit station to some farther destination, and, after painful heart searchings and spiritual Odysseys, Palestine became his final goal. Nor did he ever attempt to improve himself

[1] Men without any training or definite occupation.

economically. Such was his sense of self-identification with his brethren, to whom he had maintained throughout an intense love-hate relationship, that his own advantage would have meant nothing to him as long as they were leading lives of unrelieved misery. Even in his outward appearance he wished to be one of them. Always shabbily dressed, he refused to put on a hat or wear a collar and tie.

For a short time he seems to have broken out of his self-imposed isolation and made certain steps which may be interpreted as an attempt at *rapprochement* to the Jewish community at large. He contributed several articles on Jewish literature to the Hebrew section of the *Jewish Chronicle,* took active part in the affairs of the Jewish Labor Party *Poalei Zion,* and lectured to Hebrew teachers in the East End. It is difficult to assess the impact of these activities on the Jewish community. It may be assumed that they were too short-lived to leave a permanent mark. Before he became widely known in Jewish circles he withdrew from all public activities, never again to appear on the Anglo-Jewish scene.

After the failure of the first Russian revolution in 1905 news of anti-Jewish riots in hundreds of Russian towns and villages were reaching London. The Hebrew periodicals *Hatsefirah* of Warsaw, *Hazman* of Vilna, and *Hashiloach* had closed down, and Zionist activities were forbidden. In the eyes of Brenner this was the death blow to the Hebrew language and literature. A terrible gloom fell upon him. In his macabre imagination he saw not only the disappearance of Hebrew as a living language but the total destruction of Jewish culture everywhere. Out of this despair (it is well to recall that despair and fear of total destruction of Jewish life are powerful motives in modern

Hebrew literature) was born Brenner's resolution to start in London the publication of a Hebrew monthly called *Hame'orer*. Its name, *The Awakener,* epitomizes the main aim of this remarkable Hebrew periodical: to awaken the Jewish people from its lethargy caused by persecution, to stir them to new life, to kindle in their hearts the hope for a national rebirth, and to sustain them in their faith in a Hebrew revival. Brenner's passionate spirit dominates its pages. Compared with the stormy style of *Hame'orer* all previous Hebrew periodicals seem cold and academic. Brenner's way of writing stands in sharp contrast to the detached writing of *Hatsefirah* and to the intellectual tranquility of *Hashiloach*. In *Hame'orer* Brenner pours out his heart in endless epistles addressed to the reader, as well as in published excerpts from his diary, in which he tries to win the reader's confidence, attempting in turn to rouse him, coax, frighten, and threaten. It was almost exclusively Brenner's spirit that impressed itself upon the pages of this journal. The circle of contributors was very small indeed, even at the start of publication, and it gradually dwindled as time went on. The practical management of the paper rested entirely on Brenner's shoulders. He was its editor, staff of contributors (writing always under different pen names) publisher, typesetter, printer, and even distributor. He must have presented a pathetic and moving sight walking through the streets of Whitechapel with a heavy sack containing a new issue of his periodical over his shoulder and rushing it to the post office.

Brenner's devotion to the cause of the Hebrew language stands without parallel in the history of Hebrew literature. His love of Hebrew and his sense of urgency about keeping it alive appeared to some as "mystic, above logic and the

possibility of intellectual analysis." [2] Most of the readers
of *Hame'orer* were in Eastern Europe. The number of its
readers in England must have been small and its spirit
somewhat alien to them. To a detached observer it must
have been clear right from the beginning of its publication
that *Hame'orer* would not last very long. Brenner was too
far away from the circle of its readers, and Russia in a state
of turmoil which militated against regular contact between
the journal and its subscribers. Many copies did not reach
their destination, others were returned unread, and subscriptions were irregularly paid. Brenner had to subsidize
his publication from the wages received as compositor in
the East End Yiddish daily where he had worked. Moreover, he did not receive a sufficient number of contributions, and the fact that he was often compelled to publish
second- and third-rate material caused great suffering to
him. With the ninth issue in the second year its publication ceased in September 1907. The following extraordinary notice addressed to the readers appeared in the last
issue of *Hame'orer*: "I have to inform you herewith that,
instead of issues 10, 11, and 12, which I am unable to publish for lack of literary contributions, you will receive, not
later than the month of December, a collection of the writings of G. Shofmann. . . . Please accept this book with my
sincere apologies. I fervently hope not to trouble you
again." [3]

His important single literary achievement during the
London period is *Me'ever Lagvulin* (*From beyond the
Borders*), a drama in five scenes. He wrote it in a state of

[2] See Rabbi Benjamin's article on Brenner published in *Joseph Hayim
Brenner*, ed. Ha-Kibbutz Hameuchad (Tel Aviv), p. 77.
[3] *Ibid.* (A. Beilin's article), p. 106.

high emotional strain and completed it in eleven days. At that time Brenner considered *Me'ever Lagvulin* to be his last word, and far above everything else he had written before.

The drama is important because it is a faithful mirror of Brenner's mind during the London period, the most complete artistic reflection of the problems, conflicts, and dilemmas which troubled him during that time. He published it in *Hame'orer.*

The most characteristic feature of the drama is the fact that it ends with the almost complete dispersal of all its chief protagonists. One of them makes the absurd decision of returning to Galicia, another goes back to Russia, the third emigrates to the United States, and there remains in London only the hero of the play, the poet Johanan; but even he is thinking of emigrating to Palestine. The break-up of the entire milieu depicted by Brenner is indicative of his attitude to the existence of the Jewish people in the Diaspora—one of absolute "negation of the Diaspora." His aim is to show the glaring anomaly of Jewish life in the Diaspora exhibited in miniature in the case of the Jews of Whitechapel.

Brenner's attitude to traditional Judaism is to some extent reflected in a peculiar incident described in *Me'ever Lagvulin,* which presumably had some foundation in actual fact and which he has woven into the plot of his drama. A group of revolutionary Jews organized a public banquet on the Day of Atonement, and this outrageous provocation led to violent retribution on the part of Orthodox Jews; stones were thrown on both sides, leading to blows. The affair ended with court action.

Though generally in sympathy with the irreligious by

conviction, Brenner expressed his contempt for both parties of the strife. He despised the first because, as Johanan puts it in the play, they find pleasure in displaying in such a provocative way their lack of religious faith, and the second because they used force to impose their will on others.

That he generally should have been in sympathy with the irreligious is understandable in view of his complete estrangement from traditional Judaism even before he had come to England. As a youth he was already swept away by that wave of antitraditional revolt which he so vividly described in his autobiographical novel *Misaviv Lanekuda* (*Round about the Point*).

Yet in fairness it must be stated that at least during his London period he had shown no hatred of traditional Judaism. On the contrary, he respected the saintliness of the older generations, to whom he usually refers in his writings as "our saintly fathers." A representative of the old world in *Me'ever Lagvulin*, Rabbi Haim Yehuda, is a definitely positive figure, depicted without the least touch of satire or irony. His fate arouses sympathy, and there can be no doubt that Brenner sympathized with him. Brenner never remained indifferent when he witnessed a true manifestation of traditional Jewish life, and it often touched him to the depth of his heart. Brenner's friend A. Beilin tells us that on a Day of Atonement, when he heard the voice of prayer from a neighboring synagogue resounding in his room he was so deeply stirred that he left the ghetto and wandered aimlessly in the north of London. There he entered a park where children were playing, supervised by their nurses. His estrangement from religious Judaism and the Jewish community evoked within him such a feeling of loneliness that he considered himself to be as forsaken as an orphan, and he started weeping openly. Two young girls who were sitting nearby gave each other a sign and disappeared, leaving Brenner weeping alone in the park.

As he no longer regarded religion as an essential element of Jewish culture it is natural that he clung to the Hebrew language with an almost mystical fervor. With the same determination with which previous generations adhered to the Law as the sole guide of their lives, Brenner clung to the Hebrew language, and his shy admiration for Jewish religious thinkers of the past was to a large extent due to the fact that they had expressed their most creative and essential thought through the medium of that language. To help create a new secular Hebrew literature was his highest ambition. Though essentially of a modest character, he did not lack the consciousness of being one of the foremost builders of a new Hebraic literary movement. In London he completely abandoned Yiddish as a medium of expression, both in speech and writing, although it was his mother tongue. The reason is not far to seek. The Yiddish spoken by East End Jewry was an impure and corrupt jargon, containing an abundance of English idiom which was not properly assimilated. In Brenner's eyes this was just an illustration of its complete unsuitability as a national tongue. It was plastic and receptive and as "defenseless against foreign influence as an unwalled city."

It is natural enough that Brenner was unable to judge objectively the Anglo-Jewish community. He knew only Whitechapel, which he viewed with unrelieved gloom, and the rest of the Jewish community he knew mainly through its publications, or rather those publications which appeared in Yiddish. It must be admitted that these were not of a high quality. It is difficult to say whether Brenner knew sufficient English to be able to read the Anglo-Jewish press and other Anglo-Jewish publications of a literary character. Moreover, if we consider the effete condition of the Zionist movement in England at that time and the reluctance of English Jews to fight Sir William Evan Gordon's Aliens Bill (which was defended even by Weizmann) we can understand, though not approve, of such of Brenner's outbursts of hostility toward English Jewry as defy translation into English. But some of his critical remarks about Anglo-Jewry seem sufficiently justified. He rightly sensed its essentially materialistic spirit, its lack of spirituality and Jewish creativeness, and the low state of its popular Hebrew education, the main aim of which was— as Brenner puts it—"to find the right place in the Prayer Book during a Service."

It is a great pity that he never met Weizmann while he was staying in London. He was no admirer of the Hebrew essayist Asher Ginsberg, known by the pen name Achad Ha'am; and Achad Ha'am, on his part, does not seem to have been particularly interested in Brenner. Only once did Achad Ha'am invite Brenner to visit him, having been urged by Bialik to do so, and Brenner was not at all eager to answer Achad Ha'am's call. It needed a great deal of persuasion on the part of his friend Beilin to persuade Brenner to visit him, and this only after Beilin had promised to join him. They arrived at Achad Ha'am's house in Great Russell Street near the British Museum an hour late, and knocked at the door. When the tiny face of Achad Ha'am, with its small, triangular beard, peeped out of the window, Brenner pulled Beilin by the jacket and said: "We must immediately run away from here," and he actually began to withdraw. Beilin had to use force to make him wait until Achad Ha'am opened the door. He was very displeased that they had come so late and took out his watch and said that he would only be able to talk to them for a few minutes, as he was already expecting another caller. Throughout the visit Brenner lolled carelessly in an easy chair, and actually started whistling absent-mindedly to himself, and the conversation had to be carried on between Achad Ha'am and Beilin. Brenner felt insulted because Achad Ha'am had asked him whether *Hame'orer* still appeared. This question showed Brenner that Achad Ha'am did not consider this publication important enough to find out for himself.

Why did Achad Ha'am take so little interest in Brenner? With his high standing in the world of Hebrew letters and his great influence among the Zionst intelligentsia in Britain and abroad, Achad Ha'am was the man who might have befriended Brenner, rescued him from his isolation and obscurity, and helped him with the publication of *Hame'orer.* Did he not rightly assess Brenner's noble character and his great potentialities as a Hebrew writer? It is possible that the coolness between the two men was the result of Brenner's having lampooned Achad Ha'am. In Brenner's autobiographical novel *Misaviv Lanekuda,* written before he came to London, there appears a minor figure by the name of David ben Yishay Sheindelinsky who, peculiarly enough, is once called "Achad Ha'am" by Brenner. He appears there as a slight and superficial man, a Zionist political busybody, and the point in his character most satirized by Brenner is his streak of false modesty. It is difficult to believe that this Sheindelinsky was really intended to be a satirical representation of Achad Ha'am, particularly in view of the fact that Brenner in his youth had admired him, though he later changed his opinion. However this may be, lack of friendship between the two is in any case understandable enough. The differences in social standing, Zionist policy, and general outlook between the two men were quite fundamental. Brenner was proletarian by conviction and free choice (Beilin denies that Brenner had always been poor, saying that even in London he might have lived more comfortably had he not staked his whole fortune on *Hame'orer,* which was bound to become a complete failure); Achad Ha'am, on the other hand, was a bourgeois whose economic independence and comparative prosperity must have appeared suspect to Brenner. Moreover, Achad Ha'am rejected Brenner's doctrine of Negation of the Diaspora, always believing in the coexistence of the Zionist spiritual center in Palestine and the Jewish communities of the Diaspora. Finally, and this is a point of the utmost importance, there were very profound differences of opinion between the two men on the essential character of Hebrew culture, its relation to the Bible, and traditional Judaism in general. This difference of opinion came to a head some years later when Brenner had left England and settled in Palestine. In 1911 he published an article in the Jaffa *Hapoel Hatsair,* in which he gave vent to his "free national consciousness," which, in his own words, was completely secular, atheistic, and antitheological. Hebrew culture must, in his view, free itself from its traditional attachment to religion and break in a most radical way with the past. The only characteristic of the new Hebrew civilization is, according to Brenner, the fact of the revived Hebrew language—a purely formal cri-

terion. Brenner wished to emancipate himself from what
he once called the "hypnosis" of the twenty-four books
which constitute the Bible, and stated that many secular
books of later centuries were nearer to him, greater and
deeper. Moreover, "the same importance which I attach
to the Old Testament on account of its remnants of mem-
ories from days long past, and as the embodiment of the
spirit of our people and the spirit of humanity in the
course of many periods and generations, that same importance attaches also to the New Testament, which is our
book, bone of our bones, and flesh of our flesh." [4] He fails
to see any fundamental difference between the humble and
ascetic attitude of the prophet of Anatot and the prophet
of Nazareth.

This article was brilliantly answered by Achad Ha'am,
who published his reply under the ironic title of "Torah
from Zion." In this article Achad Ha'am finally settles accounts with Brenner, strangely enough without even mentioning him by name. He considered Brenner's attitude
suicidal from the national point of view, and his free national consciousness as "an absurd thing such as has never
been heard by any other nation and in any other language." "Nothing existing can free itself from the natural
conditions of its existence, unless it is freed from existence
itself. Can a tree free itself from its roots, which rest deep
in the earth and deny it free movement? The roots of our
national consciousness rest deep in our historic past from
which it draws nourishment and life, and if it is freed from
them, it will cease to exist." [5] Achad Ha'am justifies the

[4] J. C. Brenner, *Ketavim,* Vol. III, *Am Oved* (Tel Aviv: 1951), 34-35.
[5] *Kol Kitvei Achad Ha'am* (Tel Aviv: Dvir, 1950), p. 407.

action taken by the Odessa circle, which decided to withdraw the subsidy granted to *Hapoel Hatsair* after it had published Brenner's article. He does not mince words in his denunciation of Brenner's views, applying to him and his circle the quotation, "May the snake bite the man who breaks the fence."

It is typical of Brenner that he never recoiled from the consequences of his thoughts. His was a one-track mind, and his most outstanding characteristics were intellectual consistency, integrity, and total commitment to his ideas. In this he was the typical Russian intellectual of the beginning of the twentieth century, for whom, as Isaiah Berlin says, "the essential thing was to offer oneself without calculation, to give all one has for the sake of the light within (whatever it may illuminate) from pure motives. For only motives count. . . . The more difficult, the more paradoxical, the more unpalatable a conclusion, the greater is the degree of passion and enthusiasm with which some Russians at any rate tend to embrace it." [6] And it is an ironic reflection that the man who considered himself the initiator of a new Hebraic renascence of spirit should have so much resembled the Russian intelligentsia and thus himself appear as a typical child of the Diaspora. Achad Ha'am, at least in spirit, was a Western intellectual in whose mind many ideas had crossed and who therefore could never become obsessed with any single one. "Ideas which in the West competed with a large number of other doctrines and attitudes," says Isaiah Berlin, "so that to become dominant they had to emerge victorious from a fierce struggle for survival, in Russia came to lodge in the minds of gifted individuals and indeed obsessed them, often

[6] Isaiah Berlin "A Marvellous Decade," *Encounter*, June, 1955.

enough simply for lack of other ideas to satisfy their intellectual needs." [7]

With his essentially Western orientation, Achad Ha'am exercised a moderating influence, and owing to his propensity for detached analysis of thought, his empirical approach, his attitude of accommodation at the price of absolute consistency, he succeeded in checking those extremists among the Hebrew national thinkers who, in their pursuit to the very end of one single idea, were ready to jeopardize the spiritual future of the Jewish people.

Strangely enough, Brenner's stay in the East End of London only tended to harden his passionate rejection of Diaspora life, and the fact, as he saw it, that there was no hope for the Jewish people in the West, just as there was none in the East, made him pin all his hopes on the Jewish homeland. Paradoxical as it may appear, his London period became a decisive factor in the creation of that desperate attitude of "no alternative" which he never abandoned throughout his pioneering life in Palestine.

A corollary of this attitude is Brenner's unhesitating decision in favor of Hebrew and his rejection of Yiddish as the Jewish national tongue.

II

Brenner's pessimism regarding the revival of Hebrew proved unjustified. In 1907, when Brenner's *Hame'orer* (*The Awakener*) ceased to appear, there was held in The Hague a conference of the Zionist Organization *Ivriah,* whose function it was to declare their attitude toward the conflict of languages—Hebrew *vs.* Yiddish—and to take

[7] *Ibid.*

practical steps to advance the dissemination of Hebrew as a language spoken by the Jewish people.

The deliberations and final decisions of that conference are of great importance, not the least of which has been their influence on the educational policy of Jewish schools in Eastern Europe. Among the Jewish masses in Poland three groups representing diverse schools of thought were fighting for recognition. 1) There were those who may be called "moderate Hebrew nationalists," who, though firmly convinced that only Hebrew could become the language of the Jewish people in its homeland, adopted an extremely tolerant attitude toward Yiddish and on various grounds justified its continued use in the Diaspora. Consequently, they favored for the Diaspora bilingual Jewish schools in which Hebrew would be the language of instruction in Judaic subjects (Bible, *Mishnah,* etc.), whereas all other subjects would be taught in either the language of the country or, as suggested by some, in Yiddish. 2) Then there were the "radicals," whose main spokesman was the Jewish revisionist leader Vladimir Jabotinsky, who fought for a completely Hebraized school, to the exclusion of any other language unless taught as a foreign tongue. 3) Finally, there were the Yiddishists, led by the popular philosopher Dr. Zhidlovsky and by Dr. Nathan Birnbaum, who were in favor of Yiddish being accepted as the official language of the Jewish minorities in Eastern Europe, and therefore as the language of instruction in Jewish schools.

Ch. N. Bialik took his stand on this issue at the *Ivriah* conference and never moved from it. His was an extremely moderate attitude. His moderation was the result of two factors, one personal and the other objective. Firstly, his emotional ties with his mother tongue, Yiddish, and his love for it were so strong that he viewed with apprehension the deprecation of Yiddish by the Zionist intelligentsia. Secondly, as a profound Hebrew scholar and poet, he, better than anyone else, could assess the potentialities of Hebrew, with its roots reaching back into antiquity and with its enormously rich and varied literature. He was sure, therefore, that in the conflict between the two languages Hebrew would gain the ascendancy over Yiddish, which had no such deep roots nor any literature which could stand in comparison with that in Hebrew. Consequently he believed that there was no need to fight Yiddish or to adopt an intolerant attitude toward it. His stand on this point stemmed from inner certainty, whereas other Zionists were apprehensive as to the eventual outcome of this contest, and their intolerant attitude was motivated by the fear that Yiddish might possibly "swamp" the Hebrew tongue.

Though Bialik's love of Yiddish was instinctive and innate, he put forward interesting arguments for its continued use in the Diaspora. Yiddish, he maintained, was the devoted nurse of Hebrew, the Ruth to Naomi. It has protected Hebrew from eventual corruption and decay just because the teaching of Hebrew texts, prayers, and Holy Writ, which at the same time served as a vehicle for the acquisition of the Hebrew language, was always accompanied by a translation into Yiddish. The Jewish child learned his first prayers in Hebrew but translated them into Yiddish; he learned the Hebrew Bible by translating it, verse by verse, into Yiddish; and it was specifically this method of translating from the one tongue into the other that appealed to him. Moreover, if Hebrew had been the spoken language in the Diaspora, it would have been exposed to the influence of all the European languages spoken by the Jews, and this would have brought about its corruption and ultimate ruin. "The Lord has shown us mercy in that we did not speak Hebrew in the Diaspora, but Yiddish." Thus Hebrew preserved its purity, and Yiddish, while acting as a "buffer" and absorbing all the foreign influences, on the one hand, also gave Hebrew vitality, on the other. The Hebrew language, which had hitherto been a literary language, drew fresh life force from its close association with Yiddish, which is a homely, colloquial tongue. It became impregnated by the "living" Yiddish idiom, drawing life blood from the continuous warm and close contact with it.

Bialik felt that there was an element of artificiality in the Zionist leaders' attempt to make Hebrew the spoken language of the Jewish masses in the Diaspora. He argued that there was no objective need for the use of Hebrew as an everyday language in the Diaspora, and he, not unlike Sholem Aleichem, ridiculed the attempts of certain Zionist leaders to "declare" Hebrew the official language. A spoken language has to develop gradually and naturally from within, and cannot be imposed upon a people. He could not see any historical or sociological forces that would compel the Jews to adopt Hebrew as their native tongue as long as they remained in the Diaspora.

Naturally, Bialik's espousal of the cause of Yiddish meant only for the Diaspora; but even in Palestine he was opposed to a militant attitude toward the speaking of Yiddish, because he was so certain of the ultimate victory of Hebrew over Yiddish there.

The attitude of Achad Ha'am was somewhat similar to that of Bialik, although it savored of condescension toward Yiddish; nor was it free from an element of snobbishness.

He relegated the use of Yiddish to the *am ha'aretz* (ignoramus), who had no knowledge of Hebrew or its literature. In his view, the only justification for Yiddish as a vehicle of thought and culture was the fact that it was the language of the Jewish masses, and the writer who wished to reach them must do so through the medium of Yiddish. Later on his attitude hardened, and he insisted that a clear stand be taken in this matter. He likened the situation of Eastern European Jewry to that of the early Jewish Christians, who at first vacillated between declaring for or against Christianity but who ultimately had to come to a decision and take a final stand. "Art thou for us or for our adversaries?" was the challenge he threw out to the antagonists engaged in the Hebrew *vs.* Yiddish contest. Sometimes the reader gains the impression that Achad Ha'am was altogether losing patience over the language controversy. "I must admit," he says, "that this question concerning our national tongue, arousing as it recently has done, heated discussions in journals and from the platform of meetings, seems to be a suitable subject for a light *feuilleton.* Imagine, a nation thousands of years old doesn't know which is its national tongue! Some say it is this, others maintain it is that, and in between there are a number of peacemakers suggesting a compromise. 'Let's accept them both,' they say, 'and let there not be quarreling among brothers.' Open the history books of all nations and languages, and look diligently to see if you can find such a peculiar situation elsewhere." [8]

It is not surprising that the general Zionist leader, Yizhak Gruenbaum, who was always close to Yiddish-speaking Jewish masses and who in the years between the two World

[8] *Kol Kitvei Achad Ha'am* (Tel Aviv: Dvir, 2nd ed., 1949), p. 404.

Wars represented Polish Jewry in the Polish *Sejm,* should have adopted a tolerant attitude toward Yiddish. He even put forward further arguments in justification of Yiddish as the popular spoken language of the Jews. He was afraid that if Hebrew became the sole vehicle of Jewish thought and speech the Zionist intelligentsia would become alienated from the Jewish masses. That is why he proposed at the Zionist Conference convened in Vienna in 1913 that Yiddish be given a place in the Jewish schools of Eastern Europe. Gruenbaum feared a division of Jews into Hebrew- and Yiddish-speaking factions—a division which might further accentuate the existing class distinctions among the Jewish people. He pointed out that it was Yiddish that had created the right "atmosphere" or framework within which Hebrew could develop most naturally and with great ease. In an environment created by languages entirely alien to Jews this would not be possible. Far from being the enemy of Hebrew, Yiddish should be regarded as its natural ally.

On the other hand, Gruenbaum recognized the short-comings of Yiddish if considered as the prospective Jewish national tongue. He himself was a convinced Hebraist. Like Brenner, he felt that Yiddish was too soft and plastic a tongue and apt to absorb foreign idiom too quickly. In his view, this was due to the fact that it never commanded the respect that is accorded a national tongue, even among Yiddish-speaking Jews, but was merely regarded as a homely "jargon." In his view, one of the characteristics of a national tongue is that it develops together with its people from early antiquity, and this cannot be said of Yiddish. Moreover, had it been properly respected as a national tongue men would have risen to protect it from undue foreign influence. (In the eighteenth century Dr. Johnson, among others, felt that English was absorbing too many foreign idioms and expressions and set about the task of writing his famous dictionary, in which he attempted to keep within bounds the foreign element which he thought was corrupting his native tongue. The absence of a Yiddish counterpart to Dr. Johnson is rather characteristic in this respect.)

Moreover, Gruenbaum felt that Yiddish could not be regarded as the universal language of the Jewish people or as a force uniting it, because it was only spoken by the Jews of the Polish-German territories of Central and Eastern Europe, whereas outside this area there were many sections of the Diaspora where it was not known at all.

At a conference held in Czernowitz in 1908, where the chairmanship was shared by Dr. Zhidlowski, Dr. Nathan Birnbaum, and the Yiddish writer J. L. Peretz, the Yiddishists put forward their ideas very forcefully. They declared that Hebrew was nonexistent as a living tongue and pointed to the difficulty of reviving it artificially (as they felt). Why should not the language spoken by the Jewish masses be declared the national tongue of the Jewish people? This approach was of course an oversimplification of the issue. Nor did they answer the serious objections raised by the Hebraists against the recognition of Yiddish as the Jewish national tongue. When considering the qualifications of the three above-mentioned protagonists of Yiddish one cannot help feeling that there was a certain piquancy in the fact that Nathan Birnbaum, whose mother tongue was German and who was steeped in German culture, became one of the leaders of the Yiddishist movement. He was the "showpiece" of the Yiddishists, as he had deliberately and consciously rejected German and become an adherent of their movement.

It is hardly surprising that Sholem Aleichem, himself a Yiddish writer of genius, should have discerned the incongruity of the proceedings at the Czernowitz conference. He was particularly amused by the opening speech of Dr. Birnbaum, which the latter read out in Yiddish from prepared notes and which actually sounded German; nor could he refrain from making satirical comments on the dramatic kiss bestowed by Sholem Asch upon the Yiddish poet Abraham Reisin, intended to symbolize the final "decision" in favor of Yiddish. It seemed ridiculous to him that a group of writers should believe that they could formally "settle," to the accompaniment of melodramatic gestures, issues of far-reaching historic importance affecting millions of people. He keenly sensed the absurdity of a formal declaration that this or that language should become the Jewish national tongue. In his inimitable satirical vein he writes as follows: "While lying on my sickbed in the well-known town of Baranovich, I succeeded in transporting myself to Czernowitz, the seat of the conference; that is to say, my sinful body actually remained here, but my soul wandered there to free Bukowina, to the first conference sponsoring Yiddish as the official language of the Jews. Throughout the week of the conference I was in a state of feverish excitement. My temperature rose from day to day, the cough I had developed became worse, I lost my appetite, and my doctor was very worried about me. While listening to Dr. Birnbaum's opening speech which he delivered in his "mother tongue," my temperature rose by another ten degrees. Then during the lively debate on the question as to which is our national tongue, Hebrew or Yiddish, my temperature continued rising steadily. . . . When I heard that resounding kiss bestowed by my friend Sholem Asch on Abraham Reisin the thermometer jumped to almost 40 degrees, so that my doctor became alarmed. When the conference closed, and the delegates had gone home I immediately recovered. Then the idea came into my mind that I might follow the example of Scholem Asch [who had translated the Book of Ruth into Yiddish] and myself attempt to translate Ecclesiastes into our mother tongue. . . ."

His translation of Ecclesiastes was of course a brilliant satirical performance, which unfortunately cannot be rendered in English.[9] What Sholem Aleichem tried to bring out in his "translation" was the extreme difficulty, if not impossibility, of rendering the majestic, flowing cadences of the Bible into a language which is merely a colloquial and homely folk tongue. In his opinion, both sides in the language contest were equally wrong—those who fought Yiddish and those who opposed the introduction of Hebrew as a spoken language. He thought the issue should be allowed to settle itself. Those who fought Yiddish, especially Yiddish literature, did an injustice to the people who needed a literature which was understandable to them; while opposition to Hebrew was, in his view, merely childish. Hebrew was a language in which a great tradition was enshrined and could not be considered "dead" without

[9] *Dos iz die reid fun Koheles, der zun fun David, der kenig fun Yerushalaim. 2. Blotte she-beblotte, sogt Koheles, blotte she-beblotte-es iz allsding blotte, a nechtiger tog. 3. Wos kummt herois dem menschen fun sein ganzen tararam, wos er schlogt sich kopp in wand? 4. Ein dor geit aweg, der anderer kummt un, un die welt bleibt a welt.* (See S. Rosenheck, *Bein Ha-Ketzavoth,* published in Hebrew Yearbook, *Carmelit,* 1960, p. 269.)

doing violence to historical fact. Altogether, he thought that it was a great pity that so much time was wasted on arguing on this issue. Instead, he thought, it would have been far more profitable if Jewish writers produced more literature for the people in any language, as long as it was understood by them.

The most radical champion of Hebrew, as far as Jewish schools were concerned, was Vladimir Jabotinsky. The conviction that Hebrew was to be the language of instruction in Jewish schools came to him gradually. There was a time when he preached his famous "two-fifths program," i.e., that two fifths of the instruction given in Jewish schools was to be in Hebrew, but later, he abandoned this view and came to be the champion of an all-out Hebrew educational program. This is rather surprising in view of his background, which was entirely assimilationist. Between 1910 and 1913 he wandered from one Russian Jewish Community to another, repeating with variations his famous speech on *Sfat ha'Tarbut ha'Ivrit* (The Language of Hebrew Culture). He took great personal pride in that speech, which proved extremely effective and had great influence. For the student of Jewish education this speech is of particular interest since it is to some extent based on educational principles.

The speech was mainly aimed against the "moderates," those who supported the introduction of a bilingual system in the Jewish schools. Moreover, in order to understand his way of argument we have to bear in mind that there were fundamental differences of opinion on the essence of Jewish culture between him and men such as Bialik and Achad Ha'am.

Like Brenner, Jabotinsky maintained that Hebrew culture is characterized by a purely formal criterion—its vehicle of expression, the Hebrew language itself; and that the same criterion applied to Jewish education. In Jewish national education the language is the main thing and the content irrelevant—mere chaff, as he put it. What distinguished Hebrew culture from any other is just that fact— that Hebrew is the vehicle of its expression. Bialik and Achad Ha'am would have reversed this statement. Their view was that spiritual content is the main distinguishing feature of Jewish culture, and not merely language.

According to Jabotinsky it follows that a school curriculum that confines the use of Hebrew to the teaching of Judaic subjects only is transmitting Hebrew culture only in part. He took objection to the bilingual character of the Jewish school, calling it by the derogatory appellation *shaatnes*—a compound of heterogeneous elements.

Moreover, asks Jabotinsky, what are the most formative influences in the development of a child? Jabotinsky argues that these are not derived from specifically Jewish sources, such as the prayer book and Holy Writ. The first questions a child asks are not those pertaining to specifically religious or national matters; his curiosity is aroused by entirely different things. A child will ask: "Why don't horses drag locomotives? Why are street lights so bright? Why is it cold in winter and warm in summer?" Note down all the questions that a child asks you within a month and you will quickly realize that only a small part of them relates to matters specifically Jewish, whereas the great majority pertain to general matters closely akin to secular studies. Therefore, the language which exercises the decisive influence on the child is the one in which secular subjects are taught. (Analogically, it may be mentioned that there is a view widely held by teachers today that pupils learn their mother tongue at school not so much from the person who teaches it as a subject as from the teachers who use it merely as a medium of instruction in other subjects.)

It is surprising that Jabotinsky should have been so successful in his campaign on behalf of the Hebrew language despite the fact that the Jewish people whom he addressed did not share his views concerning the nature of Jewish culture and were more inclined to accept the views expressed by Bialik and Achad Ha'am. His amazing success can therefore only be attributed to his magnetic personality and great powers of oratory. However, although the Jewish masses accepted his policy, it was for quite different reasons and on different grounds from those he formulated.

These reasons had their roots in the nature of their existence in the Diaspora, which was most precarious both economically and socially, due to the anti-Semitism rampant in all walks of life. The Jewish masses as a whole found it impossible to become assimilated to their hostile surroundings, and when they accepted Jabotinsky's advocacy of Hebrew education for their children they probably had in mind a future in Palestine. They did not think of the Hebrew schools as preparing their children as future citizens of Poland or Russia, but regarded a Hebrew education as the best *Hachshara* (training) for future immigration to Palestine.

The difference of opinion between Bialik and Jabotinsky on matters of educational policy in the Diaspora can be entirely explained by their totally different backgrounds. Bialik was steeped in Jewish culture and had spent his whole youth studying Talmud in the *Yeshiva*. He could therefore properly appreciate the enormous potentialities of Jewish literature as a source from which modern Hebrew could draw and develop. (It was, of course, Bialik's tacit assumption that this literature is studied with the diligence and devotion characteristic of a Yeshiva student.) Jabotinsky did not know this, coming as he did from an assimilated atmosphere. To Bialik it did not greatly matter in what language it was explained to a child "why trains were not pulled by horses," as even from a purely linguistic point of view a person steeped in ancient Jewish literature could find sufficiently rich sources of material to feed and develop the spoken tongue. This is proved by the fact that the builders of modern Hebrew were men with a traditional Jewish (i.e., Hebrew) background, such as Ben Yehuda, Bialik, and Agnon, and not those who lacked such an education.

It would, of course, be a misrepresentation of history if the foundation of the Hebrew *Tarbut* schools were to be attributed merely to the efforts of this or that individual. The establishment of these schools was the culmination of a movement toward the revival of the Hebrew language—a movement in which many prominent Jewish writers and thinkers participated. It was in particular the *Haskalah* that gave a fresh impetus to the study of Hebrew and gave rise to the publication of the first Hebrew periodicals, which contributed to the dissemination of modern Hebrew. Even Mendelssohn, who was essentially a German writer, had contributed to Hebrew journals of his time such as *Koheleth Mussar* and *Hameaseph*. Since the *Haskalah* period there has been an almost continuous stream of Hebrew magazines published in Eastern Europe, and these gained an ever-widening circle of readers.

Without deprecating the part played by individual

Hebraists in the movement which led to the establishment of Hebrew Day schools in Eastern Europe, we have to point out that their contribution, though important, was not the main factor in the revival of Hebrew. The main impetus to the revival of Hebrew in the Diaspora came, of course, from the Zionist movement as a whole. Besides, even before the first all-Hebrew schools in Poland were founded, schools which used Hebrew as the medium of instruction were already flourishing in Palestine, where Hebrew was naturally and automatically becoming the spoken language of the country. It was in Palestine, too, that Eliezer Ben Yehuda was endeavoring to establish Hebrew as a modern spoken tongue. Needless to say, the supporters of all-Hebrew day schools in Poland derived inspiration from the example of Palestine.

Born of a traditional Jewish family in Lithuania in 1858, Ben Yehuda was at first a *Yeshiva* student but ran away to a secular Gymnasium. Upon finishing the Gymnasium he went to study medicine in Paris. After immigrating to Palestine he taught in the Alliance school, and was a member of the staff of Frumkin's Hebrew periodical, *Havatzelet*. In 1885 he became the publisher and editor of the Hebrew weekly *Hazvi*, which later became a daily paper and appeared up to the outbreak of the First World War. He was one of the foremost Hebrew linguists of his time engaging in research on the Hebrew language, which he found inadequate for modern life and which he wished to develop further. To this end he traveled widely in Europe and America, gathering extensive material for his famous dictionary, the *Milon Halashon Haivrit Hayeshana Vehachadasha*, which he started to publish in 1910. In the year 1890 he also founded the *Vaad Ha'Lashon* (Language Committee), which was to become the forerunner of the present-day Language Academy and of which Ben Yehuda was president to the day of his death.

Eliezer Ben Yehuda may be called the central figure in the movement for the revival of the Hebrew tongue in Palestine. It was the aim of his life to make Hebrew into a living, modern, spoken language; and with this aim in view he revived old Hebrew words with diligence and devoted zeal. His dictionary contained many words which no linguist had ever used before, which he drew from all levels and periods of Jewish literature—from the Bible, the *Mishnah,* the Talmud. He was also courageous enough to eliminate from the Hebrew language many foreign words of non-Semitic origin.

As far as Europe was concerned, up to 1917 Russia had been the center of the movement for the revival of Hebrew. But after the communist revolution many Hebrew writers and teachers moved to Poland and to those parts of Lithuania which had been ceded to Poland by Russia. Thus, although its Jewish population was only half of that in Russia, Poland became the spiritual heir and focal point of the Hebraist movement in Europe.

The foundation of the *Tarbut* schools was the result of gradual development, the culmination of the efforts of many individuals aided by the influence of many organized movements. The main goal of these schools was the preparation of young people for immigration to Palestine, as there was no future for them in Poland. The first stage in the development of the Hebrew school was the so-called *cheder metukan* or reformed *cheder.* This gave way to the bilingual school, and finally the first Hebrew secondary school was established in Vilna in 1915. This was followed by the establishment of the first all-Hebrew elementary school at Gonjentz in the Bialystok district in 1916. This primary school was meant to "feed" pupils to the secondary school, to prepare them for further study, with Hebrew as the language of instruction.

In 1922 the *Tarbut* organization was formed, and gave its name to the Hebrew schools which were founded under its auspices. This organization incorporated all other existing associations fostering the spread of Hebrew culture and set the tone for the aims and aspirations of its schools. There the pupils were educated to Zionism and pioneering, and were imbued with the conviction that the redemption of the Jewish people was only possible in their homeland, Palestine. The Hebrew language was of course the medium of instruction, and, although these schools were secular and did not teach religious observance, their spirit was not anti-traditional in a militant way, but rather neutral in matters of tradition. They rejected the educational and organizational setup of the traditional *cheder* and wished to supersede it. There were various opinions on the point of Jewish tradition, ranging from a completely negative attitude to a pronouncedly sympathetic one. According to Dr. Ormian,[10] the schools in the smaller villages acquired a distinctly religious spirit. On the whole, the *Tarbut* schools sought to implant in their pupils a recognition of their link with the past and with the spirit of Jewish tradition and ethics; but it was not considered necessary to include the recital of prayers as part of school activities. Religion was not a subject taught in the schools, and if it did appear in the syllabus of some schools this was merely a concession to the

[10] Dr. H. Ormian, *ha-Machshavah ha-chinuchit shel Yahadut Polania* (Tel Aviv: 1939), p. 172.

requirements of the Polish Government authorities, who insisted that religion be taught in all schools. On the other hand, the study of the Bible occupied a prominent place, whereas the Oral Law was taught in a half-hearted way. This is the reason why many traditionalists accused these schools of fostering a *Karaite* spirit. According to statistics quoted by Rosenheck,[11] in the year 1937-38 the *Tarbut* schools in Poland numbered 269 and were attended by 44,780 pupils.

The revival of Hebrew as a living spoken tongue and the establishment of Hebrew schools in Eastern Europe was by no means an artificially created process. The Jewish people had always been inculcated from earliest childhood with the traditional Hebrew prayers and Holy Writ, so that Hebrew had deep roots in their consciousness. Moreover, even in the Middle Ages, Hebrew, in addition to being the language of prayer and of Jewish studies, was also the language used for learned correspondence. It was the sole medium of the medieval Rabbinical *Responsa* literature, of which there is an enormous quantity extant. Thus, in a wider sense, Hebrew has never been an entirely "dead" language, and its adoption as the national tongue of the Jewish people in Israel was both natural and logical.

[11] S. Rosenheck's article on "Jewish Education in Poland between the Two World Wars" appears in *Beth Israel be-Polin, Youth Dept. of the Zionist Organization,* 1953.

6

Some Aspects of Kibbutz *Education*

I

The most striking feature of *kibbutz* education is that *kibbutz* parents forego their natural desire to rear and educate their offspring, and, instead, hand them over to the "Children's House" of the *kibbutz,* to be educated by professionals (specially appointed nurses and educators). What makes this voluntary renunciation more astounding is the fact that children are generally withdrawn from the care of their parents at an extremely tender age—in many *kibbutzim,* immediately after birth. It is difficult to find a parallel to this practice in the history of European education. One has to look into the realm of Utopias—such as Plato's *Republic*—to find something remotely resembling this practice. (In Sir Thomas More's *Utopia,* children are raised and educated by their own parents; only in cases where the family had more children than it could cope with were the surplus offspring distributed among other families.)

Kibbutz education presents four questions of particular interest to the student of the philosophy of education:

1) What were the motives that prompted the founders of the Palestinian *kibbutzim* to introduce such a novel and

146

revolutionary system of child education, particularly in view of the traditional attachment of Jewish mothers to their children—an attachment which had indeed become proverbial?

2) What arguments in favor of this system have been put forward by the propounders of *kibbutz* ideology?

3) In the light of the experience gained during the last half-century, and in consideration of development in *kibbutz* education, what are the advantages of this system as it stands?

4) What are the more recent developments and trends in *kibbutz* education?

Viewed historically, there can be no doubt that the collective education of children in a *kibbutz* was the result of the adaptation of the first communal settlers in Palestine to the pioneering way of life. The system of collective education must have appealed to the first pioneers on purely economic grounds. It released the mothers from the exacting duties of rearing and looking after their own children and made it possible for them to work side by side with the men. The labor force of the *kibbutz* was thus augmented, since a very small staff was required to look after the children. Finally, it enabled the members of the *kibbutz* to offer their children conditions of material comfort which they, as individuals, could not afford to give them. This is particularly true of the early *kibbutz* settlers, who lived in tents or primitive huts, and, since better housing could not be provided for all, it was natural that the first permanent buildings were allotted to the children.

Arguments of a purely educational and ideological nature in favor of collective education were evolved at a later stage of *kibbutz* life, though sometimes we find pronouncements of *kibbutz* education in which ideological considerations are linked with economic ones. Typical in this respect is the following passage written by one of the leading settlers of Degania fifty years ago: "The duty to take care of all children rests not only on the mother, but on all the women of the group, even on the unmarried ones. If all the women would take a share in the rearing of the children, the mothers would be able to do other forms of work, too. As for the expense of rearing and educating the children, this should be shared by all the members of the group, as should the care of the future generation. No one should be exempt merely because he himself has no children. All such distinctions undermine the basis of the collective idea." [1]

Here the practical necessity of collective education comes out very clearly. ("If all the women would take a share," etc.) Yet at the same time the collective responsibility of the *kibbutz* toward each child is presented as stemming from the idea of the commune as such.

Later, with the development and consolidation of the *kibbutz*, the economic motive behind collective education gradually recedes, and ideological and educational considerations gain prominence.

1) It is pointed out that the *kibbutz* way of life makes for complete equality between the sexes. Outside the *kibbutz* in a capitalist society the woman who works bears a double burden—that of the home and that of her job. In the *kibbutz* she is freed from this double burden, and her emancipation is real and complete.

2) *Kibbutz* educators maintain that the education of children in special Children's Houses is the best way of perpetuating the *kibbutz* way of life. The *Mossad Yeladim*

[1] *A New Way of Life* (London: Shindler and Golomb, 1949), pp. 29-30.

is a *kibbutz* in miniature, where children are reared from their earliest childhood in the atmosphere of a commune. Thus they become conditioned to *kibbutz* life and accept it as a matter of course, which they would not do if they were brought up by their parents. Parallels to this practice are found in totalitarian countries, where children from the earliest age are introduced to the way of life considered desirable for them. It is therefore not surprising that those who join the *kibbutz* later and who have not had the *kibbutzic* way of life instilled into them from early infancy comprise the majority of members leaving a *kibbutz,* whereas such instances are rare among settlers who were born there. In justification of collective education from an early age, one of the *kibbutz* teachers has made the following pithy remark: "You cannot teach a child to swim outside the water."

3) Collective education is more democratic than the traditional education within the family, and more in keeping with the spirit of co-operative living. Indeed, it is the practical realization of the idea of educational equality, which is a corollary of social and economic equality.

4) Collective education is more "scientific" than education within the family, inasmuch as children are reared and trained by experts, i.e., qualified nurses, kindergarten teachers, and other educators. Their approach to children is more objective than that of parents and more in keeping with educational principles. Parents, especially Jewish ones, are often apt to be either overambitious for their children, and, consequently, overexacting or overindulgent. Moreover, the atmosphere of the home often lacks harmony because of strained relationships between the parents, and fails to provide a favorable educational background for

children. All these adverse factors are, *a priori,* eliminated
in the Children's House of the *kibbutz.*

II

The first generation of settlers came from Eastern and
Central Europe, where they had absorbed the revolutionary
ideas emanating from the Russian revolution. There was
also a sprinkling of Eastern European Jews who had studied
in Germany and had there absorbed the revolutionary educational ideas propounded by the German youth movements and by educational theoreticians such as Gustav
Wyneken and Herman Lietz, whose teachings caught the
imagination of sensitive and intelligent Jewish youth with
leftist sympathies. Theirs was a twofold rebellion. Firstly,
the young pioneers rebelled against the traditional character of the Jewish family. In most cases the parents were
observant Jews and their children regarded the commandments of Judaism simply as fetters forged by the Diaspora.
Secondly, they rebelled against the whole structure of the
Jewish family, in which the children were financially dependent upon their petit bourgeois parents, who in most
cases objected to the "free" Zionist and socialist tendencies
of their children.

In Wyneken's educational pronouncements great emphasis was laid on the youthful autonomy and the desire
to lead a life in accordance with the nature of youth, independent of the prevailing views of adult society. "Youth,
hitherto merely an appendage of the older generation, excluded from the life of the community and given only the
passive role of learning and with opportunities only for a
dilettante form of social life, is beginning to become con-

scious of itself. It is trying to mold its own life in order to become independent of the lazy habits of its elders and of the commands of ugly convention. It is striving for a way of life which corresponds to the nature of youth, but which at the same time will enable it to take itself and its activity seriously and to bind itself as a special factor to the general cultural activity." [2]

Educational ideas such as those expressed in the famous Meissner Proclamation of the Free German Youth in 1913 inspired many of the young Jews who had made their way into the newly established communes of Palestine. That German desire for the "autonomous youth culture" way of life became amalgamated with their Zionist and socialist consciousness, and the combined impact made itself felt on those early settlers of Palestine. Because they themselves were rebels they were prone to absorb revolutionary ideas.

Moreover, the system of education adopted by the Palestine *kibbutzim* assumed a pronounced Freudian character in the course of time. It is not difficult to conjecture why the *kibbutz* educators adhered to Freud's theories and accepted him as the patron saint of their school system. It must be borne in mind that during the first decades of this century there was a powerful Freudian vogue in central Europe, and propounders of an *avant-garde* system of education found it desirable to be in accord with Freudian ideas. Furthermore, the revolutionary character of the pioneers demanded, by dint of its inner logic, acceptance of a philosophy of education contrasting as sharply as possible with that of traditional Judaism. Freudian ideas and teachings, not only in the field of education but also in the

[2] Samuel and Thomas, *Education and Society in Modern Germany* (Routledge and Kegan Paul, 1949), pp. 29-30.

fields of religion and culture in general, fulfilled this requirement ideally.

According to Freud, education within the family unit, in contrast to collective education, is fraught with certain dangers, which in the views of *kibbutz* educators could be eliminated or at least diminished if the child were transferred from its parents' care to that of strangers. The dangers inherent in educating the child within the family unit are as follows:

a) The repression of desires resulting from an Oedipus complex may create anxieties and phobias which often undermine a child's mental stability and general development. This danger is diminished if a child's first emotional ties and attachments fasten on strangers rather than parents. Also, the parent-child relationship is not aggravated by educational demands made upon children by their parents, since it is the strangers who undertake the disciplinary and socializing functions.

b) According to Freud, the task of educating children is particularly difficult for parents who had once rebelled against their own parents. The reason for this peculiar phenomenon is clearly explained in the following passage: "For us, the super-ego is the representative of all moral restrictions, the advocate of the impulse towards perfection, in short, it is as much as we have been able to apprehend psychologically of what people call the higher things in human life. Since it itself can be traced back to the influence of parents, teachers, and so on, we shall learn more of its significance if we turn our attention to these sources. In general, parents and similar authorities follow the dictates of their own super-egos in the up-bringing of children. On whatever terms their ego may be with their super-ego, in the education of the child they are severe and exacting. They have forgotten the difficulties of their own childhood, and are glad to be able to identify themselves fully at last with their own parents, who in their day subjected them to such severe restraints. The result is that the super-ego of the child is not really built upon the model of the parents, but on that of the parents' super-ego; it takes over the same contents, it becomes the vehicle of tradition and of all the age-long values which have been handed down in this way from generation to generation." [3]

Thus parents who had once rebelled against the authority of their own parents are aware of the fact that they derive their own moral consciousness from that of their parents; but they refuse to become the vehicle of tradition and reject that function of their own super-egos. The best way to escape this dilemma is therefore to transfer to strangers the responsibility for educating their children.

c) According to the opinion of Freudian educators there is a third difficulty inherent in education within the family. Parents bestow love upon their children, but at the same time have to discipline, control, and if necessary punish them. This twofold role evokes an ambivalent attitude on the part of children toward their parents, a feeling of love and gratitude not infrequently mixed with fear and even hatred. The relationship between parents and their chil-

[3] Sigmund Freud, *New Introductory Lectures on Psycho-Analysis* (New York: W. W. Norton and Co., 1933), p. 95. (In his book *Children of the Kibbutz* (Cambridge, Mass.: Harvard University Press, 1958), p. 14, Mr. Spiro praises the "very perceptive paper of Elizabeth E. Irvine," in which she suggests the above-mentioned point as an explanation for the desire of rebellious parents to hand over their children to be educated by strangers. Credit for this idea should indeed go to Freud, and both Miss Irvine and Mr. Spiro evidently overlooked this source when making their point.)

dren will become more harmonious if the two parental functions are separated and the parents' disciplinary role is transferred to "objective" educators.

We have so far shown the various advantages of collective education over education in the family as they appear to the Freudian educator. However, the adoption of Freudian principles in *kibbutz* education goes further still. The literature produced by *kibbutz* ideologists and teachers shows that they accept the Freudian conception of the main task of education. Freud has formulated it in the following way: "Let us get a clear idea of what the primary business of education is. The child has to learn to control its instincts. To grant it complete freedom, so that it obeys all its impulses without any restriction, is impossible. It would be a very instructive experiment for child-psychologists, but it would make life impossible for the parents and would do serious damage to the children themselves, as would be seen partly at the time, and partly during subsequent years. The function of education therefore, is to inhibit, forbid and suppress, and it has at all times carried out this function admirably. But we have learnt from analysis that it is this very suppression of instincts that involves the danger of neurotic illness. . . . Education has therefore to steer its way between the Scylla of giving the instinct free play and the Charybdis of frustrating them. Unless the problem is altogether insoluble, an optimum of education must be discovered, which will do the most good and the least harm. It is a matter of finding out how much one may forbid, at which times and by what methods." [4]

It is interesting to note that Freud himself merely poses the problem and leaves its solution to the educators.

[4] *Ibid.*, pp. 203-4.

Equally significant is Freud's admission that this is altogether a most difficult task, possibly even beyond the power of the educator. *Kibbutz* education has directed its main efforts toward the solution of this problem and these efforts are faithfully mirrored in their educational literature. In this literature the problems of child management, discipline, the legitimate use of reward and punishment, the educator's attitude to the child's impulses and bodily desires, and the attempt to sublimate them rank rather prominently. These problems are dealt with in the light of Freud's warning that an outright authoritarian approach on the part of the educator may be harmful to the child. The constant striving for new methods to replace the authoritarian approach of the traditional educator is characteristic of their literature and practice. It is hardly surprising that *kibbutz* educators have not succeeded in solving this problem entirely satisfactorily.

In view of Freud's warning against repression, *kibbutz* education has been, on the whole, permissive and opposed to unmotivated prohibitions, at least in theory. It does not inculcate a consciousness of sin nor does it believe in taboos. Rather than advocate the suppression of physical desires, it believes in directing the child's energies to positive and acceptable channels, though it is less clear how this is to be done in practice. It does not regard any instinctual behavior as intrinsically evil or wicked and rejects corporal punishment as morally wrong and harmful to the child. Indeed, *kibbutz* educators view punishment of any sort as undesirable from an educational point of view. The social behavior of the child is fostered by rewards rather than by punishment or even threats of punishment. Some *kibbutz* educators even view with misgiving the withdrawal

of love on the part of the educator as a reaction to a child's
unsocial behavior, as may be seen from the following passage taken from a *kibbutz* journal: "We do not throw the
child into depths of fear for loss of love of his educators
when he cannot withstand the pressure of his instincts, but
we base our education on the love of the child, and not on
his fear, as the principal restraint. . . . Our system dimin-
ishes in the child the necessity of escaping from the se-
ductions of his instincts by repressing them. . . ." [5] *Kibbutz* education has taken greater heed of Freud's warning
against causing repression of instincts, and thus neurotic
illness, than of his assertion that education entails restriction, prohibition, and suppression.

How does the *kibbutz* educator cope with the problem of
disciplining children? A brief review of relevant literature
on the subject as well as educational practice in the *kibbutz*
show that the measure most frequently used in relation to
children above infancy is an appeal to their conscience, to
their loyalty to *kibbutz* values, and to the general standards
of conduct prevailing in the *kibbutz* community. The following characteristic admonitions are frequently heard:
"This is not the way people in the *kibbutz* behave," or
"The *mossad* could not exist if everyone behaved like you."
The teacher often appeals to the group, or the class, in
order to obtain support in his endeavor to make certain
values and rules of conduct accepted, or to obtain the
condemnation of the behavior of the child who violates a
rule or principle of conduct.[6]

Needless to say, sometimes the parents are also called
upon to aid in the disciplining of their children. This view-

[5] *Ibid.*, p. 410.
[6] The same point is made by Spiro, *op. cit.*, p. 412.

point—that professionals and not parents are the main educators of *kibbutz* children—has varying degrees and shades of strictness in execution, generally depending on the affiliation of the *kibbutz* to one of the nation-wide organizations. The most orthodox in this respect, and therefore the most insistent on the decisive role of the professional educator, are the *kibbutzim* affiliated to the *Kibbutz Artzi* movement of *haShomer haTzair*. Slightly more lenient in this respect are the *kibbutzim* of the *haKibbutz haMeuchad* organization of *Achdut haAvodah*, while the least inhibited by ideological principles are the *Mapai kibbutzim* belonging to the *Ichud haKibbutzim vehaKvutzot*. In religious *kibbutzim* the parents play a more decisive role in the upbringing of their children and the children's *mossad* is more in the nature of a boarding school and merely releases the mother for work in the *kibbutz*.

Broadly speaking it is true to say that *kibbutz* children develop a conscience based on the desire to conform to the moral of the society to which they belong, or, to use the Freudian nomenclature which Mr. Sipro adopts, they develop a "shame-oriented super-ego," a conscience based on fear of condemnation by their colleagues.[7]

[7] Mr. Spiro argues that the *kibbutz* child does not identify himself with his nurses or teachers because "the transiency and plurality of nurses precludes such identification." This being so, the child cannot "internalize" their values. His conscience is therefore based on his desire to conform with his equals. This conclusion seems right, though not the arguments he puts forward in its support. Mr. Spiro believes that an entire group of people who influence a child—nurses, teachers, parents —cannot be "introjected" in the Freudian sense. According to him, "introjection" is only possible if one or two people exercise an influence which is lasting and permanent. If Freud is Mr. Spiro's authority, it must be pointed out that Freud takes a different view. He admits the fact that a group of people can be "introjected" into a child's consciousness. Freud states expressly: ". . . During the course of its growth, the super-ego takes over the influence of those *persons* who have taken the place of

III

A critical appraisal of the theoretical foundations of *kibbutz* education should be immanent, and therefore in keeping with Freudian principles. First of all, it must be asked whether collective education really eliminates the difficulties arising from the Oedipus complex. Furthermore, is collective education really conducive to a healthy emotional development of children; is the incidence of psychic disturbances among *kibbutz* children rarer than in the case of children brought up in the traditional manner? As far as the Oedipus situation is concerned, Mr. Spiro has investigated this matter and found that Oedipus feelings do exist among *kibbutz* children. On the other hand, the annual *Review of Psychology*, 1960, Vol. II, quotes a paper by Rabin, who found that "judging from the responses to the Blackey test, ten-year-old *kibbutz* boys manifest less Oedipal intensity than do other boys of the same age."

However this may be, anyone who had lived in a *kibbutz* for an appreciable length of time and is acquainted with *kibbutz* education at first hand knows that psychic disturbances, as well as instances of enuresis and disturbed sleep and even neurotic states of a more serious nature, occur frequently enough among *kibbutz* children. *Kibbutz* chil-

the parents, that is to say of persons who have been concerned in the child's upbringing, and whom it has regarded as ideal models." (Sigmund Freud, *New Introductory Lectures on Psycho-Analysis*, p. 92.) We see here that Freud speaks of *persons* in the plural. However, apart from the question of the right interpretation of Freud's text, it is a fact that every child "introjects" more than one person. Parents, grandparents, various relatives, and educators in turn serve as models, the "models" varying with the different phases of the child's life.

dren have quite frequently to be treated by psychiatrists, although exact statistics on the incidence of psychic disturbance do not appear to be available. Spiro draws attention to the harmful effect on *kibbutz* children of the frequent change of nurses, which engenders a feeling of insecurity in the children, and which in turn has an adverse effect on personality development. He attributes to this circumstance a number of character traits which *kibbutz* children develop in their later lives, such as an exaggerated need for approval, lack of self-reliance, a feeling of inferiority, and even hostility toward strangers.

This contention of Mr. Spiro deserves comment and qualification. Mr. Spiro bases his conclusions concerning the character traits of *kibbutz* children on an investigation carried out on a relatively small number of children in a single *kibbutz*. He ignores the specific ideological differences between the various *kibbutz* organizations, whose educational concepts vary to an appreciable extent. He has not investigated a wider, more representative cross section of children taken from all types of *kibbutzim* in the country. It seems plausible enough that the frequent change of nurses and educators in *kibbutz* schools has indeed an adverse effect on the later development of some *kibbutz* children. However, had Mr. Spiro investigated a larger cross section of the *kibbutz* child population he might have found that there are children who develop a resistance to influences which in some cases may appear harmful. It is altogether rather surprising that he fails to discern a variety of types among *kibbutz* children.

S. Golan, an Israeli educator of repute and experience, discerns four different types among *kibbutz* children: the "positive" type of country child, the "simple" country child, the refined, intellectual child, and the "infantile" type.[8]

The "positive" country type, to which a very large number of *kibbutz* children belong is independent, practical, adaptable, and alert; these children are extremely devoted to their *kibbutz* home and alive to its problems. They take *kibbutz* society completely for granted, and derive profound personal satisfaction from agricultural work. They are also loyal to the political movement, to which their *kibbutz* belongs.

The "simple" country child is not essentially different from the first type, although his psychic make-up is simpler. He is also deeply rooted in the land, and his attitude to life is practical. He has the simplicity and naiveté of the peasant, and something of his shrewdness, too. He is entirely unproblematical, straightforward, and attached to his political movement without going deeply into its ideology; altogether, there is a certain superficiality in his character. Although good-hearted, his behavior to others is sometimes rather rough and uncouth; he tends to avoid responsibility and shows signs of what Golan calls "ethical relativism." His intellectual capacity is only average. He regards schooling as a burden, but shows keen interest in his work on the farm.

The refined intellectual type of *kibbutz* child stands out mostly because of his desire for individual self-expression. He is as healthy in mind and body as the other types, as deeply rooted in the land and as well orientated as they are, but displays characteristic intellectual and emotional traits. He shows a tendency toward introversion or escape

[8] Shmuel Golan, *"Sugiyot Ba-Kibbutz," Sifriat Poalim,* 1961, pp. 178 ff.

from the outer world, is reserved, subject to inner struggles, and has a certain emotional instability caused by his frequently changing moods. Although he desires to stand out in company, he shrinks from social contact with the "herd" and resorts to solitude. On the other hand, he tends to attach himself to certain "selected" individuals. He displays lively intellectual activity and is greatly interested in all fields of culture.

The infantile type of *kibbutz* child is characterized by slow development and a prolonged period of childhood and adolescence, while his mental maturity does not keep pace with his physical development. This type of child not infrequently displays a number of negative character traits, and usually acts not as an individual but with the "herd." He is noisy, insolent, given to mischief and showing off, and usually lacks self-control. He also takes little interest in intellectual or social activities. According to Golan, the place of this type of child is usually "on the periphery" of the *kibbutz* child population, impeding its development as a homogeneous educational unit.

Needless to say, some differentiation of *kibbutz* children, depending on native ability and temperament, whether or not conforming to the types described by Golan, is only to be expected. The *kibbutz* provides an ideal climate for the genesis of different types of children since it is not as closed a society as an outsider may assume. *Kibbutz* children spring from a variety of origins and backgrounds. There are children born in the *kibbutz;* those who come from abroad, generally through *Youth Aliya;* city children who for some reason or other are brought up in the *kibbutz;* orphaned children; and children from broken homes. Also, a *kibbutz* arouses the interest of the outsider because it embodies an ideal and a peculiar way of life. Hence city people from Israel and abroad are frequent visitors in *kibbutzim*. It is obvious that some children are more sensitive than others to the various influences brought to bear upon them. Some are more capable of assimilating the ideological values inherent in the *kibbutz* way of life, while others merely absorb the rural surroundings and the pleasant outward features which characterize it. All these facts should cause us to expect a great deal of individual variety in the character of *kibbutz* children. It is therefore rather unlikely that the *kibbutz* school consists of a more or less uniform type labeled by Mr. Spiro as *"the Sabra."* Indeed, those negative character traits which Mr. Spiro perceives in the *kibbutz* children as a whole Golan finds mainly in the infantile type.

IV

We have mentioned the criticism leveled by theoreticians of the *kibbutz* at the allegedly patriarchal or traditional character of the Jewish family in Europe. It seems more likely that in the Jewish family in Europe it was usually the educationally more competent person or the parent of stronger personality, be it father or mother, who assumed the leadership in the family and whose opinion in matters of child education was decisive, not necessarily depending on his earning capacity.

The philosopher Emil Utitz asserts that in his time, the early twentieth century, it was the mothers of the Prague Jewish community who more frequently than not assumed the leadership in the family, in spite of the fact that the fathers were always the breadwinners. But even if we accept the view that the source of authority in the family is linked with the parent's earning capacity it must be pointed out that in many Jewish families of Eastern Europe it was the mother who was the breadwinner, and not the father, who not infrequently was for the greater part of the working day engaged in Torah study. However this may be, it may be said with some justification that the *kibbutz* did not succeed in liberating itself from patriarchal influence of another form, i.e., the influence of the *kibbutz* secretary or the leadership of the party to which the *kibbutz* happened to belong. Berl Katznelson, the well-known labor leader, writes as follows: "The theory of the commune prevalent in the *kibbutzim* gives rise to another form of patriarchal rule. The place of the father of the family, or the tribal chief, is taken by the 'secretariat,' a collective body which is the symbol of the unity and authority of the tribe. And just as under patriarchal rule it was impossible (not forbidden, but simply impossible) to overstep the boundary of what is legitimate and accepted, so the *kibbutz* member who lives in a commune based on collective principles, cannot become intellectually self-reliant, but more frequently than not must remain merely a cog in the wheel." [9]

In spite of the desire of *kibbutz* theoreticians to free the child from the numerous thou-shalt-nots and so-called taboos of bourgeois society and to allow it to grow in an atmosphere of freedom, the *kibbutz* had to create many new taboos resulting from the fact that a large number of children cannot be brought up together without the institution of a number of rules and regulations governing their lives. Shoshana Muskatblüth, herself a *kibbutz* educator,

[9] Berl Katznelson, *haKibbutz vehaKvutzah* (Tel Aviv: Havaad Hapoel, 1950), p. 36.

complains about the growing tendency of *kibbutz* educators to complicate the life of children by the promulgation of an undue number of thou-shalt-nots. She points out that the undue number of things prohibited is remindful of the thou-shalts and thou-shalt-nots of traditional Jewish education. "We cannot help but ponder upon the question whether and to what extent we have succeeded in realizing our ideal which we hold so dear, namely, to give the child as much freedom of action and thought as possible, and to diminish the influence of the taboo which merely restricts and represses. It is our duty to review critically all the accepted prohibitions from time to time, and after careful consideration we have to reduce their number to the minimum, dictated by the need for the children's safety and consideration of fundamental educational demands." [10]

The same criticism is echoed by Golan, who feels that the many demands made upon *kibbutz* children by their community leads in later life to a desire to shirk responsibility and evade the duties imposed upon them by the collective.[11]

The most serious objection that may be raised against *kibbutz* education is its fostering of what Mr. Spiro calls the "shame-oriented super-ego." This is as much as to admit that the moral consciousness of the *kibbutz* child is not based mainly on the acceptance of certain moral or religious principles nor modeled on great personalities who are held up as examples to be emulated, but depends merely on conformity with the society in which they live. But is this a sufficient basis for the moral education of

[10] Shoshana Muskablüth, *"Mibaayot Hachinuch Hameshutaf," Urim—Hamercaz leHinuch veIrgun Ovdim,* pp. 40-41.

[11] S. Golan, *Hachinuch Hameshutaf* (Sifriat Hapoalim), p. 276.

children? One cannot always hold up society as an example, because it may deteriorate or be affected by internal crises. Although the *kibbutz* is certainly imbued with certain moral values, and life in the *kibbutz,* to a far greater extent than in any other group of society, is based on social justice, it, too, may sometimes show signs of decay—as, for instance, during the crisis leading to the split in the *kibbutz* movement, which occurred several years ago.

Indeed, the same criticism may be leveled at any type of modern education which is merely based on "life adjustment." Moral education should strive for the inculcation of certain principles which should serve as an accepted criterion for society. What society needs are not people who are trained to conform but those with independent minds, ready to criticize society or its leadership when events warrant it.

The inadequacy of the type of education that trains children to conform is well illustrated by a certain aspect of *kibbutz* education which is treated by Mr. Spiro with great frankness—namely, the lack of discipline in *kibbutz* schools.

"(Early morning class in Marxism—male teacher.) Twenty minutes after class begins, two boys of the twelfth grade walk in, talking, laughing, stopping to talk to other students as they make their way to their desks. . . . Some students are sleeping, some bored, some are talking, two are reading newspapers, some are catching flies, others are fighting, or laughing. . . . Suddenly they all decide to participate in discussion. The result is bedlam, everyone shouting at once." [12]

It is interesting to note that this should be the reaction

[12] Spiro, *op. cit.,* p. 321.

of the children to a lesson in Marxism, which forms the main ideological content of leftist *kibbutz* education and constitutes its accepted philosophy. The individual in this case has no feeling of shame at all, because the group as a whole does not disapprove of his conduct. Furthermore, when children leave the *kibbutz* they have to readjust themselves to a different way of life. In that event, should they also adopt uncritically the standards of the society in which they live?

Golan, like Spiro, admits that the group is of great importance as an educational unit, but unlike Spiro, he also stresses the importance of the individual educator and his relationship to the children. Golan holds that the moral influence upon the child does not emanate exclusively from the group, but also from the individual educator. Notwithstanding all theoretical doubts as to whether a plurality of educators can be "introjected" in the Freudian sense, Golan asserts on the basis of considerable experience that educational influence is exerted both by the educator and the child's parents, and more especially the former.[13] His is the power that encourages, activates; it is the educator who makes claims upon the child, who draws his attention to every detail and implants in the children's hearts the striving for morality and idealism. In the eyes of the children the educator embodies the model and example of the ideal *kibbutz* member—a model that is so frequently held up to them. This ideal *kibbutznik* is sociable, attached to the *kibbutz*, a good worker or craftsman, a brave fighter, a man of good education, loyal to his political movement, a man of integrity and conscience and imbued with a sense of collective responsibility. To sum up, Golan does not

[13] Golan, *op. cit.*, p. 252.

accept the opinion that the group is the only factor in the moral behavior of children, as Mr. Spiro seems to conclude on the basis of his very restricted investigations.

V

The achievements of *kibbutz* education are considerable. The *kibbutzim* have produced a healthy generation deeply rooted in Israel's soil and with a strong inclination for agricultural work and respect for physical toil in general. We have mentioned that they have actually achieved their main aim, which is the perpetuation of the *kibbutz* way of life. This is the ultimate criterion by which they wish to be judged. On the other hand, it must be admitted that they have been less successful as missionaries in spreading their ideas and way of life; nor have they been able to integrate an adequate proportion of Israel's immigrant population.

The period of service in the Israel Defense Army, when *kibbutz* youths are away from their own society for a long time, is for many of them a time of crisis in their development. In the army they come into contact with different types of youth and are exposed to the allurements of city life. There they can measure their education and attainments against the achievements of their colleagues in the army. Nevertheless, the percentage of *kibbutz*-born young people leaving the *kibbutz* after army service remains extremely small, ranging from 6 to 9 per cent. It is also interesting to note that although they constitute merely 4.2 per cent of Israel youth, *kibbutz* youths are doing outstandingly well in the army, and the number of officers, pilots, and other leaders from *kibbutzim* far exceeds this per-

centage. Moreover, *kibbutz* graduates occupy leading posi-
tions in various youth movements, act as guides and in-
structors to new immigrants in the reception camps, and
are sent abroad on various missions.

Nowadays the *kibbutz* is no longer merely an agricultural unit. It very often has a mixed economy, industrial
as well as agricultural. Consequently there is also evidence
among the younger members of a fresh approach to educational matters. The former prejudice of *kibbutz* educators
against academic studies is decreasing, and there is a certain
relaxation of restrictions which were prevalent in this field.
This change is evident in the variety of subjects now studied by the young people. The *kibbutz* needs engineers,
technologists, agronomists, and other professional men in
increasing numbers, to meet the needs of its complex economy. Nevertheless, the accepted studies are not confined
to engineering and agriculture, but students are also finding their way to the humanities. (As these lines were being
written a Ph.D. degree in History was awarded to the first
kibbutz-born student at the Hebrew University.) Of course,
it is understood that on completion of their studies they
will return to the *kibbutz*.

It is generally admitted that the younger generation of
kibbutz youth is perhaps less sophisticated, less interested
in politics, and less imbued with ideologies than were their
elders. The older generation regards this development with
a certain apprehension. However, there is bound to be a
marked difference between the youth who accept the *kibbutz* as their natural home, and therefore something which
does not require justification on ideological grounds, and
their parents, whose ideological principles formed the very
basis of their new lives. Unlike their parents, they are no

longer instilled with a spirit of rebelliousness against those who have reared them.

The matter-of-fact acceptance of the *kibbutz* by the young generation may even prove beneficial. A weakening of ideological indoctrination may gradually lead to a weakening of party affiliation and perhaps pave the way to greater unity. There is also a marked liberalizing tendency in matters of educational policy and practice. If the problem of child management loomed large in the past, today it is more the relationship between the parents and the educator that occupies the members' minds. Many members feel that the rights of parents to have a decisive say in the upbringing of their children is not sufficiently respected, and instances of families leaving a *kibbutz* are often attributable to parents who are dissatisfied with the educational policy of the commune. It is a fact that the right balance in the allocation of educational responsibilities between parents and educators has not yet been found. Nowadays the general tendency is for the parents to come into their own and take an ever-increasing share of the responsibility for the education of their children. One of the *kibbutz* educators expresses a feeling which is now generally held when he writes that ". . . nothing should be allowed to happen that might impair the feeling of happiness of parents in their healthy relationship with their children." [14]

Gone are the days when parents hardly dared to enter the Children's House or when children were not permitted to call their parents by any other than their first names—when there were no "parents" but merely *chaverim* (members of the *kibbutz*). Questions such as those of mixed

[14] *Hachinuch,* pub. by the Israel Teachers' Federation, 1960, p. 380.

showers, mixed sleeping quarters for children, or even the question of permitting children to sleep in their parents' apartments, are no longer regarded as matters of high principle from which no deviation is possible. The *kibbutz* is essentially a democratic institution, and its educational policy will always be influenced by the majority wish of the parents. This majority wish is swinging toward a greater emphasis on parental responsibility for the education of children.

Kibbutz teachers are alert and sensitive to criticism. Their educational literature exceeds, both in quantity and quality, that of other educational circles in Israel. Their open minds are reflected in their frank discussion of all controversial points connected with *kibbutz* education. With such a body of teachers it may justifiably be expected that with the passage of time the outstanding problems of *kibbutz* education will be satisfactorily solved.

7

Janusz Korczak

Janusz Korczak (formerly Henryk Goldschmidt) was born in Warsaw on July 22, 1878, the son of a wealthy and assimilated Jewish lawyer. Janusz was a highly sensitive child who sought solitude, indulged in day-dreams, and seems to have suffered a great deal, both at home and in school. At home he suffered because of the sickness of his father, who had frequently to undergo treatment in a mental home; at school, because of the severe discipline and the fear of corporal punishment with which the children were continually being threatened. As a boy he wrote poetry, and was most happy when he could fill the drawers of his writing desk with papers on which he jotted down the first fruits of his poetic endeavors.

He decided to study medicine, mainly because of his strong humanitarian leanings, and eventually became a specialist in children's diseases. He wrote a *Diary,* of which no Hebrew translation is to hand. A biographical novel, *Hadoktor Nish'ar (The Doctor Remains),* by Paulina Appenshlak, was published in 1953 by Kiryat Sefer, Ltd., Jerusalem. But as the dividing line between the facts and imagination is somewhat obscure this book cannot be used as a reliable basis for a biography of Korczak.

Korczak at first practiced medicine as a children's specialist and had a flourishing practice. Then he decided to give up practicing—it must have been in 1908—and to dedicate his whole life to the care of neglected and homeless Jewish children. He founded an orphanage in Krochmalna St., Warsaw, as well as summer-resort camps for his wards, and seems to have been able to raise enough funds to run these institutions at what was then considered a lavish standard. In fact, he was quite often criticized for creating too luxurious conditions for the Jewish children in his orphanage. He also retained part of his former practice, receiving patients one afternoon a week and devoting the proceeds to the orphanage. His institution aroused the interest of the Polish authorities, and upon his initiative a similar home for Polish gentile children was established in Proshkov.

In Warsaw Korczak became popular and famous as an educational writer and broadcaster. His frequent talks over the radio were of an educational nature; very often he spoke directly to children. Later on, probably because of rising anti-Semitism, he stopped broadcasting. Under the impact of Nazi persecution his Jewish consciousness became stronger; he became the representative of the non-Zionist section of Polish Jewry in the Jewish Agency. He visited Palestine in 1934 for the first time and stayed in Ein Harod. He took a great deal of interest in *kibbutz* life and in particular in *kibbutz* education. His letters and articles from that period show how deeply impressed he was by the new life which was then being created in Palestine.

During the Second World War he served as a doctor in the Polish army and protected the orphanage as long as was humanly possible. It would appear that the Germans respected him and offered to set him free if he would abandon the children of the orphanage, who were to be deported to an extermination camp. He refused to do so and was last seen at the head of a procession of children —two he carried in his arms—on his way to the appointed place of concentration for the Jews, from where they were loaded onto trucks headed for the gas chambers of Treblinka. He was never seen or heard of again.[1]

I

Korczak's educational writing is rich and varied. He wrote children's stories, a novel containing autobiographical material, *Yeled Ha'traklin* (*The Drawing-room Child*), *Mati the King*, and a children's book based on the life of Pasteur. His articles and other writings, which appeared in his own children's newspapers and other journals, have been collected and translated into Hebrew by the Hebrew poet Shimshon Meltzer and Professor Dov Sadan of the Hebrew University under the title *Ktavim Pedagogiim* (*Pedagogical Writings*). This and another book of his, *Keizad le'ehov Yeladim* (*How To Love Children*) were published by the *Kibbutz Hameuchad*. Here in Israel he is well known, especially in *kibbutz* circles, as one who devoted his whole life to the cause of education.

Korczak never married; he chose to renounce the joys of a home and family of his own in order to devote himself more completely to the orphans in his care. He seems

[1] Report in *Time and Tide*, December 19, 1942.

to have taken the decision not to marry while on a visit in England, "in a park near London." It is quite possible that he was also prompted by his fear of having inherited a schizophrenic disposition. The tragedy of his life has stirred even non-Jews, and a play based on Korczak's life, written by the German dramatist Erwin Silvanus, was staged with great success throughout Germany. Silvanus, himself a former inmate of a Nazi labor camp and an invalid as a result, was profoundly moved by the selflessness and self-sacrifice of the great Polish-Jewish humanist Korczak. The fact that his play has met with such success with German audiences is proof of the respect and admiration Korczak commands from Jew and gentile alike.

Korczak founded his orphanage in the year 1908, and remained its principal until July 1942. The organization and management of the orphanage were quite unlike those in any similar institution. The children themselves played a major part in running it, and were to a large extent responsible for its smooth functioning. Every new boy had to have a sponsor, a resident "old boy," who would introduce him to the institution. He did not become a member of the institution until admitted by general vote, which was held after a month. On the basis of the children's vote the newcomers were divided into three groups. The first consisted of the "plus" children, i.e., those who were pleasant, accepted by the others, and whose presence in the institution was considered desirable and beneficial. The "minus" children were usually those disliked by the permanent residents. The third group, classified as "zero," consisted of children to whom the others were more or less indifferent. After a year a second vote was taken and then every boy or girl was given a so-called "status." He could be: 1) a full member; 2) a temporary resident; 3) a boy to whom the others remained indifferent; 4) a difficult child who was likely to become a burden to the orphanage. There was of course a possibility of upgrading in the "status" of the children, while if the general assembly felt for a whole year that a boy was a burden and showed no improvement he was expelled. He could, however, after an interval of three months, be re-admitted and given another chance to prove himself fit to become a member of the children's community. These arrangements reflect Korczak's peculiar genius for complicated organization.

A boy who was a full member had more rights and more duties than those who were not. He could be elected to the Governing Board of the institution, which was composed entirely of children. He was usually a boy who displayed initiative and responsibility, could organize the children's play and recreation, and was entrusted with the valuable games and equipment of the orphanage. Such a boy was free to come and go as he pleased, and his views on all organizational matters carried some weight.

If a child was a temporary resident only he could not be given much responsibility in the running of the orphanage. The children in the other two groups could not be elected to the self-governing body. This seems to show that Korczak did not believe in indiscriminate equality among the boys in their democratic system of self-government. Moreover, when the institution distributed clothes to the boys, those who took care of them and kept themselves clean and neat were given the best suits, while careless and untidy boys received only the simple clothes they deserved.

There was also a "Tribunal" composed of five boys, whose duty it was to sit in judgment on offenders. Only boys who had clean and unblemished records were negligible, and the secretary of the Tribunal, who was usually the teacher or educator, was not one of its members and had no right to vote. Complaints against any one of the children, or even against one of the adults in the institution, had to be lodged at fixed times only. The "judges" would hear all the evidence, withdraw for consultation, and then pronounce their verdict, which was also published in the institution's weekly magazine. Korczak had a curious predilection for keeping records of the boys' conduct by indicating it on a graph.

The Council of the institution consisted of ten boys and the educator, who acted as its chairman, and only those boys who were full members and who had good records were eligible for the Council. The task of the council was to probe more deeply than the Tribunal and to investigate the causes that led to the offenses, and then to suggest ways and means for correction of errors or improvements in administration. It had also from time to time to review the rules of the institution in the light of experience gained, and make any alterations considered necessary. If the boys needed help or advice they could turn to the Council, which was also responsible for cleanliness and order in the orphanage.

The boys were required to assist in the work of the institution, which was divided into half-hour units. The boys had to work in shifts, which were changed once a month, and to complete a certain number of work units each day. The wishes of the individual boys were taken into consideration when the work was distributed. Thus the orphanage could be run with a comparatively small staff, which consisted of a matron, a housemaster or educator, a cook, and a maid. These were all assisted by groups of children in rotation.

Every week just before *Shabbat* the weekly magazine appeared. Korczak himself was its editor and frequently contributed to it. He was assisted by his devoted colleague Mrs. S. Wiliczinska; its pages contained accounts of all events and happenings at the orphanage, including school games and other features.

Despite the somewhat overelaborate organization of the orphanage and the high measure of self-government enjoyed by the children, Korczak's fatherly figure—like that of Pestalozzi in Stanz—dominated the institution. His was the decision in all matters, great and small. There was something of the Good Samaritan in Korczak's activities as an educator. Often he did not spare himself the most menial and unpleasant task, such as the washing of children's handkerchiefs and underwear, which some member of the orphanage staff had refused to perform. He would take into his own bed children who suffered from pain or nightmares, hoping that his physical proximity would cause them to calm down and fall asleep. In an article on Korczak, Ada Poznansky mentions that once he even kissed the sores on the iodine-smeared head of a boy, so that the child should not feel himself a pariah. Dov Sadan mentions that this type of conduct is in accordance with Chassidic tradition, and specifically quotes Rabbi Moshe Lev of Sassow, who said that "he who cannot lick the sores of an ailing child has not the slightest love for humanity."

II

Janusz Korczak was first and foremost a man of action in the field of education, a man permeated by ideals and a sense of mission. Throughout the history of Jewish education it is difficult to find another educator who devoted himself to his work so completely, bringing to it the force of his entire personality, as Janusz Korczak did.

Korczak's literary work may be regarded as a commentary on his practical work in education. Almost every article that he wrote and every talk on children that he broadcast on the Polish radio was closely bound up with the pedagogical experience that he had gained during the years of his work in education. Apart from his contribution to children's literature—I refer to the books previously mentioned, such as *King Mati, Yotam the Magician,* and *The Stubborn Child*—his pedagogical writings constitute a collection of realistic descriptions of children, the fruit of his penetrating observation of their lives and of their relationship to each other and to the adult world.

Indeed, the writings of Korczak, precisely because of their simplicity, their freedom from theoretical and abstract assertions, give the uniformed reader the impression of being a collection of disconnected gleanings of little value on various educational subjects; but a closer study reveals to the reader how rich was his experience in the care of children, how profound and penetrating his observation, and how original his approach to the educational problems he dealt with.

His style of writing bears the mark of a strong individuality. The reader can immediately recognize an article or talk by Korczak by its simplicity, succinct phraseology, its predilection for pithy aphoristic sayings which are characteristic of his literary work. At times, especially when reflecting on the sufferings of children, his prose rises to the heights of poetry, and then immediately returns, apologetically as it were, to its usual tone. A humorous and ironical vein is also discernible in his writings; it is most pronounced in his essay on *"Hapedagogia ha'mevadachat"* ("Humorous reflections on Pedagogics"). Korczak wins the heart of the reader by his perfect sincerity, the ardor of his faith in children, and his touching modesty.

Korczak's work for the welfare of the child, with his strong insistence upon the rights of children to consideration and a respect of those rights by adults, is characteristic of the attitude adopted by modern educators, beginning with Rousseau and continuing with Pestalozzi, Froebel, and Dewey. Modern educators attribute most of the difficulties encountered by teachers in their relations with their pupils to their total lack of understanding of children. Wherever one opens the writings of Korczak one finds this theme of defense of children's rights and his advocacy of a respectful and considerate attitude toward children.

The following extract is typical of Korczak's writings: "Children are not fools; the fools among them are no more numerous than among adults. Frequently we wrap ourselves in a mantle of authority and hand out orders which lack understanding or consideration, and are sometimes even impossible to carry out. Many a time an intelligent child stands taken aback and confused before the foolish, offending, and inconsiderate orders of the grownups." [2]

[2] Korczak, *Keizad le'ehov Yeladim* (*Ho'zaat Ha'kibbutz Ha'meuchad*, 1960), p. 53.

We find similar passages in all of Korczak's writings. He is never weary of defending children against treatment that is offensive, injurious, and cruel. In his opinion, the children's weakness and complete dependence on the adult makes their protection absolutely essential. It is not because the child is so different from an adult that it is difficult for the educator to understand him. Korczak stresses again and again that the child, and particularly the adolescent, has the same basic traits, inclinations, feelings as the adult, but, as it were, on a smaller scale. On this point Korczak differs from the famous educators who preceded him, as the latter viewed the age of childhood and that of adolescence as distinct and separate stages of growth each with a character of its own.

In his interesting book *How To Love Children,* which surpasses all his other writings in its concentrated thought and its wide and comprehensive perception of educational problems, Korczak, in defense of child behavior says *inter alia:* "Do all the children love to fight? No, they are generally innocent, kind-hearted, give in easily. Observe closely the conditions in which they work and the way they live together. Just try to put forty clerks in one room, seat them on uncomfortable benches, and keep them doing responsible work for a period of five hours, under the pedantic supervision of a person of authority. They will soon scratch each others' eyes out." [3]

In the same book, Korczak's extraordinary conception of the child is revealed in the following passage: "The assumption that pedagogy is the study of the child, and not of man, is one of the most irritating of errors. An aggressive child, when it is annoyed, hits another. An

[3] *Ibid.,* p. 53.

adult in a rage commits murder. You can take away a toy from a good-hearted child by a trick, and an adult will use cunning to get a signature on a check. A flighty child will buy sweets for the sixpence he was given to buy an exercise book, while the adult will lose all his property at cards. There are no children as such; there are *people* who have different criteria and standards and concepts, stores of varying experiences, people who differ in their feelings and characteristics." [4]

These passages illustrating Korczak's concept of the child as "an adult in miniature" need thorough clarification, because they contain one of the main theories running through his educational teaching. (In general, Korczak was most sparing in the formulation of theories and free from the tendency to generalize.) We hear that basically the child does not differ from the adult. He has the same urges, the same desires and feelings as the adult, and the difference between child and adult is mainly quantitative. The child is smaller, weaker; his life is not as full of danger; his aspirations and demands are, as it were, on a smaller scale.

The reader will no doubt be astonished at these ideas and consider them out of date. It may be asked what all the writings on child psychology deal with if not with the differences in characteristics, emotions, and aspirations between the child and the adult? Korczak gives two answers to this question:

a) The border line between childhood and adulthood cannot be clearly defined. "Ask an old man," says Korczak; "in his eyes even a man in his forties is not yet grown up. In our daily life we meet entire groups or

[4] *Ibid.*, p. 13.

classes of people who cannot be termed adult because of their intellectual weakness. Moreover, there are entire nations and peoples whom we consider underdeveloped and immature. Where therefore is the boundary between childhood and maturity?"

b) Korczak did not attach much importance to the findings of psychology and other sciences in the field of education. In his view, these sciences deal mainly with generalities which can neither be applied to the child as an individual nor to the concrete situations which the educator faces in his daily work.

In addition to these two reasons given by Korczak, which do not seem to be very convincing, we may point out that, as a Polish writer with a socialist turn of mind, it may be assumed that he was acquainted with the Marxist theories of education, which differ profoundly from those accepted in the West. Russian psychologists have a pronounced tendency to minimize the specific differences between child and adolescent behavior, on the one hand, and that of adults, on the other. Whereas Western educators attribute many of the peculiar manifestations of adolescents, such as rebelliousness, a propensity for daydreaming, estrangement from parents, withdrawal to solitude, etc., to biological and psychological factors accompanying the process which leads to physical maturity, their Russian counterparts attribute these phenomena to social factors, i.e., the spontaneous rejection by youth of the social order in bourgeois countries, which young people consider unjust, reactionary, and therefore unacceptable.

The issue between the Marxist and Western educators in Korczak's time is the relevance of psychology to education. Are the previously mentioned behavior patterns of young people attributable to biological or psychological processes, and therefore inherent in the period of adolescence, or are they mainly the result of the interaction between the individual and a particular kind of society? It would appear likely that Korczak's attempt to reduce the specific differences between child and adult behavior can be traced to the influence of Russian psychologists and educators. The latter reject the accepted theories of adolescence and puberty. It is not insignificant that they call adolescents *Podrostki,* persons not quite grown to maturity, thus denying them, as it were, a special status in their growth to maturity.

In his treatment of children at the Warsaw orphanage and in the summer camps under his direction, Korczak did not rely on the abstract assertions of psychologists but upon his own penetrating observation of children, their behavior and reactions in various situations. The power of perception he acquired was the fruit of his pedagogical intuition, supported by extensive experience gained during long years of educational work. His profound understanding of the child's soul was also the fruit of his efforts to identify himself completely with his wards, and to apply the method called by Professor Simon "methodical psychological regression," i.e. the attempt to probe his own past and recall experiences of childhood and adolescence, thus becoming, as it were, a child living among children. His book *When I Became a Child Again* is a fruit of these efforts, which to some extent are also reflected in his other writings. He admonishes the teacher: "Do not attempt to be a serious educator full of psychological pedantries in your heart and a head full of pedagogical rules; you have an ally in the experience of your own youth, and you should be helped by this experience." [5]

The term "methodical psychological regression" seems to me most appropriate to apply to Korczak's system. However, it would be misleading to interpret it as a scientific method; in fact, it is more probable that the "regressive" ability grows out of artistic leanings, a fact which Korczak's interpreters chose to ignore. Nor is this ability the result of a conscious struggle against forgetfulness but the fruit of the increased ability of the artist to see and relive his whole past with unusual clarity. Thus, the artist does not free himself from his past but carries it with him and makes it an integral part of his personality. It must be borne in mind that the artistic element in Korczak is rather prominent, and it is to this power that we should attribute his ability to identify himself with the life of children, to understand and describe them in a way that only an artist can do.

His sceptical attitude to conventional "teacher training" in general, and especially to the benefit a teacher can derive from the science of psychology, is expressed not only in his "Humorous reflections on Pedagogics" but in several of his pedagogical talks. These reflections must therefore be regarded as truly representative of Korczak's views. When settlers in the Emek asked him about the establishment of a teachers' training college for the villages he retorted: "Why do you need a college? The field, sheep pen, poultry runs, these are your pedagogical books." In another passage of his writings he says: "I fear the urban pedagogues; I have my misgivings about

[5] *Ibid.*, p. 14.

the teachers' training colleges. The teacher would do much better to engage in chicken farming and from raising chickens proceed to raising children, instead of doing so with the qualification of a diploma testifying to the completion of her studies." [6]

Such pronouncements are aphoristic and somewhat exaggerated, but nevertheless contain a serious idea. Korczak regarded education as a mission, and one which is almost wholly a function of the teacher's personality and character—not something that can be "learned" in teachers' training colleges. Moreover, he valued highly the personal experience which every teacher must acquire in the course of his work; he even stressed that if teachers relied too strongly upon the experience of their colleagues it would do them more harm than good.

Korczak writes as follows in the opening chapters of his book *How To Love Children*: "I fear that the reader will find it sufficient to place his faith in me; if that is the case, this book can only do him harm. And so I hasten to say that the way I have chosen in education, although not the shortest and most convenient, is the best one for my personality, because it is my own. I discovered it after much painstaking effort, and only when I realized that all the books I had read, and all the knowledge and experience of others meant nothing at all to me." [7] This passage is a further example of his propensity for overstatement, understandable enough in a man of strong individuality who feels that he can pursue his way in edu-

[6] Korczak, *Pedagogical Writings—Ktavim Pedagogiim* (Hotzaat Ha'kibbutz Ha'meuchad, 1956), p. 133.

[7] *Keizad le'ehov Yeladim*, p. 8.

cation independently, learning from his own experience
and not from that of others. Korczak demanded that the
educator know each one of his pupils individually, their
family background and specific problems; in addition he
demanded from the teacher boundless love and devoted
friendship for the child. A teacher who acquires these
qualities will gain a profound understanding of his pupil
which will be of great value to him in solving the problems that crop up in his daily dealings with the children.

Korczak was gifted with an extraordinary intuitive understanding of children, which he claimed every devoted
teacher could acquire by broadening and enriching his
experience. The abstract study of psychology cannot possibly be a substitute for experience. In his pedagogical
writings there are descriptions of countless situations in
which he was helped to find the right solution of a problem not by a knowledge of psychology but by his recognition of the influence that that particular child's background could have upon his conduct and by his ability
to identify himself with the child. I shall illustrate this
point by quoting two passages from his writings: "I was
astonished when one of the boys, who was by nature dry,
reserved, and closed up within himself, as well as somewhat of a misanthropist, suddenly displayed the heartiest
friendliness toward me, was the first to laugh at my jokes,
and tried to anticipate my every wish. He did this deliberately, with the obvious aim of drawing attention to
his actions. This lasted for quite a long time, and I con-
cealed my feeling of distaste . . . when finally he came
out with a request—that his younger brother be admitted
into the orphanage. I felt my eyes fill with tears. "Poor
child," I thought; "how much effort it had cost him to

play the part of another person, somebody who was not his real self!" [8]

In the same chapter he makes the following observation about one of the boys in the orphanage: "Do you know why the boy wanted to take his raincoat on a sunny day? Because he has an ugly darn on the knee of his stocking, and in the park he will meet a girl whom he loves. . . ." [9]

It is evident that in such cases the teacher cannot be helped by his knowledge of psychological literature, but only by his love and devotion for the child and an intimate knowledge of his background and personal circumstances.

It is somewhat paradoxical that this same Korczak, who had such little faith in the educational sciences, adopted such a completely scientific approach to the children under his care. His medical knowledge and experience helped him greatly in his educational work, and the same objective, experimental, groping approach characteristic of a doctor was discernible in his educational approach to the child. "Those who think that I betrayed the medical profession by turning away from hospital work and devoting my life to the orphanage are wrong." [10] As a doctor, he looked for the hidden symptoms of an illness, and these symptoms helped him in determining his diagnosis. This was also his approach in educational matters. He examined the conduct of children with great care, taking into consideration the personal circumstances of each of his pupils, pondered upon the meaning of disturbing manifestations of child behavior, without getting angry or

[8] *Ibid.*, p. 77.
[9] *Ibid.*, p. 39.
[10] *Ibid.*, p. 85.

excited, and then drew his conclusions. He laid great emphasis on the emotional calm which should accompany the work of the educator, who, when faced with a problem, should assume the role of an objective investigator. This was his approach in theory, though in practice he could not always conform to this demand, and sometimes did become excited and raised his voice in anger. It is interesting to note that after losing his temper he always tried to justify himself. In his book *How To Love Children,* Korczak found it necessary in self-justification to quote Pestalozzi's letter from Stanz, in which the latter confesses to sometimes losing his own emotional equilibrium.

Korczak's knowledge of medicine and physiology helped him to recognize many manifestations of child behavior which the ordinary educator would find hard to understand. He regarded the orphanage as a kind of laboratory where he investigated the great changes that accompany the critical years preceding adolescence, and their influence on the child's mind and behavior. There was no detail of child behavior that he regarded as unimportant, and he sometimes complained of the fact that, whereas extensive literature has been written about the most trivial details in medicine, whole aspects of boarding-school life have not been investigated at all. As a doctor, he had a marked propensity to explain peculiar instances of child behavior as resulting from purely physiological processes.

III

What were Korczak's aims in education? It is very probable that such a question would have caused him embar-

rassment, because he was very sparing of programmatical
declarations and abstract pronouncements regarding the
aims of education. He sometimes seemed to regret his
silence on these matters, and made sporadic attempts to
clarify the fundamental problems upon which education is
based. His reluctance to make theoretical declarations on
the ideals of education was most probably due to a lack
of propensity for philosophy and a certain indifference on
the question of religious observance, although he respected religious attitudes that differed from his own.
Moreover, it is very likely that his doubts and hesitations
in religious matters have their source in the fact that
Korczak never fully recognized the implications of his
Jewish origin. In his mind Judaism was identified with
humanism, and thus the reader does not generally find
any specifically Jewish bias in his writings. In a moment
of self-analysis Korczak confesses regretfully that the
"problem of man," his past and his future on earth, still
slightly obscures the problem of "the Jew." [11]

Although he draws the conclusion, based upon his pedagogical experience, that the Jewish child differs from the
Polish child, this is still a far cry from feeling the need
for specifically Jewish education for Jewish children and
the formulation of different aims. He knew very well the
extraordinary sensitiveness of the Jewish children in the
Polish Diaspora, and describes it in the following words:
"There are rare instances of children who do not carry
merely the ten years of their life, but are burdened with
the sorrow of many generations. In their minds are gathered the grief and suffering of hundreds of years, and at
the slightest provocation this pent-up load is suddenly

[11] *Ktavim Pedagogiim,* p. 186.

released—the pain, the sorrow, anger, rebellion—and you feel the lack of all proportion between this stormy reaction and the incident that set it off." [12]

Professor Simon's comment that Korczak's long life experience led him "from extreme assimilation to ardent attachment to his Jewish origin" [13] seems to me somewhat exaggerated, although there are here and there in Korczak's later writings signs of a tentative approach to religion. "One can raise children without religion, but not without God. How can one explain birth, death, the march of generations, without God?" [14] However, I have not found in his writings an expression of that "ardent attachment" to God, and it is far more probable that his attitude to matters of religion remained somewhat hesitant and vague. Even in his later years he owns to being unable to pray, though he taught his children to do so: "If I had kept in my heart a simple faith in God, I should have prayed that he hasten the moment of redemption; for the world is suffering, and first and foremost to suffer are the children." [15]

Korczak's story "The Children of the Bible," which is a poetic presentation of the life of the child Moses, constitutes evidence of his drawing closer to the Bible and the sources of Judaism. Simon rightly asserts: "It is indeed surprising that an ignoramus in matters Jewish, and a man unlearned in the knowledge of the Jewish religion, should have managed to use the technique of the homilies of the Hebrew sages. As they did, he too makes use of the brief pithy sayings of the Bible which in places are not ex-

[12] *Keizad le'ehov Yeladim*, p. 96.
[13] Simon, *Pestalozzi and Korczak* (Tel Aviv: Urim, 1949), p. 30.
[14] *Ktavim Pedagogiim*, 1957, p. 132.
[15] *Ibid.*, p. 188.

plicit enough, and fills them out by bringing into play the force of his imagination, as a true poet should do." [16]

There can be no doubt that Korczak's attitude to the Jewish religion was one of profound respect. In his letters to the orphanage he supports the Jewish children in their refusal to attend the Christian school on the Jewish Sabbath; and his advice to the unobservant children was not to declare to the teachers that keeping the Sabbath was a matter of indifference to them, for "he who does not honor his own religion forfeits the respect of decent people." [17] Nevertheless, the atmosphere at the orphanage was decidedly assimilationist, and Jewish observance and custom were conspicuously absent. Dov Sadan quotes a letter from a former pupil of the orphanage, a certain Hirsch Steinhardt: ". . . I and my younger brother were for some time pupils in Dr. Janusz Korczak's orphanage, where we received no Jewish education whatsoever. Every pupil of the orphanage was completely assimilated. My younger brother has been unable to recover some measure of Jewishness. He speaks Yiddish only because our family used to speak it, but he is unable to read or write it. The orphanage was a factory for assimilation. For the sake of truth I must admit that Dr. Janusz Korczak was an exceptional man, an outstanding personality, a great physician, a gifted writer of children's stories, a man with a wonderfully kind heart. He gave his whole heart and soul to his miserable orphans. But he was the biggest assimilationist that I ever met in my life. . . ." Dov Sadan feels that the boy has exaggerated, but there is no doubt as to the genuineness of his complaint. The orphanage

[16] Simon, *op. cit.*, p. 35.
[17] *Ktavim Pedagogiim*, p. 185.

certainly was a hothouse of assimilation. To some extent this was due to the influence of Steffa Wiliczinska, Korczak's assistant, who was a completely assimilated Jewess brought up on Polish culture and devoid of all knowledge of things Jewish. We do hear about a certain gentleman called "old Mr. Guttman" who came to the orphanage to teach the children Hebrew and give them religious instruction, but the children were not encouraged to attend these lessons. Janusz Korczak's religion may be described as highly personal. He did not attach himself to any synagogue nor did he observe religious custom. On the other hand, we hear from one of his pupils that he composed prayers in the Polish language and taught the children to pray. When criticized by his free-thinking colleagues because of his religious leanings he retorted rather laconically: "Faith is necessary for the lonely and the sad. What will you give the children instead of prayers?"

When a new building was being erected for a Polish Christian orphanage in the district of Bielani Korczak insisted on the inclusion of a small chapel. He mantained that an orphan who is deprived of the loving care of a mother is in need of a place where he can contemplate, pour out his heart, assuage his grief, weep in solitude, complain of his bitter fate, and converse with God intimately, face to face. All these facts indicate a certain pragmatic attitude to religion, although we cannot be absolutely certain on this point. It is possible that Korczak's argumentation in favor of religion was merely *ad hominem*. It must be borne in mind that most of his colleagues were completely irreligious but that he himself felt very deeply on this subject—a fact that is hinted at by Ernst Simon in a passage we have previously quoted.

It is evident that in his work at the orphanage and in the summer camps which he directed he laid special emphasis on the work of education, as distinct from teaching. The children in the institution attended the Polish Christian school in the vicinity; thus he was freed from the duty of dealing in detail with problems connected with school instruction. The shaping of the children's character occupied first place in his program. The following passage sums up his aspirations in this respect: "I feel that I have an obligation toward the child. . . . I have endeavored to make the children's organization rest upon mutual love and justice, to remove them as long as possible from the evil influence emanating from the adult world, to give the children years of independence and tranquility, and the creation of an appropriate atmosphere for growth. I have tried to teach them not to become a burden to others, not to be neglectful, not to do wrong." [18]

There is an outstanding similarity between the personality and socio-pedagogical activities of Korczak and those of Pestalozzi, and the former has, with justification, been described as a "reincarnation of Pestalozzi sprung from the Jewish people living on Polish territory." On the other hand, the pronounced difference between the two distinguished educators should not be overlooked. Besides being active in the practical field of education, Pestalozzi was also a brilliant theoretician who built up a complete system of educational philosophy, and was

[18] *Ibid.*, pp. 191-92.

the originator of a revolutionary theory concerning teaching methods, whereas Korczak did not excel in abstract theory at all.

There are also many parallels between the writings of Korczak and those of his Russian counterpart Makarenko. Both viewed pedagogical writings as a kind of interpretation of and commentary on their practical work, and both attached little importance to the educational sciences. However, Makarenko was imbued with communist ideology, which left its mark on all his writings, while Korczak remained officially uncommitted to any ideological trend in education. Moreover, Makarenko believed in the regimentation of school life, whereas Korczak supported democratic school management. The latter also did not share Makarenko's antireligious views.

A number of additional questions arise when considering Korczak's writings. Whence comes his persistent championship of the child? Whence comes the feeling that the child is always neglected and maltreated? Does this feeling stem from his own supersensitivity? Who were these children who needed so much protection? It must be borne in mind that most of Korczak's writings belong to the pre-Hitler era, when Polish Jewry was not subjected to the harsher forms of persecution. In those years the Polish-Jewish family was closely knit and devoted to its children who were seldom, if ever, neglected. Jewish tradition enjoins special provision for orphans, and the history of the Jewish communities in Europe shows that this sacred injunction was faithfully carried out. The fact that usually university students were attracted to Korczak's orphanage and worked there in return for board and lodging bears witness to the previously mentioned fact that conditions there were reasonably comfortable, and that the institution was well financed. Korczak seems to have been able to devote a good deal of his time to educational writing, and, up to the outbreak of World War II, to have had no unusual difficulty in raising the funds required for his institution. We can therefore only assume that the neglected children Korczak had in mind were not necessarily specifically Jewish, but the suffering children of humanity as a whole.

Korczak's criticisms are often paradoxical and sometimes cancel each other out. If, as he says, the child is not so dissimilar from the adult, why does he assert that adults do not understand children? This assertion is difficult to reconcile with the fact that he always tried to narrow down the differences in character and disposition between the adult and the child, maintaining that these differences are only quantitative. Moreover, what age group did Korczak have in mind when making these assertions? It is difficult to assume that he referred to adolescents, because the children in his care were of a much lower age level, mainly between the ages of seven and fourteen.

The fact that Korczak thought so little of psychology as an aid to education is unjustifiable, in view of the modern educational trend to base pedagogy on psychology, and particularly in view of the fact that the first decades of the twentieth century witnessed great advances in child psychology. It is nowadays completely unnecessary to emphasize the importance for the teacher of a general training in this subject. It is indeed strange that Korczak, who had scientific leanings and collected data concerning child

behavior all his life, should have questioned the usefulness of a conventional training in psychology for the educator. Korczak gathered a vast amount of scientific data
based on his many years of observation of and contact
with children, and was helped in this task by Steffa Wiliczinska. Unfortunately, however, the material was lost
during the upheaval caused by the Nazi occupation. The
main subjects of his research were a) problems connected
with coeducation and the relations between the sexes in
general; b) the children's habits of making collections of
various objects and exchanging ("swapping") them; c)
traffic accidents involving children; and d) the incidence
of quarrels among children.

Korczak did not evolve a scientific or methodical theory
of education. Some of his writings are journalistic in character; others still bear the imprint of homely talks addressed to children, which served their purpose at the
time but are of no permanent interest. Nevertheless, the
modern educator can derive great benefit from his writings, especially from his book *How To Love Children,*
which is based on his experience in the institution under
his care. This book is reminiscent of Pestalozzi's letter from
Stanz, containing as it does a moving and realistic account
of how he educated the children in his orphanage. Nor
should it be overlooked that Korczak's contributions in the
field of children's literature were significant, and definitely
place him in the front rank of Jewish writers of children's
stories.

Korczak bases education on the simplest principles—the
educator, the child, and their mutual relationship. Moreover, in his insistence on the educator being imbued with
love for the child, a sense of mission, and the ability to

identify himself with his pupil he somewhat resembles such other Jewish educational thinkers as M. Buber and A. D. Gordon.

Korczak's fame does not rest solely upon his writings, of which we cannot yet make a final assessment since they have not all been translated into Hebrew. However, it is safe to say that his fame rests mainly on his devoted service to the Jewish children in his care and on the influence he exercised on Polish education in general. He will be remembered first and foremost as a man who sacrificed his life for the sake of his wards, refusing to abandon them in their hour of need and displaying a courage and heroism which may well serve as an example to educators everywhere.

Because of his close association with *kibbutz* life and education he has created a permanent bond with Israel, where the *kibbutz* settlers cherish his memory and have perpetuated it by publishing a Hebrew translation of his collected writings.

8

Franz Rosenzweig as an Educationist

Franz Rosenzweig's work in the field of Jewish education may be interpreted as a reaction to the rapid and sustained process of German-Jewish assimilation which had started with Mendelssohn and Weisel and continued throughout the nineteenth century and well into the twentieth. Viewed biographically, it may be regarded as a reflection of Rosenzweig's spiritual development, leading from complete estrangement from Judaism toward an ever-deeper personal involvement in matters of Jewish faith and religious practice.

He spent his most formative years in an atmosphere of assimilation engendered by emancipation, enlightenment, and German idealist philosophy which was still in vogue in his student days. The conscious attempt of German Jews to water down the distinguishing features of their Jewishness and identify themselves with the non-Jewish culture surrounding them had been part of the Rosenzweigs' family tradition. Franz Rosenzweig's great-grandfather, S. M. Ehrenberg, was the headmaster of the Jewish Free School at Wolfenbuettel, which was run on progressive lines in the spirit of Naphtali Hertz Weisel, the "liberator" and archreformer of Jewish education in Germany. Zunz, a pupil of Ehrenberg, characterized that school in the following words: "The institution was originally a Talmudic school in which a few general disciplines were tolerated, later a scholarly institution in which Talmud was tolerated, and finally a high school without Talmud instruction." [1]

His home was cultured, but it lacked a Jewish atmosphere. The Judaism of his parents was a veneer, lacking roots and depth. His parents' ignorance of things Jewish is best characterized by Franz Rosenzweig's literary attempt at a satirical or rather tragi-comical presentation of his own circumcision ceremony. His parents did not appear to have been aware of the fact that the baby had to be given a Hebrew name on that occasion, nor did they remember the Hebrew names of their own forebears, a fact which caused great embarrassment. Some thirty years later, when he was a young officer in the German army, Franz Rosenzweig's diet was reinforced by a regular supply of bacon and ham sandwiches dispatched to him by his own mother.

In view of such a home background, it is not surprising that the young Franz Rosenzweig, under the influence of his friend Eugen Rosenstock, a Christian of Jewish descent, decided to embrace Christianity. However, it is rather paradoxical that he wished to enter Christianity as a Jew, with a fuller experience of Judaism than he had previously possessed. Because of this wish he decided to visit a synagogue on the Day of Atonement, 1913, prior to accepting baptism. According to Nahum Glatzer, this visit was of decisive importance in his spiritual develop-

[1] Nahum N. Glatzer, *Franz Rosenzweig* (A Shocken Book, 1953), p. xii.

ment. "He was halted on his way and called back into Judaism. This event came about with that suddenness and in that spirit of absolute finality reported in great conversions." [2]

Glatzer bases the story of Rosenzweig's conversion on the version of Rosenzweig's mother, who had confided it to him, but adds that "this contention could only be convincing if confirmed by some internal evidence."

However, the internal evidence of Rosenzweig's writings does not corroborate Glatzer's supposition, and Glatzer himself would appear to have doubted the validity of this assumption. Rosenzweig was not a mystic. In a letter addressed to Mawrik Kahn on October 19, 1918, he speaks strongly against the acceptance of mystical experience as the basis of one's faith. This he regards as a characteristically Christian approach. The Jewish approach to religion, in his view, is practical and pragmatic. Judaism has to be "tried," studied, and lived. *Nulla dies sine linea Hebraica* (No day without a line of Hebrew) was his motto. Mystical experience lies far in the past, at the birth of the Jewish people. (A possible hint at God's revelation to the forefathers and the Covenant on Mount Sinai.) Quoting from the Passover *Hagada* that "In every generation it is the duty of each individual to regard himself as though he had gone forth out of Egypt," he insists that the Jewish approach to religion is "to remember," to enter into the collective experiences of our people, and to identify oneself with them, rather than to wait for an individual revelation. Moreover, a personal "revelation" and religious ecstasy do not prove anything. On this point Rosenzweig clearly dissociates himself from the teaching

[2] *Ibid.,* p. xvii.

of "Rabbi Martin of Heppenheim" (a rather ironical appellation for Martin Buber, Rosenzweig's admired teacher and friend, who had then taken up residence in the suburb Heppenheim, near Frankfurt-on-Main). It was Buber who, with his rediscovery of Chassidism, had made the talk about mystical experience and religious ecstasy fashionable in Jewish circles, but Rosenzweig clearly rejected Buber's approach. (*"Hinaus* also *ueber Buber."*)

Even if we allow for a certain development in Rosenzweig's Jewish philosophy and admit a gradual *rapprochement* in theological matters between him and Buber, Glatzer's contention of Rosenzweig's sudden conversion to Judaism as the result of religious experience would still seem to be unacceptable. The letter to Mawrik Kahn, with its pronounced devaluation of mystical experience, could not have been written by a man who only a few years previously had had a decisive mystical experience which had resulted in his own rediscovery of Judaism.[8]

A real factor in the story of Rosenzweig's conversion to Judaism was his first contact with Eastern European Jewry. At the end of the First World War he visited Warsaw and spent a few weeks there. He was strongly impressed by the pulsating Jewish life which he found in the Jewish quarters of Warsaw. "I can well understand that the average German Jew, just because of his Philistine and bourgeois character, no longer feels any kinship with the Eastern European Jew, but I, and people like myself, feel it very strongly and immediately." Rosenzweig admired the matter-of-course Jewishness of the

[8] Nevertheless, the story of Rosenzweig's sudden "conversion" is reiterated by Professor S. H. Bergmann in his Hebrew introduction to the Hebrew anthology of Rosenweig's writings called *Naharayim*, published by Mossad Bialik, 1960.

Ostjuden, who would never dream of hiding that they were Jews. He was deeply moved by their prayers ("Such praying I have never known before"), their religious chanting, and their celebration of the "Third Meal" before nightfall on the Sabbath. His keen interest in Jewish education led him to the Warsaw *Hadarim,* the Jewish schools, where he engaged the children in lively conversation. Contrary to the denigrating observations about the *Heder* of men such as Weisel and other *Haskalah* writers, Rosenzweig had only praise for the Jewish education given in the Eastern European *Heder.* "In its actual effect the *Heder* is closer to the ideal of an educational institution than the Western European school. The latter produces fragmentary people, totally lacking orientation, but from the *Heder* there springs the constant renewal of a whole people." In the same letter there is an ironic remark aimed at his own great-grandfather. "I fully understand that S. M. Ehrenberg did not like the *Heder.* For people who wish to have baptized grandchildren, the *Heder* is a totally unsuitable institution." [4]

It is interesting to note that Rosenzweig had written these appreciative comments on the *Heder* about ten years before Eliezer Lifschitz published in *HaTekufah* his famous vindication of the *Heder* and nearly thirty years before Nathan Morris, an Anglo-Jewish educationist, made the following remarks: "The old *Heder,* an institution which was much abused by ill-informed writers of the *Haskalah,* but which would repay more serious study than has yet been given it by historians and educationists, followed in most cases the readings of the Synagogue. . . . It adopted a kind of grand universal syllabus and

[4] Franz Rosenzweig, *Briefe* (Schocken, 1935), pp. 326-27.

time-table, based on the synagogue and followed by the whole people wherever they were. . . . The philosophy of this method, as indeed of historic Jewish education as a whole, can be expressed in entirely modern terms like this: The child is not only to be prepared for life, but from the beginning helped to live the life which is regarded as desirable. . . ." [5]

In our attempt to account for Rosenzweig's return to Judaism mention has to be made of Nehemias Nobel, Rabbi of the Conservative Jewish Congregation of Frankfurt-on-Main, who exercised on him a strong and lasting influence. Rosenzweig admired Rabbi Nobel's personality, his imposing Jewish scholarship, and his qualities as a preacher and expounder of Judaism. It was Rabbi Nobel who guided Rosenzweig's first steps in the study of the Talmud and opened the treasures of Rabbinic literature to him. In his letters Rosenzweig speaks with deep gratitude and admiration of his "great teacher Nobel." Needless to say, these letters do not indicate Rabbi Nobel's feeling towards Rosenzweig, nor do we know whether he fully appreciated Rosenzweig's singular qualities and his importance for German Jewry; but the mere fact that Rabbi Nobel intended to ordain Rosenzweig as a Rabbi and actually prepared him for his Rabbinical ordination shows that he had a high regard for him.

After Nobel's sudden and untimely death Rosenzweig felt like an orphaned son. "His life was so intimately bound up with mine that I feel my own life fading away without him."

Definite limits, however, are set to any attempt at "ex-

[5] Nathan Morris, *Curriculum and Method in the Hebrew Class* (London: *Jewish Educational Publication*, 1946), p. 7.

plaining" the religious conversion of a man. Many a German Jew must have come into contact with Eastern European Jewry without being influenced one way or another; and as for Rabbi Nobel, it is clear from Franz Rosenzweig's letters that Buber, too, had made his acquaintance but was not impressed by him. Ultimately the deepest cause of Rosenzweig's return to Judaism lies in his unique personality, the receptiveness of his soul, his religious susceptibilities and idiosyncrasies, or, in one word, his religious genius. To his mother his interest in Judaism and Jews appeared as something in the nature of an obsession. To us it appears as a marvel of Jewish vitality, resilience, renewal of heart, and capacity for *teshuvah* (repentance).

II

Rosenzweig probed the theoretical foundations of the three streams of the Judaism of his time—Liberalism, Zionism, and Orthodoxy—with the acumen and intellectual fastidiousness of a trained philosopher. It is not surprising that he could not quite identify himself with any of them, though he felt nearest to Liberal Judaism, as he expressly stated in a letter addressed to the historian Maximilian Landau as late as February, 1924. This, however, did not prevent him from criticizing Liberalism on many points. He rejected the equation of Judaism with prophetic teaching because he saw in this attempt an oversimplification and an unjustifiable contraction of the vast framework of the Jewish heritage. Neither could he accept the interpretation of Judaism as mere "religion," or, as he put it, "religion" when applied to Rabbis, and "persuasion" or "confession," when applied to the rest of the Jews, since in his view the latter did not possess any religion at all. "God forbid that we again put on this gramophone record, which no longer renders a single pure tone—has it ever done so?" [6]

Moreover, he had doubts as to the validity of the philosophical superstructure of Liberal Judaism and in particular he criticized its attempt to create a new system of Judaism and formulate new principles according to which the modern Jew should live. "Liberalism failed because it tried to postulate new principles according to which we are required to act. These principles are like officers without an army, like parents without children." [7]

It has already been pointed out that Rosenzweig's attitude to Judaism was essentially practical and pragmatic. In his opinion the laws of the Torah have to be freely chosen, adopted, and "tried out," and the ultimate responsibility for the choice rests with each individual. "We start with action [he means the fulfillment of *Mitzvoth*]; let us hope that one day, we, or others, will find out the underlying principles of the laws." [8] After the publication of his *Star of Redemption* the problem of the Law was foremost in his mind and he intended devoting a book to it. However, he was prevented from carrying out this plan, partly because of the untimely death of Rabbi Nobel, who had been his guide in the study of Halachah, partly because of the serious illness that had overtaken him.

It is rather paradoxical that in spite of Rosenzweig's

[6] Franz Rosenzweig, *Kleinere Schriften* (Schocken, 1937), p. 81.
[7] *Briefe*, p. 425.
[8] *Ibid.*

affinity to Jewish Liberalism his approach to Judaism is the opposite to that of religious reform. The latter started with preconceived principles, endeavored to build a system, and imposed this system upon historic Judaism. It selected from the Corpus of Jewish law such *Mitzvoth* as seemed in accordance with its principles. Rosenzweig started with "action"—that is to say, the free adoption of *Mitzvoth*, and postponed the system building to a later stage.

Rosenzweig's anti-Zionist convictions were deeply rooted in his Jewish philosophy. For him, to be a Jew implied living in the Diaspora. He saw the whole of Jewish history as moving from one exile to another; and the spirit of the exile, the people's estrangement from the soil as part of the Jewish destiny, was deeply engraved in his mind. He believed that a higher spiritual life is only possible if a people is free from territorial limitations and thus not involved in international strife, rivalries, and wars which are frequently the natural concomitants of normal nationhood. Moreover, in his view, the concept of Jewish nationhood is removed from the process of history which does not impinge upon it. Here Rosenzweig's thought is somewhat contiguous to the ideas expressed by Orthodox philosophers such as Samson Raphael Hirsch and notably Isaac Breuer, who regarded not only Jewish nationhood but also the Law of the Torah as withdrawn from the process of history. Nor should it be ruled out that Rosenzweig was directly influenced by some of the writings of Isaac Breuer, a fact which has not been admitted by expounders of Rosenzweig's teaching but which nevertheless seems likely to be true. Rosenzweig read Breuer's *Judenproblem* with the most enthusiastic assent (*die heftigsten*

Zustimmungsausbrueche) and he found that that book contained an "amazing amount of truth, much that I should have formulated in exactly the same way." [9] According to Rosenzweig, Zionism is an excellent diagnostician inasmuch as it truly recognizes the weakness of the Jewish people in the Diaspora, but it is a poor therapeutist because it overemphasizes the provisional character of Jewish life in the Diaspora and therefore cannot free itself from the tendency of postponing "serious treatment" to an uncertain future. The fundamental mistake of Zionism is to equate the concept of Jewish nationhood with that of other nations. In a lighter vein, he once likened the difference between Jewish and secular nationhood to the difference between a *shofar* and a trumpet. He tells the story of a *chazan* who was once asked by a judge to give a definition of a *shofar*. The *chazan* gave a long and learned exposition of the subject, based on Scriptural passages; but, after noticing the judge's dissatisfaction and visible impatience, simply said that the *shofar* was a trumpet. Thereupon the judge became very angry and asked the *chazan* why he had not said so at once instead of engaging in a long and tiresome exposition. "But is it really a trumpet?" retorted the *chazan*.

Rosenzweig's attitude to Orthodoxy is extremely intricate and to some extent ambivalent. He affirmed the election of Israel and therefore fully accepted the implications of this fact in the spirit of the blessing, "Who hast chosen us from all peoples and given us Thy Torah." His own spiritual development had led him to the acceptance of the Judaic Law as a whole; that is to say, he asserted and understood its *raison d'être*. On the other hand, how-

[9] *Ibid.*, footnote to p. 496.

ever, he did not find it possible to accept a number of specific *Mitzvoth* which remained "alien" to him. (*Gerade zum Ganzen hat uns unser Weg wieder gefuehrt, aber das Einzelne suchen wir.*) In his later years he came very near to traditional Judaism in actual religious observance. "An outsider looking on the observance of the Sabbath in Franz Rosenzweig's home, with prayer, benediction, song and scrupulous abstinence from all proscribed manner of work, would expect to find a strictly Orthodox Jew";[10] but this fact must not blind us to the profound difference between his conception of Judaism and that of Orthodoxy, particularly as far as matters of doctrine are concerned. He did not reject Western Orthodoxy merely because, as Mr. Glatzer likes to put it, "it overstressed the legal aspects of the law." (*Sic!*) Like Buber, Rosenzweig did not believe in revelation in the sense of "verbal inspiration." In a letter to Jacob Rosenheim he says: "Where we differ from Orthodoxy is in our reluctance to draw from our belief in the holiness or Uniqueness of the Torah and in its revelationary character, any conclusions as to its literary genesis and philological value of the text as it has come down to us. If all of Wellhausen's theories were correct and the Samaritans really had the better text, our faith would not be shaken in the least. This is the profound difference between you [Orthodoxy] and us—a difference which, it seems to me, may be bridged by mutual esteem, but not by understanding." In the same letter he continues: "For us, too, the Torah is the work of one spirit; we do not know who its author was; we cannot believe that it was Moses. Whoever it was, and whatever sources

[10] Glatzer, *op. cit.*, pp. ix-x.

he may have used, he was our teacher and his theology is our teaching." [11]

From these presuppositions there follow important consequences for Rosenzweig's attitude to religious observance. According to Rosenzweig, Judaism contains, strictly speaking, no laws, but merely precepts (*Gebote*), i.e., *Mitzvoth*, which should be freely accepted. It has already been mentioned that the ultimate decision as to the acceptance or nonacceptance of *Mitzvoth* rests solely with the individual and the only criterion is his "choice of ability" (*die Auswahl des Koennens*), i.e., the inner readiness or ability of the individual Jew to take upon himself religious observance. Once, when asked whether he put on the phylacteries, he answered, "Not yet," which of course implied, "but soon I will." The outstanding feature of this attitude is its individualism. Even Rosenzweig's admirers admit the danger inherent in this individualism, which, if accepted, may eventually lead to the disintegration of the Jewish people as a religious community. Rosenzweig's answer to this serious difficulty can hardly be considered satisfactory. "The danger of individualism exists only for the individual Jew, but not for the whole people. For the choice of *Mitzvoth* according to one's ability is made from the spiritual stock of the whole people, and only inability is individual." [12] In other words, the objective existence of the entire corpus of tradition, unimpaired by the individual's choice, is the guarantee against disintegration. Professor S. H. Bergmann answers this point with an act of faith. "He Who has promised us that 'My words which

[11] *Briefe*, pp. 581-82.
[12] *Ibid.*, p. 522.

I have put in thy mouth shall not depart out of thy mouth, nor out of the mouth of thy seed, nor out of the mouth of thy seed's seed from henceforth and for ever' will not allow us to become disunited." [13]

(This prophecy of Isaiah is most reassuring. However, Professor Bergmann does not raise the question of the possible preconditions of such a promise. It may very well presuppose the continued existence of Jews who, unlike Rosenzweig, accept the Judaic law *in toto*, in obedience to the Scriptural injunction, "According to the sentence of the law which they shall teach thee, and according to the judgment which they shall tell thee, thou shalt not decline from the sentence which they shall shew thee, to the right hand nor to the left.")

Rosenzweig criticized the dichotomy inherent in the modern Orthodox solution suggested by Samson Raphael Hirsch, with its concomitant fragmentation of life epitomized by the dualism of *Mensch-Jisroel,* Torah and *Derech Eretz,* Judaism and secular culture, the division of life into two spheres, one dominated by Halachah and the other free from it. He had a vision of a Judaism embracing our complete lives. "On principle, no sphere of life may be regarded as being outside Judaism," he says expressly in his essay "The Builders." The spirit of the Law, Jewish custom, and folklore have to be applied to that sphere of life to which Judaism does not appear to have any application.

This criticism, however, may be rather hard on S. R. Hirsch, who, certainly no less than Rosenzweig, stood for a complete Judaism, embracing all our lives.

[13] S. H. Bergmann, *On Franz Rosenzweig* (Jerusalem: A Beth Hillel Publication, 1956), p. 53.

III

Rosenzweig's keen interest in educational matters and his qualities as an educational thinker are displayed in his essay *"Volksschule und Reichsschule,"* published in 1916. However, the topics covered in this essay do not appear to have a direct bearing on his views on Jewish education, except his conception of *Bildung,* which he explains in the following way: *"Bildung* means the power to act, it is the ability to understand, it is never mere mastery over material, but the ability to rise above the material; it is always personal, always man himself and not man as 'possessing' something. It is not mere knowledge about things but their meaning and rationale [*Sinn*]." [14] A variation of this conception of *Bildung* reappears in Rosenzweig's outline of the function of Jewish education, as will be shown later.

Rosenzweig chose the Jewish *Gemeinde,* on which all trends of Judaism were represented, as a suitable platform from which to start his educational activities. As a first step, he prepared a plan for the reform of Jewish religious education on a country-wide scale and submitted it in a letter to the distinguished philosopher and exponent of Liberal Judaism, Hermann Cohen. (In Rosenzweig's *Kleinere Schriften* this letter appears under the title "The Time has come. . . .")

The plan is based on the admission that the German-Jewish home has lost its Jewish character in the course of three successive generations and therefore could no longer be considered a factor in Jewish education. The

[14] *Kleinere Schriften,* pp. 432-33.

only living center of Judaism is the synagogue; hence the need to build around it the new syllabus of elementary and secondary education. The starting point must be the prayer book. "A Jew to whom the *Siddur* and the *Machzorim* (Festival Prayer Books) are not closed books has more than a grasp of the essence of Judaism; Judaism is still part of his life, he possesses a 'Jewish world.' " [15]

Rosenzweig did not envisage separate Jewish day schools for the Jewish children of Germany. He took the existing educational structure for granted and accepted the fact that the vast majority of German Jewish youth were educated in non-Jewish schools. He was therefore mainly interested in the reorganization of the *Religiousunterricht,* i.e., Jewish religious instruction given for two hours a week for nine successive years between the ages of nine and eighteen. Into this inadequate vessel Rosenzweig intended to pour the rich content of Jewish education.

For the first three years Hebrew should be taught according to the old translation method, with no more than the bare essentials of Hebrew grammar. The texts selected for study must be connected with the synagogue and the Jewish Calendar. Hebrew should be taught not as a dead grammatical language but as a living tongue practiced daily in prayer and study. Hebrew as a sacred tongue must dominate the *Religionsunterricht*. Rosenzweig opposed Jewish catechizing (suggested for the first time by Naphtali Hertz Weisel), as well as the study of the Bible in German. "Language and meaning are closely interconnected. We would greatly underestimate the intimate connection between Christianity and the German language since the days of Luther, if we believed that it is

[15] *Ibid.,* pp. 57-58.

possible to render Jewish thought in German unmarred by alien idiosyncrasies." [16]

As for the fourth year, the teacher should aim at completing the Pentateuch in Hebrew as well as the main parts of the prayer book and the *Machzorim*. With *Bar Mitzvah* approaching, synagogue attendance on the Sabbath should become part of the *Religionsunterricht*. Rosenzweig opposed the "artificially framed" youth service. Young and old should worship together, as had been the case throughout Jewish history.

After the age of thirteen, Torah should be studied with Rashi. Thus the pupil is introduced into the spiritual world of the Talmud and *Midrashim*. At the same time, the student should get accustomed to reading unpointed Hebrew. The following two years mark the end of the school career for those pupils who do not go in for higher education. They should not leave school without a first direct introduction to the Babylonian Talmud. Nor is the study of the Bible to be discontinued. Rosenzweig suggests the study of the *Haftaroth*, the Psalms, and the Ethics of the Fathers. The connection with the prayer book should be maintained throughout the school career.

The Hebrew studies of the following year center around the Talmud and *Midrashim*, on the one hand, and the prophetic teaching of Judaism, on the other. The eighth year should aim at surveying the complete exilic literature up to Mendelssohn and Zunz. The last year is almost completely devoted to the study of Jewish philosophy, based on texts such as the *Kuzari* or Maimonides' *Moreh Nevuchim*, or the study of the Moralists, such as Bachyah or Luzzatto.

[16] *Ibid.*, p. 61.

This, in outline, was Rosenzweig's plan. It is of course an overambitious and overcrowded curriculum, unless one may presuppose that students possess intellects like that of Rosenzweig himself. In the face of criticism, Rosenzweig had to make certain reductions and concessions, and finally left the detailed "editing" of the plan to the experts. From a historical point of view the plan is very interesting, because *it marks a definite break with the theoretical assumptions of Haskalah education, a break made by a Liberal Jew.* The plan had more than a traditional flavor; indeed, it is a somewhat modernized curriculum of the *Heder* and the *Talmud Torah* which Rosenzweig had seen in Warsaw.

Although Rosenzweig's attempts to reform Jewish primary and secondary education remained ineffective from a practical point of view, his work in the field of adult education proved of great importance for the Jewish communities of Germany. Before we describe his activities in this field we have to mention his plan for the creation of a body of Jewish scholars, who, supported by German Jewry as a whole, were to dedicate their lives to Jewish scholarship and teaching. This plan and his plan for the reform of the *Religionsunterricht* dovetail, since he hoped that out of the ranks of these scholars would come the teachers required for the implementation of his plan.

Rosenzweig deplored the inadequacy of German-Jewish scholarship, which, in his time, was concentrated in theological seminaries which aimed solely at the training of Rabbis. There was no body of lay scholars to mediate between the Rabbis and the Jewish rank and file. In the Jewish communities of Eastern Europe, and indeed also in Germany in former times, the Rabbi was merely a *primus inter pares*, a scholar living in a community of scholars. Rosenzweig felt very strongly the absence of such a body of scholars in Germany and devoted all his energy to creating it anew. This plan, too, he outlined in his letter addressed to Hermann Cohen.

The *Freies Juedisches Lehrhaus* he founded in Frankfurt-on-Main was a unique institution. It was "free" in the sense that no previous qualifications were required from any one who wished to be enrolled. Rosenzweig laid special emphasis on the fact that this was not to be a mere "People's High School of Judaism." In conformity with his conception of *Bildung* in general, he demanded that this school become not merely an institution for the dissemination of Jewish knowledge but must aim at turning Jewish knowledge into a living force which would make itself felt in the everyday life of the community. The main aim of the school may be summed up by the motto "Back to Judaism," or, to be more precise, "Back to the sources of Judaism."

Another fact that distinguished the *Lehrhaus* from other People's Colleges in Germany was the different social origin of the students. Whereas the initiators of German adult education intended serving the German working classes, Rosenzweig's students were, as he himself once put it, the *Crêpe de Chine* Jewish public of Frankfurt. This was by no means intended by Rosenzweig but was rather the accidental result of the sociological grouping of German Jewry.

Rosenzweig attributed the success of this institution to the fact that it was "anti-ghetto" in spirit, not dominated by Rabbis (though there was indeed a sprinkling of Rabbis on the teaching staff), unpolemical, not apologetic for Judaism, and "universal" in its general Jewish orientation. It was informal as far as teaching methods were concerned, favored free discussion rather than lecturing. Even when lectures were given there was always the possibility of interposing questions. The emphasis was on teaching rather than on lecturing. Among the teachers of the *Lehrhaus* there were, apart from Rosenzweig himself, who served as its head, men such as Buber, Rabbi Nobel, E. Strauss, Ernst Simon, and Nahum Glatzer. Also Agnon sometimes gave readings in Modern Hebrew. Buber considered the *Lehrhaus* "the only Jewish school of real standing in Western Jewry."

Another characteristic feature of the *Lehrhaus*, particularly mentioned by Ernst Simon, was the fact that some of the teachers were themselves students, and it happened that the difference in knowledge between teacher and student was rather narrow. In fact, Rosenzweig favored the appointment of lecturers who were ignorami in the Jewish field but prominent in some other. "Every program should include at least one *am-haaretz*," Rosenzweig wrote in a long and humorous letter to his successor, Rudolf Hallo (Rosenzweig was then too ill to continue acting as the Head of the *Lehrhaus*) and "if possible always another *am-haaretz* on each program. Ignorance of things Jewish is, of course, no proof of suitability for lecturing, but the *am-haaretz* must be a man who has made a name for himself in another field. His reputation coupled with the so-called "will for Judaism" represents the right qualifications for a *Lehrhaus* teacher. Of course you have to be careful not to let him talk about Judaism too much." [17]

[17] *Briefe,* p. 458.

Rosenzweig ran the *Lehrhaus* in a businesslike spirit and possessed a keen eye for propaganda (rare attributes in a philosopher). The *Lehrhaus* prospered and the number of students enrolled steadily increased. It survived its founder by about nine years. Its activities ceased with the destruction of Jewish life under Hitler.

At first, Rosenzweig's influence was mainly confined to the circle of his personal friends and to the people around the *Lehrhaus,* but thence it spread to other German Jewish communities. Outside German Jewry his influence is not strong, least of all in Israel. This is rather a pity. An intelligent perusal by Israeli educationists of Rosenzweig's plan for the reorganization of Jewish education in Germany would have done Israeli education a world of good. At least Israeli children would have known the difference between a *talith* and a bathing towel long before the official introduction of "Jewish consciousness" in Israeli schools.

It is possible that his anti-Zionist attitude (explained away by his disciples as a reaction to Klatzkin's extreme nationalistic doctrine, equated by Rosenzweig with Zionism) stands somewhat in the way. On the other hand, it has been explained to the Hebrew reading public that Rosenzweig is more fairly described as a non-Zionist than an anti-Zionist. His letters show that he took great pride in the development of the Jewish settlement in Palestine. It must also be borne in mind that only part of his writings have been translated into Hebrew. (Apart from Mr. Glatzer's short anthology of Rosenzweig's writings, there has recently appeared another Hebrew anthology called *Naharayim.*) His *chef d'oeuvre, The Star of Redemption,* is probably untranslatable. Moreover, its vagueness, obfuscation, and frequent oscillations between poetry and philosophy, as well as its highly involved style, make the book unreadable even to a person who has a full command of German. Rosenzweig had hoped that this book would be regarded as a gift of the German spirit to the Jewish people. It is a tragic fact—I may be pardoned if I say so in an outright manner—that it is this German spirit which mars the book and prevents it from taking its place among the classics of Jewish thought. *The Star of Redemption* furnishes the proof, if proof were necessary, that it is almost impossible for anyone—even a man of genius such as Rosenzweig—to enter the maze of German post-Kantian idealistic philosophy (Rosenzweig wrote his thesis on Hegel) without having his ability for plain, lucid writing somewhat impaired. Nor should it be accepted as a self-evident fact that depth of thought must necessarily be accompanied by vagueness of expression and all-around incomprehensibility. Though I know full well that the philosophy of Wittgenstein and that of Rosenzweig are worlds apart, I am nevertheless tempted to call the former as a witness against the latter—"What can be said at all can be said clearly: and about what one cannot speak one must be silent."

Rosenzweig's *Kleinere Schriften* and his fascinating *Briefe* are likely to remain with us. They testify to his religious genius, his keen perception of educational problems, and, as far as his character is concerned, to his warm-heartedness, generosity, breadth of sympathies, and unusual capacity for friendship. He was entirely free from vanity and jealousy, qualities that frequently mar the character of the scholar—and, altogether, a man as free from blemish as a human being can possibly be. However, at least for the time being, it is true to say that Rosenzweig the educational thinker is certainly no less alive today than Rosenzweig the philosopher.

9

Buber on Education

Buber's lecture "On Education" (*"Über das Erzieheri-sche"*), delivered at the Third International Pedagogical Conference in Heidelberg in 1925, represents his main contribution in the field of educational philosophy. Both in originality of thought and depth of insight into the essence of the educative process, it surpasses his later lectures on educational topics such as *"Bildung und Weltanschauung,"* a lecture delivered in 1935, in the *Freies Jüdisches Lehrhaus* in Frankfurt-on-Main, and "The Education of Character," delivered at a conference of Palestinian teachers in 1939 in Tel Aviv. This first lecture, "On Education," will be the main subject of our analysis and interpretation. The other two will be dealt with more briefly.

It is a tribute to the vitality of Buber's thought that his first lecture, delivered more than thirty-five years ago, still retains its freshness and relevance. Though it is relatively brief and concentrates on a limited number of educational topics, it may be regarded as a classic of educational literature. It transcends, in its far-reaching significance, the well-defined bounds of Jewish education and assumes universal importance.

Buber starts with a criticism of the basic assumption of the Conference which had invited him to deliver his lecture and which conceived of education as the development of the creative powers of the child. The first question Buber asks is, "What are the creative powers of the child?" The elucidation of this point leads Buber to a critical appraisal of the psychology of Freud and Alfred Adler, with certain aspects of which he is in entire disagreement. "Modern psychologists are inclined to derive the multiform human soul from a single primal element —the 'libido,' 'the will of power' and the like. But this is really only the generalization of certain degenerate states in which a single instinct not merely dominates, but also spreads parasitically through the others. . . . In opposition to these doctrines . . . which impoverish the soul, we must continually point out that human inwardness is, in origin, a polyphony in which no voice can be reduced to another, and in which the unity cannot be grasped analytically, but only heard in the present harmony. One of the leading voices is the instinct of origination." [1]

This instinct of origination is an original force, not to be derived from any other. It emanates from the soul, impresses itself upon an external object, where, as it were, it peters out. It is essentially individual, and does not lead the child into communion with his fellow human beings, and, therefore, as long as a person acts as a creator, he remains essentially solitary. In Buber's own words, "Only

[1] Buber, "On Education," *Between Man and Man* (Boston: Beacon Press, 1955) pp. 85-86.

if someone grasps his [the child's] hand, not as a 'creator,' but as a fellow creature lost in the world, to be his comrade, friend or lover beyond the arts, does he have an awareness and a share of mutuality. An education based only on the training of the instinct of origination would prepare a new human solitariness, which would be the most painful of all." [2]

It follows, therefore, that the development of the creative abilities of the child, that is to say the child's instinct of origination, cannot possibly represent the whole task of education. It would leave out of consideration the essential teacher-pupil relationship, which, according to Buber, is the heart and core of the educative process, and, indeed, of human relationships in general.

When speaking of human relationships we touch immediately upon Buber's principle of "dialogue," the exposition of which requires the elucidation of his fundamental distinction between the "I-Thou" and "I-It" relationship. In his later notes upon his own writings Buber lays great stress on the fact that this distinction is not to be understood as one involving mystical experience but is essentially an epistemological distinction which concerns ways of perception and cognition of objects.

Buber's distinction between the "I-It" and "I-Thou" ways of perception may be illustrated in the following ways:

1) I may form in my mind a clear idea of London, but, not having previously been there, I may think of it as a geographic concept, a nerve center of a large commonwealth of nations, a demographic unit, an accumulation of economic power, the cradle of democracy, or in other

[2] *Ibid.*, p. 87.

terms. In all these cases, "London" is merely the object of my perception; it does not speak to me in a personal way; it is, as it were, separate from myself and from other potential objects of my perception. It does not affect me personally, nor does it necessarily touch upon anything that is a part of my own life. But my way of thinking of "London" may be different if I have spent a lifetime in that city, and am now, by force of circumstances, far away from it. Then the idea "London" may recall to me childhood experiences, the memory of parents and friends, recollections of growth and development, hours spent in happiness, struggle, disappointment, frustration. In this case, "London" ceases to be for me a cold concept, but speaks directly to me in a personal way. It may again influence my life and even prompt me to act in one way or another. Here, the "I-It" relationship yields to the "I-Thou" mode of conceiving of objects. The most artistic illustration of this mode of "I-Thou" relationship, if referred to cities, we find in works of poetry, such as Dr. Johnson's famous poem "London."

2) Another interesting illustration of this fundamental distinction is contained in Professor Hugo Bergmann's Hebrew essay on the dialogic thinking of Buber. A Chassidic Rabbi once said: "The Land of Israel has given me the following experience:

"When I see a bundle of straw lying on the road, then the mere fact that it lies along the road and by the pavement (and not across the road, where it would be an obstacle to passers-by) arouses in me a feeling of awe, awakening in me an awareness of the Divine Omnipresence." This Rabbi did not view the bundle of straw from the point of view of its utility, nor was it for him an object of study but something that aroused in him deep religious feeling; it spoke to him and, by way of association of ideas, brought home to him his nearness to God. This again is an example of the "I-Thou" relationship in viewing objects.

This "I-Thou" relationship characterizes, according to Buber, the genuine dialogue.

In his lecture "On Education," Buber distinguishes between three chief forms of the dialogical relation.

The first may be illustrated by a discussion at an intellectual level. The point at issue between the two parties may be a matter of general outlook, a matter of scientific attitude, or an assentment of men or ideas. Let us suppose there exists between the parties a profound difference of opinion which remains unresolved for a long time. It may happen that "in an instant—as if by the action of a messenger as anonymous as he is invisible—each becomes aware of the other's full legitimacy, wearing the insignia of necessity and meaning. What an illumination!" [3]

In that moment of "illumination" each partner sees the subjective justification of the opposite point of view. Each appears to the other like Luther the moment he pronounced the famous words: *"Hier stehe ich und kann nicht anders."* ("Here I stand; I cannot do otherwise.") Such a discussion bears the imprint of genuine dialogue, inasmuch as it is characterized by what Buber calls "inclusion" or "envelopment," whichever word we choose in order to render Buber's German term *"Umfassung."* In the case quoted above, the term *Umfassung* is most fitting, because in this case each disputant incorporates, as it were, his partner's stand in his own being, and sees the

[3] *Ibid.,* p. 99.

point at issue from the other's viewpoint. This "inclusion" is a characteristic of the "I-Thou" relationship and of genuine dialogue in general.

However, in the case of two disputants, the "inclusion" is only partial, in that it concerns merely a person's opinion or viewpoint and not his or her complete being; or, to use Buber's phrase, "it is bound to leave out the full reality of a person's being and life." But it may happen, and Buber himself gives an example out of his own life, that a violent clash of opinion and its subsequent resolution lead to a genuine dialogue in the fullest sense of the term, with mutual inclusion, and to a relationship which bears in the most complete measure the character of "I-Thou."

The incident to which Buber refers occurred before the First World War at a gathering of distinguished representatives of many countries who, sensing the approaching catastrophe, made a last-minute attempt to forestall it. One of those present, described by Buber as an ex-clergyman (presumably the German philosopher Paul Natorp), protested at the composition of the committee, which in his view included too many Jews. Buber took exception to the protest, and from there the discussion led in some way to the subject of Jesus. Buber maintained that Jews knew Jesus "from within in the impulses and stirrings of his Jewish being, in a way that remains inaccessible to the peoples submissive to him . . . in a way that remains inaccessible to you." The clergyman stood up, and so did Buber, and they "looked into the heart of one another's eyes. . . ." "It is gone," he said, "and before everyone we gave one another the kiss of brotherhood. . . ." "The discussion of the situation between Jews and Christians had been transformed into a bond between the Christian and the Jew." [4]

The second form of dialogue is found in the relationship between teacher and pupil, which is also of the "I-Thou" nature, though it is denied mutuality, as will be shown later. This relationship is characterized by "inclusion" in the sense that the teacher must be fully aware of the effect of his action on the pupil; he must feel how it is experienced from "over there." He must project his mind into that of the pupils and see himself through their eyes. This action of "inclusion" does not detract in any way from his status as a mature person, nor does his position as a teacher become weakened thereby. On the other hand, "inclusion" does not mean mere empathy, nor does the "inclusion" refer only to one aspect of the pupil's mentality—his powers of comprehension—but to his whole being and concrete existence. "Without the action of his spirit being in any way weakened he must at the same time be 'over there,' on the surface of that other spirit which is being acted upon—not some conceptual, contrived spirit, but all the time the wholly concrete spirit of this individual and unique being who is living and confronting him and who stands with him in the common situation of 'educating' and being 'educated.'" [5]

Buber goes on describing the pupil-teacher relationship, and points out that it must be uncolored by *Eros. Eros* presupposes selection; we select our friends whom we love from a multitude of persons. But it is the destiny of the teacher to accept his class as it is offered to him, with no possibility of selection. "He enters the schoolroom for the

[4] *Ibid.*, p. 6.
[5] *Ibid.*, p. 100.

first time, he sees them crouching at the desks, indiscriminately flung together, the misshapen and the well proportioned, animal faces, empty faces, and noble faces in indiscriminate confusion, like the presence of the created universe; the glance of the educator accepts and receives them all." [6]

Moreover, the "inclusion" which characterizes the educational process must, in Buber's view, remain one-sided; that is to say, the pupil must not feel the influence emanating from the teacher from the teacher's own point of view. Where there is mutuality of "inclusion," the educative relationship "bursts asunder," and is transformed into friendship, which is the third form of dialogue.

It would appear that Buber had in mind the typical classroom situation where friendship between teacher and pupil would break up the class as an educative unit. He does not, however, rule out the possibility of friendship between tutors and their pupils, or between two mature persons of whom one is the teacher and the other the pupil. Common experience, as well as instances from the world of literature, provide ample examples of friendships of this kind.

In his later writings Buber adds two more examples of an "I-Thou" relationship which is necessarily denied full mutuality of "inclusion." One is the relationship between the psychotherapist and his patient and the other that of the pastor and the member of his congregation to whom he ministers. The psychotherapist must of course practice "inclusion" and experience the effect of his action on the soul of the person he endeavors to cure. "But . . . the specific healing relation would come to an end the mo-

[6] *Ibid.*, p. 94.

ment the patient thought of and succeeded in practicing 'inclusion' and experiencing the event from the doctor's pole as well. Healing, like education, is only possible to the one who lives over against the other, and yet is detached." [7] The same applies *a fortiori* to the relationship between the pastor and the person in his spiritual charge, because mutual inclusion would in this case completely disable him from fulfilling the sacramental commission of the priest, and would, especially in the case of the Roman Catholic priest, undermine his status as a father confessor.

We have seen, so far, that Buber's educational thought centers around the character of the pupil-teacher relationship. It is this point which he illuminates by means of most delicate psychological distinctions and on which he lavishes his full powers of perception and analysis.

But true communion between human beings can only thrive in an atmosphere of freedom. By freedom Buber means both outward freedom, i.e. freedom from constraint, and inner freedom—that is, freedom of decision and choice. He poses this freedom as the prerequisite of education and not as its actual aim. It is characteristic of our world (which has been described by another great educational thinker as a "world adrift" because it has lost its power of spiritual orientation) that it sees in freedom the highest fulfillment of the educational aim. In Buber's view, freedom is merely a "springboard" and a "functional good" rather than the goal itself.

On the other hand, Buber's insistence on freedom as the prerequisite of true education does not lead him to a complete rejection of authority. The teacher has to exer-

[7] Buber, *I and Thou*, trans. Ronald Gregor Smith (New York: Charles Scribner's Sons), p. 133.

cise authority, like the master in his relation to the apprentice, but he should do so in the most delicate and subtle way, "by the raising of a finger, or a questioning glance." Any exercise of heavy-handed authority, with its concomitant demand of submission, provokes conflict "by dividing the soul in the teacher's care into an obedient and a rebellious part." [8] The teacher's authority must flow unaware from his own personality. After all, he is only one of the many factors which exercise an educational influence on the child. Buber elaborates this point further in his second lecture, "On Education of Character," where he enumerates a host of things which impress themselves upon the juvenile soul and exert an influence on it—"nature and the social context, the house and the street, language and customs, the world of history, and the world of daily news in the form of rumor, broadcast and newspaper, music and technical science, play and dream—everything together. Many of these factors exert their influence by stimulating agreement, imitation, desire, effort; others by arousing questions, doubts, dislike, and resistance. Character is formed by the interpenetration of all those multifarious opposing influences." [9]

What distinguishes the teacher from all the other influencing factors is his conscious desire to educate. This, after all, is the goal of his vocation; but this conscious will of the teacher to educate must not express itself in a high-handed show of authority. In the eyes of the child, the teacher must be like the other "elements" that impress themselves upon the child's soul and exercise an influence by their mere existence. "Though acting consciously, he

[8] "On Education," *Between Man and Man*, p. 90.
[9] Buber, "The Education of Character," *ibid.*, p. 106.

[the teacher] must nevertheless do it as though he did not." [10]

Since, within the multitude of chaotic elements that leave their imprint on the child's soul, the teacher represents the only purposeful element, it is possible clearly to determine his functions. Conscious and purposeful education is defined by Buber as "the selection by men of the effective world [*Auslese der wirkenden Welt*]." [11]

This rather vague statement calls for elucidation. The key to the understanding of the whole passage in which the function of the teacher is explained is in the first sentence, where Buber says that the master craftsman remains the model for the teacher. In more than one place in his writings Buber elaborates on this point. Buber sees in the master-apprentice relationship the ideal teacher-pupil relationship, because the apprentice shared the life of his master. Of course, he also learned from his master, but he did so in an indirect and subtle way. In learning a trade he became imbued with the spirit of his master, and, to use the words of Buber, "he learned the mystery of life." Nowadays this kind of education is no longer possible, or, rather, it has become exceptional; but it has not ceased to be the ideal of the pupil-teacher relationship. The world which surrounds the pupil is chaotic, but, channelled through the mind of the teacher, it becomes ordered and intelligible, and thus the teacher becomes the embodiment of the "selection of the effective world."

On this point of Buber's teaching Sir Fred Clark makes the following comments: "In the disciplinary relationship,

[10] "On Education," *ibid.*, p. 90.
[11] *Ibid.*, p. 89.

teacher or parent is selfless in the sense of being wholly disinterested, seeking not his own. Yet at the same time he is very much a self in the sense of being a 'concentration' of a 'world' that is likely to be 'effective' for his pupil. That is, Buber seems to say, he is, as teacher and guide, not a syllabus, not a social code, not even a system of morality, but a living embodiment of a 'world' [of experience?] not yet actual for the pupil, but both feasible for him and desirable for him in the sense that, in that world, he can be most truly and effectively himself." [12]

I find it difficult to agree with the above interpretation. If the teacher is neither a syllabus, nor a guide, nor a social code, nor even a system of morality, what then is he? Sir Fred Clarke says the teacher is the "living embodiment of the world" or of experience. Thus, he leads us back again to Buber's original words, which he admits to be "dark," and quite fails to elucidate them.

It is more likely that according to Buber the teacher represents to the pupil a world of ordered experience, a scale of values, and an embodiment of purpose. Moreover, if we are permitted to apply this particular point of Buber's thought to the classroom situation, we may also understand this phrase as implying that "selection of the effective world" which is represented by the subject matter taught at school. Out of an infinite variety and quantity of material for instruction just this or that branch is selected for study and this or that quantity of knowledge is brought to bear upon the pupil's mind.

In his lecture "On the Education of Character," Buber

---

[12] Sir Fred Clarke, *Freedom in the Educative Society* (London: University of London Press), p. 66.

draws three conclusions stemming from this central point of his theory. Firstly, the fact that the teacher is only one among a multitude of factors in the educational process should teach him humility; secondly, the fact that he consciously endeavors to shape the personality of other human beings imposes upon him a heavy responsibility; and thirdly, that in order to put into effect this conscious endeavor, he must first gain the pupil's confidence. "For the adolescent who is frightened and disappointed by an unreliable world, confidence means the liberating insight that there is human truth, the truth of human existence. When the pupil's confidence has been won his resistance against being educated gives way to a singular happening; he accepts the educator as a person. He feels he may trust this man, that this man is not making a business out of him but is taking part in his life, accepting him before desiring to influence him. And so he learns to *ask*." [13]

Here we have to pause for a while to examine further one particular point of special difficulty in Buber's thought. I refer to Buber's attitude to freedom. We have pointed out that Buber rejects pronounced self-assertion on the part of the teacher, and requires him to exercise influence only in the most subtle and unobtrusive ways by means of a questioning glance or a raised finger. In this context he joins issue both with the old type of education and the new.

Since Buber himself does not give a detailed characterization of these two systems of education, we may, for the sake of convenience, accept John Dewey's lucid characterization of the two systems as a basis for the further dis-

[13] "The Education of Character," *Between Man and Man*, p. 106.

cussion of Buber's attitude to freedom. According to Dewey, the distinctive features of the old type of education are: imposition from above, external discipline, learning from texts and teachers, the acquisition of skills and techniques by drill, static aims and materials, preparation for a more or less remote future. The new education is characterized by expression and cultivation of individuality, learning through experience, instruction which makes a direct appeal by making the most of opportunities of present-day life and encouraging acquaintance with a changing world.[14]

We have seen that Buber does not identify himself with either system of education. He finds fault with the old type of education because it places an exaggerated emphasis on authority. Neither does he approve of the new type of education, because it appears to dispense with authority altogether. He takes his stand somewhere in between the two. The teacher who properly fulfills his role is characterized by a peculiar blend of self-assertion with self-effacement. The question may now be asked whether such an attitude—symbolized by the teacher's "questioning glance" and "raised finger"—will suffice to invest the teacher with the authority and command required to conduct a class. Is not Buber's teaching too utopian and unrealistic in view of conditions prevailing in the ordinary school? Though there may be some teachers of outstanding personality who, as it were, unconsciously radiate authority—and then an element of fear enters into the teacher-pupil relationship, which Buber himself considers highly undesirable—

[14] *John Dewey's Philosophy*, "Intelligence in the Modern World" (New York: Modern Library, 1939), pp. 656-57.

this is not the case with the majority of teachers, who may find Buber's advocacy of fastidious gentleness toward the pupil impracticable.

It is problems of this kind which force us to interpret Buber's conception of authority in a wider sense. It does not appear likely that, on this particular point, Buber is very much concerned with the technicalities of school instruction. The question of normal disciplinary measures, the adoption of a syllabus, and choice of subjects to be taught at school may not constitute a problem to him.

Moreover, in his lecture "On the Education of Character" Buber seems to indicate clearly that his advocacy of freedom of the pupil, who, as he puts it, is to be restrained merely by "the raised finger and questioning glance" does not apply to school teaching. He says: "He [the teacher] has to introduce discipline and order. He has to establish a law, and he can only strive and hope for the result that discipline and order will become more inward and autonomous, and that at last the law will be written in the heart of his pupils." [15] This passage shows clearly that, as far as school teaching is concerned, more than the questioning glance of the teacher is permissible and indeed necessary if discipline and order are to be maintained. Ultimately, discipline must come from within, but this is a remote aim according to Buber. We are therefore justified in concluding that, at least at the outset, discipline and order must be imposed from above. This is a far cry from the conception of modern education upheld by the disciples of Dewey.

Dewey's advocacy of education on progressive lines has caused many of his followers to accept the absence of all

[15] "The Education of Character," *Between Man and Man*, p. 113.

authority in the classroom as axiomatic and, what makes it worse still, as a principle which should reign supreme in all spheres of school instruction. Dewey had therefore to turn against his own followers who said: "Above all let us not suggest any end or plan to the students; let us not suggest to them what they shall do, for that is an unwarranted trespass upon their sacred intellectual individuality, since the essence of such individuality is to set up ends and aims." [16] It is therefore understandable that Dewey found it necessary to justify the teacher's claim of a share in the discussion of syllabi and in the determination of the pupil's work.

It is interesting to note that Dewey, like Buber, holds up the master craftsman as an example of the ideal teacher. "There is the same presumption of the right of a teacher to make suggestions as to what to do, as there is on the part of the head carpenter to suggest to apprentices something of what they are to do. . . . If he [the pupil] does not get the suggestion from the teacher, he gets it from something or somebody in the home or the street, or from what some more vigorous fellow pupil is doing." [17] Dewey sums up his own attitude in this matter in the following words: "The implication that the teacher is the one and only person who has no 'individuality' or 'free-

[16] *John Dewey's Philosophy, op. cit.,* pp. 623-24.

[17] *Ibid.,* p. 624. Likewise Comenius: "Craftsman do not hold their apprentices down to theories; they put them to work without delay so that they may learn to forge metal by forging, to carve by carving, to paint by painting, to leap by leaping. Therefore in schools let the pupils learn to write by writing, to speak by speaking, to sing by singing, to reason by reasoning, etc., so that schools may simply be workshops in which work is done eagerly. Thus, by good practice, all will feel at last the truth of the proverb: *Fabricando fabricamur.*" (From P. Bovet, *J. Amos Comenius* (Geneva: 1943), p. 23.)

dom' 'to express' would be funny if it were not often so sad in its outworkings." [18]

Buber discusses the problem of freedom in a somewhat different context. He does not need to justify the teacher's right to suggest specific tasks to the pupil and to exercise normal disciplinary functions since he has never denied the teacher that right within the concrete situation of the classroom. Buber's demand for a subdued expression of authority symbolized by the "questioning glance" and the "raised finger" is merely a corollary of his doctrine of "inclusion." This doctrine has its proper application in the individual pupil-teacher relationship, in the sphere of character training and moral education, and wherever a teacher exerts direct influence upon his pupil and is about to actively intervene in his pupil's life. It is here that Buber cautions the teacher against any direct imposition of authority and arbitrary will, which, in his view, "is almost always due to an interruption or a temporary flagging of the act of inclusion." [19]

Buber sees in his theory of education merely a "principle of its reality" and not a statement of its maxim or aim. Only at the end of his lecture "On Education" is the aim rather abruptly revealed, and without any elucidation. Obviously this lecture is not to be read in isolation but in the light of his philosophical and theological writings.

In Buber's view the aim of education is determined by the general trend or spirit of each age, which leaves its imprint on education and gives it its ultimate direction. In this sense, there is no autonomy in the field of education.

According to Buber, our age is characterized by the dis-

[18] *Ibid.*, p. 625.
[19] "On Education," *Between Man and Man*, p. 100.

integration of traditional beliefs, by lack of spiritual orientation and the absence of a clear and common aim. All
agree that the only generally accepted aim is the desire
for material welfare. Instead of education for a way of
life we seem to be educating for a comfortable livelihood.
But we have reached a point where even this no longer
satisfies us. As John Wren Lewis stated in a recent Third
Programme Lecture, "The increase of material welfare
has become so great in the main civilized countries, that
people are no longer prepared to see the human good
merely in terms of further increase, and they begin to
look again at their relationships with one another to see
where, in them, the ultimate good lies." [20] This leads us
back again to Buber, but, as we have seen, Buber lays
emphasis on the fact that the cultivation of human relationships does not constitute the ultimate aim either.
Where then is it to be found? "Only times which know a
figure of general validity—the Christian, the gentleman,
the citizen—know an answer to that question, not necessarily in words, but pointing with the finger to the figure
which rises clear in the air, out-topping all. The forming
of this figure in all individuals, out of all materials, is the
formation of a "culture." But when all figures are shat-
tered, when no figure is able any more to dominate and
shape the present human material, what is there left to
form? Nothing but the image of God." [21]

In the same context Buber elaborates this point and
defines the aim as the "imitation of God (*imitatio Dei
absconditi sed non ignoti*)."

The reader cannot help feeling that "when all directions

[20] John Wren Lewis in *The Listener,* Oct. 13, 1960.
[21] *Between Man and Man,* p. 102.

fail" the sudden turning to God and the *imitatio Dei* will be of little avail. Neither does Herbert Read's comment on this particular point of Buber carry us any further. He calls this aim "remote" but not "impracticable," a statement which seems to suggest that he himself is not quite convinced of its validity. He further says, rather vaguely, that we may proceed toward this aim "step by step through the realm of beauty to the realm of truth." Only by considering the wider aspects of Buber's dialogical thinking can the discussion of this point proceed satisfactorily.

In his postscript to *Schriften über das Dialogische Prinzip (Essays on the Dialogic Principle)* Buber makes it clear that in a wider sense the dialogical relation between man and man points to a similar relationship between man and God. "We have realized that the Thou that goes out from man to man is the same that descends to us from the Divine and ascends back to it. This common factor is essential for us; the twin commandments of 'Love thy God' and 'Love thy neighbor' direct our glance to the transparency of the mortal Thou, but also to the loving-kindness of the infinite Thou wherever and in whichever way it may appear." [22]

Buber's reference to the twin commandments of "Love thy neighbor" and "Love thy God" is most revealing, be-

[22] *"Wir hatten erkannt, dass eben dasselbe Du, das vom Mensch geht, eben dasselbe es ist, das vom Göttlichen her zu uns niederfährt und von uns her zu ihm aufsteigt. Um dieses Gemeinsame in der äussersten Ungemeinsamkeit ging es und geht es. Jene biblische Verschwisterung von Gottesliebe und Menschenliebe im Doppelgebot lenkte unseren Blick auf die Transparenz des endlichen Du, aber auch auf die Gnade des Unendlichen, zu erscheinen, wo und wie es erscheinen will."* See Buber, *Die Schriften über das Dialogische Prinzip* (Heidelberg: Verlag Lambert Schneider, 1954), pp. 299-300.

cause in it lies the seed of his dialogic principle. Moreover, he states elsewhere that this principle finds its fullest
expression in both the divine election of the Prophets
with their answer to His call, and in Chassidic life and
teaching. This dialogic relation between man and God is
possible in the first place because of the "transparency"
of man—that is to say, man's spiritual awareness and sus-
ceptibility to Divine influence. It is made possible in the
second place by God's loving-kindness to man, expressed
in His desire to enter into a relationship with him.

In the same postscript Buber amplifies this teaching by
pointing out that when we place ourselves in a direct
relation with God we actually think of Him as a person.
Indeed, according to Buber, His being a person may be
regarded as one of the attributes of the Godhead.

Thus it is understandable that the "I-Thou" relationship to God and to man are actually two facets of the same
dialogic principle and that belief in the universal Deity
can arise spontaneously out of the experience of meeting
human beings. Hence Buber's recourse to the *imitatio Dei*
at the end of a discourse dedicated mainly to the illumination of the "I-Thou" relationship between teacher and
pupil can be well understood.

However, there are limits to what education can do. It
cannot "teach" the *imitatio Dei* as its supreme aim, nor
for that matter can it inculcate a religious outlook on life.
Yet, according to Buber, education can lead the pupil a
step farther toward God and toward a spiritual perception of the universe. To achieve this aim the student must
first be rescued from what Buber calls elsewhere the
"fiery jaws of collectivism" or what A. D. Gordon calls
the "hypnosis" engendered by mass movements; that is

to say, man has first to be freed from the uncritical attitude so characteristic of our times. He must learn to be
sceptical of the opinions, prejudices, and slogans propa-
gated by political parties or other organizations through
the various media of mass propaganda. In Buber's own
words, man must become a "person" again. He must become self-reliant and autonomous, in order to be capable
of entering into a personal relationship with the Absolute. Buber regards the all-pervasive materialism of our
time, with its concomitant insensitivity to spiritual influences, as a serious sickness of the human race. Once man
has become a person again, then, and only then, it may
happen to him that in hours of utter solitude he may withdraw within himself, ponder upon his relation to other
fellow creatures, and ultimately find a relation with God.
It is the task of the teacher to guide his pupil in that
direction.

Our interpretation of Buber's philosophy of education
is now drawing to its close. Its outstanding feature is the
fact that it centers around the most simple and essential
factor of the educational process—the teacher-pupil relationship. We have seen that his educational teaching contains a profound religious element. It is not associated
with the technicalities of teaching, the imparting of skills,
nor with its vocational aspects. God, the teacher, and the
pupil are the three focal points around which the fabric
of his educational thought is woven. It is interesting to
note that the Indian philosopher Sri Aurobindo also bases
his educational thought on these three points.

The general train of Buber's educational thought may
be regarded as an important balancing factor in the current trend in education. The modern trend emphasizes

in a most one-sided manner the multifarious aids, techniques and other "scientific" devices, sometimes of a very
trivial nature, which are associated with the practice of
teaching, such as audio-visual aids, statistical surveys,
intelligence and aptitude tests, teaching machines, etc.,
while quite failing to recognize the essential purpose of
education as opposed to mere instruction. The enormous
flow of American magazine literature on the minutest
technicalities of instruction is witness to the alarming pro-
portions that the new trend is assuming. This educational
literature presents a distorted picture of educational
values.

The conception of education as essentially an art and
not a science is inherent in Buber's philosophy of education. Modern educational trends stress its scientific aspects. In our materialistic civilization the exact sciences
and technology are preferred to philosophy and the arts.
It is therefore understandable that an ever-increasing number of educationists like to see themselves as educational
technologists working in educational "laboratories" or as
scientists engaged in "field research," thus emulating their
colleagues in the exact sciences. Against this tendency the
voice of Buber is raised in loud and lonely protest. This
state of affairs has been rightly diagnosed by Sir Fred
Clarke, who in a chapter devoted to the discussion of
Buber's impact on educational thought observes that
modern education has become so preoccupied with the
"science" of education that it has neglected to take note
of the more subtle components of the supreme artistry
that it exacts in practice.

Buber's conception of "enveloping" the pupil, if applied
to the relation between teacher and class, leads to the

creation of an atmosphere congenial to the teacher's work. At the end of a chapter devoted to Buber's contribution to education Herbert Read states the following: "My first conclusion was that good results depended on the creation, in the school or class, of a sympathetic atmosphere, and to a certain extent I still think this is true. But if by 'atmosphere' one means the amenities which money can buy, it is not true. The right atmosphere can exist in a village school, or in a dingy barracks in some industrial city. The atmosphere is the creation of the teacher, and to create an atmosphere of spontaneity, of happy childish industry, is the main and perhaps the only secret of successful teaching. To do this, the teacher may not need more than a minimum of technical or academic qualifications; but he or she does require the gift of understanding or 'enveloping' the pupil which Buber has defined."[23] This remark is pertinent and true in spite of the fact that Buber's treatment of human relationships in education is rather one-sided inasmuch as he confines himself completely to the teacher-pupil relationship and disregards the relations between the pupils themselves. It must not be forgotten that this has as much bearing on the question of creating an atmosphere as the pupil-teacher relationship itself.

The teacher who comes into contact with the world of Buber's thought, and understands it, cannot help being influenced by a philosophy whose purpose it is to refine his relations with his pupils and being imbued with gentleness and sympathy toward them. Moreover, Buber places a heavy responsibility on the teacher's shoulders and fills him with a high sense of his calling.

[23] Herbert Read, *Education through Art* (Faber and Faber), p. 288.

It is no exaggeration to say that any teacher who reads Buber's educational writings with a receptive mind cannot fail to feel elated and enriched. He will be both a better teacher and a better man.

10

Rabbi Kook
(His Influence on Jewish Education)

Rabbi Kook, who was Chief Rabbi of the Ashkenazi community of Palestine from 1919 to the year of his death, 1935, will forever be linked with the return of the people of Israel to their homeland.

Abraham Isaac Hacohen Kook was born in Greive, a small town in the district of Dvinsk, Kurland, in North Russia, in 1865, the scion of eight generations of Rabbis. His father was a pious and learned Rabbi whose home was a center of Torah learning. His son received a traditional education in the local *Heder*. The boy's exceptional piety and devotion to learning made him famous throughout the district and earned him the appellation of the *Illui* (child prodigy) of Greive. Abraham Isaac next attended *Yeshivot* in the Vilna district and continued his studies at the renowned *Volozhin Yeshiva,* where he grew to be an outstanding scholar, the favorite disciple of Rabbi Naftali Zvi Yehuda Berlin.

Abraham Isaac's great-grandfather had been a *Chassid,* a disciple of the Baal Shem Tov, but his father and grandfather were *Mitnagdim* (opponents of *Chassidism*), and so the young man was exposed to the influence of both trends within Judaism. Thus, although a *Mitnaged* himself, he was extremely sympathetic to the *Chassidic* movement. His great-uncle, one of the first settlers of Yahud near Petach Tikva, instilled in him a passionate love of Zion and a longing to settle in the Holy Land. This deep love for the land of Israel was further nourished by his contacts with the famous Rabbi of Radin, the author of *Hofetz Haim* (*He That Delighteth in Life*), and also by Rabbi Mordecai Eliasberg of Boisk, one of the earliest adherents of the *Chovevei Zion* movement.

Although Kook did not want to become a Rabbi by profession, he was finally persuaded by his teachers to do so. When in 1904 he was invited to become Rabbi of Jaffa, he unhesitatingly answered the call. The years of the First World War found him in London, but he returned in 1919 to become Chief Rabbi of the Ashkenazi community of Palestine, a post he held until his death in 1935.

I

The exposition and clarification of Rabbi Kook's ideas on Jewish education are bound up with many difficulties. First of all, his views on education do not form a systematic section of his writings but are revealed in various articles and letters, some of which were written in reply to specific questions on issues of the day. It is possible that this correspondence does not present a complete picture of his educational ideas and that his disciples and those close to him received a fuller and more comprehensive exposition of his attitude to this subject. His essay on the "World *Yeshiva* Center," in which he develops his views on higher education and about which more will be said later, is his only piece of systematic writing in the field of education known to me.

The modern reader of his principal work *Orot Hakodesh (Lights of Holiness)* or, for that matter, any other of Rabbi Kook's philosophical or theological works may —especially if unversed in Jewish mystical thought—be baffled by the vagueness and obscurity of his writings, which are steeped in Jewish mysticism. His letters, however, in spite of their elevated style, sometimes rising to poetic heights, make fairly lucid and straightforward reading. As already mentioned, these letters are the main source of information regarding Rabbi Kook's ideas on education.

The outstanding impression gained on reading his work is that Rabbi Kook has built a bridge between the religious and secular sections of the Jewish people. This could only be done by a man imbued with a great love for the Jewish people and to whom all the members of his flock were dear, even those who were neither learned nor religiously observant.

Since the time of Rabbi Levi Izhak of Berdichev, 150 years before Rabbi Kook's time, there has been no such staunch believer in the inherent goodness of every individual Jew. His *Judenliebe* was not merely emotional but was deeply rooted in his metaphysical views about the character of the Jewish people. He, like Yehuda Halevi before him, believed that Jews were endowed with a special spiritual and moral sensitivity which made them eligible to become a kingdom of priests and a holy nation.

Commenting upon the Biblical verse (Exodus 33:16), "So shall we be separated [differ], I and thy people, from all the people that are upon the face of the earth," he points out that Knowledge of God does not come to the Jew, as it were, "from outside," through contemplation upon nature or history, but stems directly from an "inner divine spark" lodged in his soul. The existence of a Divine Being is for the Jew not a subject of mere philosophic speculation but a matter of absolute existential certainty.

In Rabbi Kook's all-embracing system of philosophy all the elements of life are drawn into a unity and all dichotomies disappear. There are in his thought no absolute dividing lines; everything flows. There is no absolutely clear distinction between concepts such as body and soul, life and death, matter and spirit, faith and reason. In his view, all antinomies and conflicts are merely apparent and superficial; essentially there is harmony in all creation because all things created partake of the Divine. Hence all friction, enmity, and antagonism are merely temporary manifestations bound to resolve in ultimate harmony. Nor is there a sharp contrast between the holy and profane. "The holy is built upon the profane, the profane is the stuff of which the holy is made, and the holy gives it its form. The more solid the basic matter the more significant and enduring is the holy." [1]

According to Rabbi Kook, the physical growth and development of the Hebrew nation symbolizes the emergence of the spirit of holiness. "Despite the fact that the national resurgence of the Jewish people in the land of Israel, as well as the progress of all mankind, are manifest mainly in physical and material advance, this progress heralds

[1] Rabbi Kook, *Orot Hakodesh* (Jerusalem: 1938), p. 145.

the imminent emergence of a Kingdom of the Spirit and the light of Divine Salvation will eventually be revealed in its golden splendor." [2]

It can therefore be understood that Rabbi Kook saw in the expansion of the *Yishuv* and in its consolidation in the holy land a sign that heralded the spreading of spiritual influences; firmly believing that in God's good time the spirit of holiness would again become manifest in the land of Israel.

There is a sharp contrast between Rabbi Kook's optimism regarding the future of the Jewish *Yishuv* in Palestine and the pessimistic forecasts of those who believed that spiritual and intellectual degeneration would follow in the wake of normal Jewish statehood. Rabbi Kook believed that the dormant spiritual powers of the Jewish people would unfold through contact with the holy land, and the spiritual wealth of the people accumulated through the centuries would shed its outer covering, cast off its alien elements, and appear in all its pristine purity. This dream of his is somewhat reminiscent of Bialik's grandiose conception of the *Kinuss,* the "ingathering" of the foremost literary creations of the Jewish people through two thousand years of exile and their re-emergence in Hebrew garb in the holy land.

II

We have dwelt so far upon some of Rabbi Kook's philosophical ideas in which his views on education are founded. It may be gathered from what has been said so far that his attitude to the secular education introduced

[2] *Ibid.,* p. 155.

by the new settlers in Palestine was not entirely negative. A man like Rabbi Kook, who did so much to foster religious influence and who feared the "distortion of the spiritual countenance of Jewish education," could not approve of a system of education which did not accord to religious studies a place of prominence in school or demand the fulfillment of religious commandments. Nevertheless, when referring to secular education in Palestine he says ". . . It cannot be denied that it, too, contains much of value for living a rich life. It fosters love of the people and aspires to contributing to the strengthening and expansion of the *Yishuv*. It causes the spirit of the generation to become more and more attached to its land and its people. Despite its estrangement from religion, it still contains within itself a strong holy spark which should be further strengthened by hands that minister to it faithfully." [3] When enlarging upon the question of how religious influence should be brought to bear upon the irreligious he never tires of saying that this must be done with due respect and tact, that the sin and not the sinner must be attacked.

Rabbi Kook was opposed to Orthodoxy's barren and unconstructive criticism of the modern secular educational institutions of the *Yishuv*. He was convinced that Orthodoxy's chiding and censuring could only cause conflict within the Jewish camp. He believed that they should teach by example and set up religious schools and *Yeshivot* which would serve as models. In this way the Orthodox community could achieve constructive results.

The problem that Rabbi Kook had to face was the

[3] Rabbi Kook, *Igrot Ha'reiyah* (Jerusalem: Mosad Ha'rav Kook, 1946). II, 79-80.

foundation of a new type of religious school which would appeal to the modern European Jew. He felt that the educational institutions of the old *Yishuv,* their *Yeshivot* and Talmud Torah schools, were in a state of stagnation and no longer in keeping with the spirit of the time. They lacked modern school buildings, equipment, and other essential amenities, and altogether excluded secular studies.

The pressing need for the foundation of new schools caused Rabbi Kook to ponder the aim of Jewish education in general, as well as the difficult and controversial question of the relationship between secular and religious studies. Rabbi Kook defines the aims of Jewish education in a noble spirit and in significant and striking terms which have no parallel in other Jewish sources. "The main aim of education," he writes, "is to mold man into his 'reformed' or civilized form [*Tzura Metukenet*]." [4] Man is civilized and "reformed" if he acts justly and honestly; to educate man to just and upright living is the supreme aim of Jewish religious education. The more deeply rooted in his soul man's ability of "calling upon the name of the Lord" the more upright and righteous he becomes. Although Rabbi Kook does not appear to exclude the possibility of the existence of ethics divorced from religion (the autonomous ethics of secular humanism), he maintains that the surest way to achieve the aim of righteousness and uprightness is through a thorough religious grounding. He felt that it was the Jews' mission to teach mankind that only by "calling on the Name of the Lord" can we civilize man, as it is written in Genesis 18:19: ". . . and they shall keep the way of the Lord,

[4] *Ibid.,* I, 118-19.

to do justice and judgment. . . ." This being the ultimate aim of religious education, it follows that the Torah must have a central place in the curriculum of a Jewish school worthy of its name. Vocational education is merely a sideline and secondary aim; the main aim remains to mold, civilize, and "reform" man. Without God and religion, any system of ethical education will lack a solid basis and therefore prove a weak and precarious instrument in the process of "reforming" man. (Recent experience seems to corroborate this contention of Rabbi Kook. It may not be amiss to mention here that there were many more German ministers of religion who opposed the Nazi regime than university teachers and intellectuals in general.)

Rabbi Kook was fully aware of the fact that in modern times vocational training or an education for a livelihood in a broader sense is bound to take up a large part of the school syllabus and a child's hours of study. He insisted, however, that the "spiritual countenance" of Jewish education should not for that reason be "defaced or obliterated," particularly in the holy land, "For out of Zion shall go forth the Law and the word of the Lord from Jerusalem." However, Rabbi Kook refrains from formulating hard-and-fast rules as to the number of hours that may be devoted to secular studies in a religious school. That must depend upon the requirements and exigencies of time and place; what matters is the preservation of the right balance between religious and secular studies. That which is of paramount importance (i.e., religious studies) must not become subsidiary to that which is less important (i.e. secular studies); in other words, Jewish studies must constitute the heart and core of the religious school.

We have seen that "the proclamation of the Name of God," and making man upright and righteous, are, according to Rabbi Kook, almost synonymous concepts. In other words, in his view religious observance is inseparable from ethical conduct. Following the teaching of the Hebrew prophets, Rabbi Kook opposed a formalistic conception of religious observance and an empty ritualism divorced from spiritual and moral significance.

III

Like many other great educational thinkers who were dissatisfied with the systems of education in their countries, Rabbi Kook too criticized education in Palestine, the policies and practices of the Talmud Torah schools, *Yeshivot,* and other religious institutions of his time. This criticism is of particular importance, coming, as it does, from a man of profound educational knowledge and insight who, though in fundamental agreement with the general spirit of these schools, was by no means blind to their shortcomings.

As an educational critic, Rabbi Kook is reminiscent of Rabbi Loeb of Prague and other distinguished Rabbis who refused to regard as sacred all that went on within the confines of the religious schools of their time. First and foremost, he deplored the unsuitable and dilapidated state of the buildings in which the *Yeshivot* and other religious schools in Palestine were housed, their lack of order and organization, the fact that there were no fixed times for the lessons, the lack of cleanliness and all that that implied; the slovenly and shabby clothing of both pupils and teachers, who, according to Rabbi Kook, failed to "march with the times" and to participate in the new life that was emerging in the holy land. These defects in the old schools led to the birth of Rabbi Kook's idea of a new type of *Yeshiva,* one that would be more suited to the new life in Palestine, a school, which from the very beginning would be free from the defects and failings of the existing religious educational institutions. He grieved at the sorry plight of the religious schools, felt that the "inner light" that should burn brightly in these institutions was dimmed by their grave shortcomings, and feared that the new generation in Palestine would regard them as outdated and decrepit.

However, with true nobility of spirit Rabbi Kook defended or rather found an excuse for the old educational system by attributing most of its shortcomings to the poverty of the Jewish community, the indifference of the Mandatory Government to Jewish education, and the desolate atmosphere emanating from the ancient destruction of Jerusalem, which had set its mournful seal upon all aspects of life, including the educational institutions. "Here in Jerusalem," he said, referring to the Old City and the Wailing Wall, "where there is such a sharply pervading atmosphere of loss and mourning, where the ruins of our Temple are always before our eyes . . . this sight is bound to depress our spirit and leave its mark on education as well as on all walks of life. . . ."[5]

The new *Yishuv,* however, had a totally different character. Here he saw a spirit of renewed national life which demanded a new system of education, and he fought courageously for reform in religious education and its adaptation to the new life so rapidly developing in the

[5] *Ibid.,* I, 118.

country. On no account would he belittle the value of improved material conditions in the educational institutions, and opposed the widely held Orthodox viewpoint that to invest education with spiritual content it is necessary to reject all forms of material comfort. It was this view that, at least to some extent, was responsible for the primitive housing conditions and inadequate equipment of the religious schools.

There is great historic interest in Rabbi Kook's criticism of the syllabus of the old type *Yeshiva* and Talmud Torah school, which concentrated mainly on the study of the Talmud and the Codes, ignoring other Judaic studies. Rabbi Kook saw in this fact clear evidence of the spiritual impoverishment and stagnation pervading these institutions. He proposed to remedy this situation by establishing a central *Yeshiva* in Jerusalem which would be imbued with the spirit of the Jewish national revival. He emphasized most strongly and repeatedly that no aspect of Judaism was to be omitted from the syllabus of the new institution. Judaism in all its richness and all its splendor was to be taught there—not only the Oral and Written Law but also Jewish history and Palestinography, the *Midrashic* literature, *Hassidut, Kabbalah,* Philosophy, and *Mussar.* Rabbi Kook felt that the one-sided Talmudic orientation of the *Yeshivot,* their neglect of Jewish philosophy, *Aggada,* and Mysticism were robbing Judaism of much of its vitality, appeal, and power.

In his essay which gives details of his plan for the Central *Yeshiva,* he envisages a central seat of learning that would serve all the Jewish communities of the Diaspora as well as Palestine Jewry, and where all the above-mentioned subjects would be taught, a program in keeping with and worthy of the national resurgence taking place in the holy land. As a center of universal Jewish learning, the *Yeshiva* was intended to symbolize the fundamental unity of the Jewish people. The students who were accepted would have to display outstanding ability and character and were to be versed in at least one "Order" of the Talmud. The course of study would last six years; boys would enter the Institution at sixteen, and leave at the age of twenty-two. The period of study was thus limited, we presume, to curb the *Yeshiva* students' propensity to become "eternal students." Some graduates, at least, should go out into the world to become Rabbis and teachers. Besides a systematic study of all Judaic subjects, the syllabus was also to include a scholarly study of the Hebrew language and rhetoric. The fact that he advocated the inclusion of the latter subjects indicates that Rabbi Kook's aim was to train Rabbis who would be capable of bringing the message of Judaism to the new *Yishuv*. Outstanding scholars would be given the opportunity to continue their work in Judaic research, after the fixed period of study.

The aims outlined in this essay, as well as Rabbi Kook's general efforts to modernize Jewish education, naturally brought him into conflict with the ultra-Orthodox element, who opposed all reformist tendencies. They even showed open hostility toward him and vilified him bitterly, using invective and other forms of attack.

In his letters, Rabbi Kook makes sharp rejoinders to these attacks. He felt that in refusing to widen the scope of Yeshiva education Orthodoxy was defeating its purpose —dimming, as it were, that "inner light" inherent in Judaism and embodied in *Aggadah*, Jewish philosophy,

Mussar, Kabbalah, and *Hassiduth.* One objection of the Orthodox element to the broadening of Jewish education was that not enough knowledge about Talmud and the Codes would be imparted if studies covered too wide a field. This view Rabbi Kook completely rejected. On the contrary, he maintained that all Jewish studies are correlated and mutually complementary; the study of one subject serves to shed light upon the other. On the other hand, he was quite aware of the fact that at an advanced stage some specialization was necessary, especially in the field of research.

The narrow education provided by the old type of *Yeshivoth* had left its mark on some of the Rabbis of the old school. This greatly grieved Rabbi Kook, who knew full well that some Rabbis were hopelessly out of touch with their flock and altogether detached from the world and its realities. In a letter to the late Pinchas Cohen he expresses his complete disillusionment with Rabbinical conferences. Many contemporary Rabbis, he asserts, are "sunk in deep slumber engendered by weakness of the soul, caused by the fact that they had not partaken of spiritual food, which is the supreme living light emanating from the depth of the Torah." [6] (The allusion is probably to the fact that some refrained from delving into Jewish mysticism and from preoccupation with Jewish philosophy in general.) Drawing on his experience of such conferences he comments as follows: "They [the Rabbis] will certainly adorn the conference table with some deliberation on a point of *Halacha* of the minutest significance, which of course assumes great importance when judged by the complex casuistry applied to its

[6] *Ibid.,* I, 240.

evolvement. This reminds me of a machine constructed of many thousands of golden nuggets, producing one tiny needle of steel. . . . When dealing with a matter appertaining to *Aggadah* they will present it in a discourse embellished with moral lessons that are completely divorced from life; if the subject be *Kabbalah,* it is bound to become a jerky, stammering, disconnected performance permeated with an outmoded philosophy. All this helps to engender a stifling atmosphere and thus a new pain is added to the birth pangs of *Knesseth Israel,* writhing in agony. . . ." [7] It is, therefore, understandable that Rabbi Kook was keenly interested in the creation of a new type of *Yeshiva* which would produce a modern type of Rabbi, intellectually alert and sensitive to the requirements of modern life.

Rabbi Kook worked hard to establish the Chief Rabbinate of Palestine, which was to become the center of the spiritual life of the *Yishuv.* He hoped that the post of Chief Rabbi would help him to exercise a religious influence on the *Yishuv* as a whole, and in 1927 the Chief Rabbinate was established. It goes without saying that Rabbi Kook was free from any personal ambition or hope of material gain from the post he assumed. Indeed, it is a well-known fact that he lived all his life in a state bordering on poverty. A story is told about him which illustrates the straitened circumstances in which he lived. When asked about his income, which was known to be inadequate, he replied cryptically, *"Ani mitparnes bechavod."* The idiomatic meaning of these words, "I earn an honorable living"; their literal meaning is, "I live on honor"; that is to say, honor was all he had.

[7] *Ibid.,* I, 140.

Rabbi Kook's exceptional modesty in material matters is reflected in many of his letters. Referring to his efforts in establishing the Chief Rabbinate, he writes ". . . the Chief Rabbinate must establish itself in a manner commensurate with its dignified status. It should have sufficient means to enable its emissary to make frequent journeys to all parts of the *Yishuv*, from Judea to Galilee, and to cover printing and publishing expenses for various letters and pamphlets aimed at fostering the unity of all available forces and returning them to religion. . . ." [8] In his capacity as Chief Rabbi he requested financial help only to cover postage and travel expenses and in order to print and distribute suitable literature to all settlements of the *Yishuv*. He did not ask even for the services of a secretary. Needless to say, he envisaged the Chief Rabbinate as serving not only the religious section but the *Yishuv* as a whole.

We have mentioned Rabbi Kook's strenuous efforts to create religious secondary schools which would be in keeping with the *Yishuv's* modern outlook. It was in his time that the first secular secondary school, the *Herzliyah Gymnasium*, was founded in Jaffa, and in the absence of a seat of higher learning in Palestine it was assuming great importance as a center of Hebrew culture; besides, it was fast becoming a prototype of a school which, though Hebrew and national in spirit, was divorced from all traditional and religious influence. If even Achad Ha'am had found fault with the exclusively secular spirit of this school, how much greater was Rabbi Kook's concern at the possible influence of this type of institution on the youth of the *Yishuv* as a whole. In a postscript to a letter

[8] *Ibid.,* I, 122.

addressed to the Central Bureau of the *Mizrachi* organization he writes as follows: "It is a well-known fact that the
teachers, especially those of the Gymnasium, and in particular the teachers of Holy Writ, extract the soul of
Judaism from their pupils' hearts by their strict adherence
to the grotesque ideas of the more worthless of the Biblical
critics. I do not wish to defile my pen by recounting all
the false ideas with which these teachers mislead our
children. How can I keep silent on this matter? Let us
deliberate and decide what course of action to take. May
He who girdeth Israel with might guide us in our efforts
to remedy this wrong." [9]

On the other hand, he viewed this school as a challenge
which was to awaken religious Jewry from their lethargy
and cause them to found a parallel school which would
counteract the influence of the *Herzliyah Gymnasium.*
Rabbi Kook felt that religious parents who wished their
children to acquire a traditional education should not
have to forego all the modern amenities and improvements of the newly founded secular schools. He envisaged
a school which would have the same material amenities
and include secular subjects in its curriculum but in
which the spirit of the Torah would predominate and
permeate the entire institution. Thus the *Tachkemoni*
school was founded in Jaffa and Rabbi Kook became its
supervisor. (*Tachkemoni* is a combination of two Hebrew
words, *Torah* and *Chochmah*—wisdom. The school was
founded in 1910 and sponsored by German-Jewish Orthodoxy.)

Rabbi Kook insisted that the decision in all matters
concerning Jewish studies should be his sole responsibility.

[9] *Ibid.,* I, 317.

It must be remembered that he was under strong pressure from the ultra-Orthodox elements, and, in order to safeguard the strictly religious character of the school, he wished to retain the power of inspector and adviser in all matters concerning religious instruction. In many of his letters he complains that he is not being sufficiently consulted on matters of school policy, especially those appertaining to the appointment and dismissal of teachers and the character of the religious instruction. These letters reveal him as a practicing schoolman occupied with the day-to-day problems of instruction, administration, personnel, and even fund raising.

Besides the *Tachkemoni* school, which Rabbi Kook had taken under his aegis, he exercised a strong influence on the *Netzach Israel* Talmud Torah schools (which taught Arabic, arithmetic, and a few other secular subjects, in addition to Jewish studies) and the *Mizrachi* schools in general. He also advocated the foundation of trade schools which would, as he puts it, "be filled with Torah and religious faith, sound knowledge and common sense, and permeated by a spirit of purity which would heal the soul and body of the Jewish people."

Rabbi Kook took a keen interest in the religious education of girls, a field which had hitherto been much neglected. He aimed at the education of girls in a way that would prepare them "to become mothers in Israel who would know how to march with the times in a modern spirit, and yet be armed with courage, knowledge of the Torah and our holy faith." He strengthened the hands of all who strove to draw Orthodoxy out of its isolation and accepted enthusiastically every proposal purporting to create a religious intelligentsia of a new type, which would make a constructive contribution to the development of the *Yishuv*.

IV

A parallel can be drawn between Rabbi Kook's influence on Jewish education in Palestine and that of Rabbi Samson Raphael Hirsch of Germany, who had died more than a generation before him. Both were dedicated men possessing outstanding qualities of leadership and endowed with an intuitive understanding of educational problems. Their historical function in the field of education is very similar, the main difference being that Hirsch was facing a generation of completely assimilated Jews, who as a result of their enjoyment of equal rights with the gentiles were fast giving up their own distinctive way of life and culture and becoming alienated from Judaism. Rabbi Kook greatly admired Hirsch, and especially his activities in the field of education. He called him a "Nazarite of the Lord, a man of outstanding historical vision, who saved by his courageous action the remnant of Western Jewry by teaching them to take full advantage of every means to synthesize traditional Judaism with the spirit of the time." [10] Rabbi Kook's task was more difficult because of the bitter opposition of the ultra-Orthodox elements, who were almost nonexistent in the German-Jewish community of Hirsch's time.

However, there was a marked difference in the theoretical argumentation of the two men in support of their educational aims. Hirsch supported his *Torah im Derech Eretz* principle by his contention that Holy Writ is not

[10] *Ibid.,* I, 182.

the exclusive repository of the Divine Will. The Will of God is also manifest in history, in the wonders of nature, as well as in the spirit of man, inasmuch as man is capable of creating works of permanent value such as literature and art. Translated into educational language, this means that in a Jewish religious school there cannot possibly be a ban on the study of history and nature and man's achievements in literature and art. These studies must, therefore, supplement the teaching of the Torah.

Rabbi Kook's stand was based on his faith in the metaphysical significance of the Jewish settlement in Palestine; hence his efforts to strengthen the religious elements and integrate them into the life of the *Yishuv*. But this could only be done by liberalizing the existing system of religious education and by creating new schools which would aim at a combination of religious and secular studies. However, Rabbi Kook did not go as far as Hirsch. Though he introduced secular studies into religious schools, the main emphasis was on Jewish studies.

In recent generations no Rabbi in Israel has gained such esteem in all sections of the Jewish community as Rabbi Kook enjoyed. The expounders of his philosophy are, in the first place, his son Rabbi Zvi Yehuda, his disciples, *inter alia*, Rabbis Bar Shaul, Israeli, Neriya, and Amital. Outside the Orthodox camp it was notably Buber who paid tribute to Rabbi Kook in a well-known essay, and Professor S. H. Bergmann, whose Hebrew essay on Kook has also appeared in an English version under the heading "Rabbi Kook, or All reality Is in God." Professor Nathan Rottenstreich's exposition of Rabbi Kook's philosophy, embodied in the former's *Hamachashava Hayehudit Be'eyt Hachadashah,* is also worthy of mention.

Rabbi Kook's memory is preserved in a most fitting way in an Institute in Jerusalem bearing his name, the *Mossad Ha-Rav Kook,* which publishes important books in the field of Judaics. The Institute carries on the activity nearest to Rabbi Kook's heart, namely, literary work and publication of suitable material for the instruction of the public in matters Jewish. Altogether it is true to say that his reputation, far from declining after his death, has grown steadily.

Rabbi Kook's influence on contemporary education has been considerable. The fact that a good many of the reforms in Jewish education that he advocated have been carried out proves his foresight and vision and is also a measure of his success. Meanwhile, important changes have occurred within the religious sector in Israel—changes which are reflected in its reformed educational system; and this in turn exercises an influence on religious circles. State religious schools in Israel have accepted the organic synthesis of religious and secular studies, both at the primary and secondary school level. On the whole it may be said that a certain stabilization has been brought about within the religious camp. The question of the right relationship between secular and religious studies no longer gives rise to heated controversy, because there is such a vast variety of schools and every shade of Orthodoxy is catered to. The educational system in the religious sector has developed along the lines that Rabbi Kook visualized, as witnessed by the wide range of religious schools combining religious and secular subjects.

The number of *Yeshivoth* combining a secondary-school curriculum or some kind of vocational training, with a thorough grounding in Bible and Talmud, is steadily increasing, and this is in no small measure due to Rabbi Kook's influence.

However, the central *Yeshiva* founded by Rabbi Kook has fallen short of the hopes he placed in it; to some extent this may be due to his untimely death. In a way, the religious university in Ramat Gan may be regarded as the nearest approach to what Rabbi Kook had in mind, though it cannot be denied that this institution, too, does not fully realize his dream. He had visualized a supreme center of learning and research in all Judaic subjects rather than an ordinary graduate school run on religious lines.

On the whole, his influence is most strongly felt in the field of religious secondary and vocational education; the *Yeshivoth,* on the other hand, have been rather slow in adopting the measures advocated by Rabbi Kook. The broadening of the curricula of *Yeshivot* in Israel has proceeded at a rather slow pace. While many *Yeshivoth* still teach Talmud almost exclusively, there are some that include Bible, *Mussar* and Jewish philosophy (*Machshevet Yisrael*) in their curriculum.

To sum up, his message to Jewish religious teachers would be: First of all, ensure a thorough and solid grounding of the pupils in Jewish subjects; secondly, insist on exemplary moral conduct on the part of teachers and students alike; thirdly, answer the challenge of the time, with its fast-developing science and technology, by broadening the study of Judaism until it becomes commensurate with the progress made in the secular fields. Fourthly, the "soul of Judaism," i.e., its religious tenets and living faith, its philosophy and mysticism, must become an integral part of Jewish education. Fifthly, march with the times and combine secular and vocational training with the study of Torah. Lastly, do not allow the material amenities and outward appearances of religious schools to fall short of those in the secular schools.

When viewing the general state of Jewish religious education in Israel today one is gratified to observe that Rabbi Kook's prayer, expressed in poetic form in one of his letters, has been largely realized.

> The points of my thought
> Which grow into legions
> Will give me the letters to form into words;
> The words will become essays,
> Which shall grow into books,
> And the books shall spread
> To every city.

11

Sarah Schenirer

The neglect of the religious education of girls, which is characteristic of almost all phases of Jewish history, is deeply rooted in Jewish tradition. I am thinking particularly of certain *dicta* of the Talmud, which laid down that women were not to be instructed in the Torah; as wives and mothers whose place was in the home, there was no need to develop their intellectual abilities. No serious attempt was therefore made to instruct girls in the tenets of Judaism, and beyond teaching them the rudiments of Hebrew, the principal prayers, and those religious commandments that apply especially to women, nothing was done to further their education.

With the emergence of the *Haskalah* movement in Eastern Europe in the nineteenth century and of the spirit of "Enlightenment" it brought in its wake (in the non-Jewish world this spirit found expression, e.g., in the institution of compulsory state education for all, including Jews), the Orthodox Jewish community adopted two widely differing systems of education for its children—one for its sons and another for its daughters. While boys were given a most thorough Jewish education in *Cheder* and *Yeshiva,* girls were sent to be educated in Polish (Christian) schools and grew up in ignorance of the tenets of the Jewish faith.

Thus an incongruous situation was created, marked by the worldliness of the Jewish womenfolk, which contrasted strangely with the unwordly piety of their husbands. Such a situation was bound to be fraught with dangers of conflict, felt particularly strongly in very Orthodox families, where the men had constantly to defend themselves against the criticism of their worldly-minded and businesslike wives. It has to be borne in mind that in Eastern Europe Jewish women were often the breadwinners of the family, and conseqently developed an ample measure of practical good sense.

The person who brought about a profound change in this situation was the romantic and now almost legendary Sarah Schenirer. Born in Cracow, Poland, in 1873, the daughter of a rich merchant who was a *Chassid* and adherent of the Rabbi of Belz, Sarah was sent to a Polish school. The religious instruction that Jewish girls received was given by a Rabbi who came to the school once or twice a week for this purpose. Sarah was the only girl who took these lessons seriously, although she, too, could not help feeling that they were not very conducive to progress. She immersed herself in the popular moralist literature for women written in Judeo-German which she found at home. Beyond that her religious education was very scanty.

With the worsening of the economic situation of her parents, Sarah was obliged to learn a trade and help support her family. She learned sewing and embroidery, served her apprenticeship, and set herself up as a dress-

maker in a small room, where she soon built up a considerable clientele. Her close contact with girls and women
of all types gave Sarah food for serious thought. She observed how assiduously women pursued the adornment
of their bodies while sorely neglecting their spiritual development. She often wondered why Jewish parents who
spared no pains to promote the physical well-being of their
daughters did so little for their religious education.

With the outbreak of the First World War, the family
came as refugees to Vienna. There Sarah began to attend
the services and lectures of Rabbi Dr. Flesch who was an
adherent of the S. R. Hirsch school of thought. These ser-
mons struck Sarah as modern and progressive, though they
were in fact completely traditionalist in spirit. Sarah was
greatly influenced by Dr. Flesch and soon realized what
power there was in Judaism if only it was brought to the
people in a way they could understand and in a spirit that
was akin to theirs. "I listened intently to Dr. Flesch's inspiring sermon," she writes about the first *Chanukah* service she attended in Vienna; "The rabbi painted a vivid
picture of Judith, the heroine of Jewish history. He held
her image up as an example to the girls and women of
our days and urged them to walk in the footsteps of the
illustrious women of Israel of ancient times. I have no
words that can adequately describe the powerful impression his sermon has made upon me. I said to myself: 'How
I wish that the women of Cracow might hear who we are
and who our ancestors were.'" [1]

Sarah now regularly attended the study circles of Dr.
Flesch and read extensively on Judaism. She considered
herself untutored, and what knowledge she possessed she

[1] S. Yarchi, *Sarah Schenirer* (Sifriat Metzach), p. 10.

had acquired by her own efforts. She read more about modern German Orthodoxy and its chief exponents, such as S. R. Hirsch and Dr. Hildesheimer; she was impressed by the writings of popular German-Jewish authors such as Lehmann, because these men possessed the ability to depict Jewish life in a way that appealed to contemporary Jews. In 1917 she returned to Cracow, and there her rather vague plans concerning the education of women assumed more concrete form.

The ideas that shaped the educational activities she later undertook in Cracow were founded on three convictions, which were the fruits of her perceptive observation of the Jewish scene. Firstly, she realized the anomaly of the situation whereby only boys received a Jewish education, while girls were sent to Polish schools. As future mothers who would exercise a decisive influence on their children, the girls, no less than the boys, needed a Jewish education. Secondly, she was attracted to the ways of Western Orthodoxy, which paid a great deal of attention to the education of girls. Thirdly, she realized that if Polish became the mother tongue of the Jewish girls then their whole outlook became Polish rather than Jewish, and they were drawn into alien cultural circles. She also knew that she, as a woman of modest intellectual abilities, was unable to transmit Judaic culture to the girls through the medium of the Polish language, and she came to the conclusion that Yiddish was the most effective means of keeping the girls within the Jewish fold. She regarded the Yiddish language as an effective barrier to assimilation and, while admiring the Hirsch school of thought, which had adopted the language of the country, she felt instinctively that this was not feasible in her country. Moreover, she took into consideration the fact that since the days of Mendelssohn German Jews had spoken German, whereas the majority of Polish Jewry still spoke Yiddish as their mother tongue.

Sarah sought moral support for her ideas from the Rabbi of Belz and approached him in Marienbad, where he was attending a conference of the *Agudath Israel Organization*. The Rabbi sent her a written reply, wishing her success and giving his blessing to her efforts. She received similar encouragement from the Rabbi of Ger and from the saintly author of *Hafetz Haim*.

She now set out upon her enterprise in the small room she used for her work as a dressmaker. A blackboard and benches were brought in and she went ahead in her undertaking. At first she had attempted to draw grown girls, more or less of her own age, into her circles, but without success. They had snubbed her efforts and showed a contemptuous attitude to her attempts to bring them back to Orthodoxy. These girls, who had been educated in Roman Catholic schools, felt at home in Polish literature and culture. Although compelled at home "to conform" and observe the Jewish commandments, as demanded by their parents, they were ashamed of their Jewishness and refused to introduce their parents and brothers to their gentile friends. Thus Sarah realized that she would have to concentrate her efforts on younger children if she were to meet with any measure of success.

Sarah's modest beginnings were soon to be crowned with phenomenal success. On the 11th *Kislew* 6678 (1918), she wrote in her diary: "The school is making marked progress. My dreams are becoming reality. There are already forty girls studying here, thank God. All the difficulties are disappearing as though erased by a miraculous hand. The girls are wonderful, innocent of all sin. They attend school most willingly and every day they absorb new knowledge. They realize that a human being's life is not based only on food, drink, and a pretty dress. They know that the happiness of a Jew lies in wholehearted service to the Lord." [2]

At the end of that year the number of her pupils had already risen to eighty, and she was compelled to take a larger flat consisting of three rooms, to house her school adequately. She did not confine her activities to Cracow alone but visited other towns, addressing Jewish communities at numerous meetings and propagating her ideas with great success. From these small beginnings there grew a whole network of day schools, seminars for the training of teachers, and other evening schools spreading over the foremost Jewish communities in Europe, America, and Palestine. According to reliable statistics there were in the year 1937-38 in Poland alone 248 *Beth Jacob Institutions* providing for 35,585 children. (The appellation *Beth Jacob* alludes to the verse: "O house of Jacob, come ye, and let us walk in the light of the Lord.")

How can one explain this phenomenal success? How could this simple woman launch an educational movement that spread to so many Jewish communities and won the approval of a substantial part of Jewish Orthodoxy?

Firstly, it has to be borne in mind that Sarah Schenirer's cause spoke for itself; her schools answered a vital need. Secondly, the character and personality of Sarah Schenirer contributed in no small measure to her success. Her pupils and all those who came into contact with her were moved by her piety, her disarming sincerity, simplicity, and in-

[2] *Ibid.*, p. 16.

tegrity. Being close to the people, she could easily influence them and evoke a positive response. Finally, she did not have to crusade single-handed. Only a few years after she had set up her first school, the *Agudat Israel World Organization* began to sponsor her schools and sent contributions through its local branches. The schools also received financial support from the *Keren Hatorah,* a fund established by German-Jewish Orthodoxy in aid of Torah education.

In the absence of qualified teachers, Sarah at first had recourse to her former pupils, who were persuaded to act as teachers. The fact that these pupils could take to teaching without undergoing professional training may cause surprise. However, in these schools, permeated as they were by the fear of the Lord and dedication to the Jewish heritage, there was no need for conventional school discipline and conventional teachers. All that a teacher needed in order to be successful was religious integrity, idealism, and knowledge of Judaism.

Later on, however, a school for the training of *Beth Jacob* teachers was founded in Cracow. The erection of the big multistoried building which housed the teachers' training school was the crowning achievement of her life.

Sarah Schenirer was interested in attracting to her schools as many children as possible. When she realized that the rapid expansion of day schools was too difficult and costly an enterprise she devoted much of her time and effort to the establishment of evening schools, which offered supplementary religious instruction in after-school hours.

Besides providing the girls with a thorough religious education, the *Beth Jacob* schools taught the rudiments

of secular subjects; others provided instruction in handicrafts and trained the girls for a livelihood. This aspect
of vocational training has been particularly developed
in many of the present-day *Beth Jacob* schools in Israel,
where they have proved most beneficial. These schools
absorb a large number of immigrant girls from oriental
communities, who are taught a trade and thus given
the means of earning their living.

Sarah Schenirer lived to see her work expand beyond
her most ambitious dreams and to be acclaimed by Jewish
Orthodoxy all over the world. Just before her death at
the age of fifty-two, she wrote a will in the form of a
letter, which contains the following exhortation to her
pupils: "Do my daughters realize what great faith I and
the majority of our people place in them? Do they feel
the burden of responsibility to become examples of pure
daughters of Israel and in turn to raise a new generation
of Jewish daughters? Will they overcome the trials and
difficulties that stand in their path? A silent prayer rises
from the depth of my heart: 'O Lord of the Universe,
help my dear daughters in their holy task. . . .' And you,
my daughters who go out into the wide world, your duty
is to implant the holy spark into the souls of the pure and
innocent young children. It is your task to sanctify these
souls. . . . May you be strengthened and fortified in your
sacred work! . . ." [3]

Simplicity, modesty, and piety were the keynotes of
Sarah Schenirer's personality. In her schools, character
formation was placed before formal training. Although
miles apart in background and outlook, she and the Polish-

[3] Moshe Prager, *Sarah Schenirer Em Be-Israel* (Jerusalem: Merkaz Beth
Jacob), p. 28.

Jewish educator Janusz Korczak had in common a high sense of mission, complete dedication to their vocation as teachers, and selfless devotion to their pupils. The network of schools which continues to play a vital part in Jewish education, both in the Diaspora and in Israel, is an abiding tribute to Sarah Schenirer's dedicated work for her pupils.

12

How Jewish are Israel's General Schools?

I

Israel state schools are of two kinds: general (secular) and religious. The latter include in their curriculum, in addition to the subjects taught at secular schools, intensified courses of study in Bible and Talmud, as well as instruction in religious observance. They cater to 25.4 per cent of all children educated in state schools. In addition to these state religious schools, there are independent religious schools sponsored by the *Agudat Israel* organization, which receive substantial state aid. Altogether religious schools cater to 31.6 per cent of the total school population.

It was in September 1959 that the Ministry of Education decided to take steps to foster in Israeli youth a deeper understanding of our spiritual heritage. This decision was intended to implement the government educational program adopted by the *Knesseth* on the 18th *Cheshvan*, 1956, where it is clearly stated that ". . . the government will endeavor to contribute to the deepening of Jewish consciousness among Israeli youth in the elementary and secondary schools as well as in the institutions of higher education, to root them in the past of the Jewish people and its historic heritage, and to imbue them with the feeling of belonging to World Jewry, springing from an awareness of their common destiny and historic continuity, which unites the Jews throughout the world in all countries and throughout all generations. . . ."

A few years later this aim was reiterated and a new law was actually adopted by the *Knesseth* after a long and heated debate and much preparatory work done by prominent personalities in the field of education. Two committees were appointed to recommend ways of implementing the law. One, headed by Mr. Aranne, then Minister of Education, considered the introduction of "Jewish-Israeli consciousness" in our general schools, where the emphasis would be put on the religious aspect of the subject; the other committee, under the chairmanship of Mr. Unna, then Deputy Minister of Education, followed a parallel course in connection with the religious schools, where special stress was to be laid on fostering the national Israeli consciousness of the children. These committees summed up their findings and proposed methods for cultivating the "Jewish-Israeli consciousness" in elementary schools. A detailed program was worked out for the implementation of these proposals, suitable textbooks and other literature were published, and in most schools "Jewish-Israeli consciousness" has already been introduced.

In actual practice, teachers are to inculcate Jewish consciousness by pursuing the following three aims:

1) The pupils are to be rooted in the spiritual heritage of the Jewish people.

2) They are to be rooted in the past of the Jewish people.

3) They have to acquire a feeling of belonging to, or being part of, the Jewish people as a whole.

The first aim is to be achieved by an intensified study of Torah, i.e., by reading the weekly *Sidrah* (portion of the Law) in the intermediate and upper forms of primary school; by a systematic study of *Aggadah* (Fork Lore); by the study of *Mishnah* (the Oral Torah) for two weekly periods during one school year, either the seventh or the eighth; by the study of chapters from the Prayer Book and *Machsor* (Prayer Book for the Festivals), especially before the Jewish Holy Days; by the creation of a suitable atmosphere at school, with the object of preparing the children for the religious festivals and days of remembrance; and finally by the use of the Hebrew in place of the Christian calendar.

The second aim is to be achieved by placing renewed emphasis on certain periods, happenings, and personalities in Jewish history, in order to deepen the pupils' awareness of the continuous nature of our history and people, to enhance their powers of endurance and creative achievement, as well as to trace the growth and development of the national character.

The third aim is to be achieved by imparting to the pupils a thorough knowledge about the Jewish communities of the Diaspora, their political, economic, and cultural position, with a view to deepening the pupils' understanding of the way of life of Diaspora Jewry. These studies are to be introduced into the syllabus of the seventh and eighth forms, accompanied by suitable social and educational activities.

II

How can we explain this feeling that there is a pressing need to revise the trend of Israeli educational practice? Did the Ministry merely become a mouthpiece for the latent sentiments of teachers and educators? In other words, did this desire to deepen the Jewish consciousness of Israeli youth stem from the people or was it imposed by the authorities? The reception of the new law in the *Knesseth* was, generally speaking, a favorable one, the only exception being the extreme left-wing parties; and even these did not oppose the law as such, but suggested that emphasis be laid on the Jewish pioneering spirit rather than on imparting information concerning Jewish religious observances. The *Knesseth's* acceptance of the law, while it shows that the law had popular support, does not throw light on its origin. How was the idea formed and who were the initiators of this movement?

In his closing speech, Mr. Aranne, former Minister of Education, mentioned the difficulties encountered in the implementation of the principles as originally expounded; these difficulties may have caused the Ministry of Education to give renewed consideration to the subject of Jewish consciousness (the *Kavei Yesod* adopted by the *Knesseth* in 1956.) "From its very beginning," he said, "the Hebrew school in Israel had to face four baffling problems." These were: 1) How to foster in Israeli youth the feeling of belonging to the Jewish people, although the majority of this people lives outside the boundaries of the state. 2) How to root the youth in the history of the Jewish people, when half of that history occurred outside the boundaries of the state. 3) How to reconcile the Zionist teaching of "rejection of the Diaspora" with the authorities' wish to inculcate in Israeli youth an awareness of the unity of the Jewish people. 4) How to bring closer to children educated in secular schools a culture permeated with religion.

These were the problems Israeli educators had to deal with, problems which, according to Aranne, required further attention and clarification, the outcome of which was a program introducing "Jewish consciousness" into Israel schools. So much for the initiative of the authorities in this matter.

The indifference of Israeli youth toward Jewish tradition and its failure to recognize its bond with the past heritage of the Jewish people have long troubled Israel educators. Besides, this youth has no emotional ties with the Jews of the Diaspora, and in no way identifies itself with it. The deep spiritual bonds which united the Jewish people in the past, so aptly expressed in the saying, "All Israel are responsible for one another," have become weakened and not strengthened by the new Israeli mode of life. Whereas Diaspora Jewry see in the Jewish religion the main unifying force in their lives, Israeli youth consider the fact of having been born in Israel and speaking Hebrew the bond and basis of their national life.

As a result of this alienation of Israeli youth from the Jews of the Diaspora a situation has been created which at first sight seems paradoxical. Israelis abroad feel closer to the gentiles than to their Jewish brethren living there. This undesirable phenomenon, which has been widely recognized, caused many educators to feel that there was something wrong with Israeli education. The link be-

tween the State of Israel and the Jewish communities of
the Diaspora is essential to our very existence, and must
be preserved and strengthened. When our educators talk
of "defects in the Jewish consciousness" on the part of
Israeli youth they refer mainly to this nonidentification of
Israeli youth with the Jews of the Diaspora and the at-
tendant danger of a severance of the vital link with it.
On the other hand, we have already pointed out that the
problem of Jewish consciousness has much wider implications, and touches upon the general spiritual make-up of
the Israeli as a whole.

It may be worth-while to mention here a rumor that
was current in the Israeli press at the time when the
question of "Jewish consciousness" arose—that a group
of Israeli students in the United States had become con-
verted to Christianity. Although this rumor was later denied, it is significant that it spread and had repercussions
far and wide. In addition, it is interesting to read descriptions in the press of the visits of Israeli youth delegations
to the 1958 Moscow Youth Festival. There they came into
close contact with Jews of the Soviet Union. An Israeli
journalist, describing the group's visit to a Moscow synagogue, reports that the young Israelis confessed that that
was their very first visit to a synagogue. Consequently,
they hardly knew what to do with the prayer books and
prayer shawls that were given to them.

There are, too, illustrations of this lack of awareness of
the religious aspects of Judaism on the part of our Israeli
school children. Dr. Weizman related that when he mentioned the Scrolls of the Law to children in a *HaShomer
Hatzair Kibbutz* they did not know what he was talking

about. Professor A. H. Fraenkel, after visiting a Bible lesson in a left-wing *kibbutz,* relates that the teacher's attention was drawn to a girl stealthily reading a book which she held on her knees. On investigation, it appeared that the book she was reading in secret was the "Complete Bible," which she said she found much more interesting than the one in use in class. (That *kibbutz* used an expurgated edition of its own.) Professor Simon mentions the case of a nine-year-old *kibbutz* boy, who, when asked who created the world, replied with absolute certainty, "The workers, of course." Similarly, when a sixteen-year-old *Sabra* was asked if he considered himself a Jew, or merely an Israeli, answered, "What shall I read to find out?"

Since the emphasis on Jewish consciousness in Israeli schools stems from direct government action, it may not be uncharitable of us if we assume that, among other motives, a political one was also present. It emerged from one of the debates in the *Knesseth* that the majority party in the *Knesseth* objected to an absolutely clean-cut division of Israeli education into secular and religious categories, which would give the religious schools a monopoly of the teaching of religious values. This, the majority but secular party, did not desire, as Mr. Azania of Mapai clearly stated in his reply to Mr. Raphael of the National Religious party: "What is it you would like? Do you want the secular school . . . to be free from anything that might constitute a living link with our Jewish heritage or a bridge to it? And then, do you hope that this lack of religious content in our schools will drive to your schools [the religious ones] all those who desire a bond between the past generations and the various sections of our people? . . . This will not happen, as you imagine it will. . . ."

This motive acquired great importance with the increase of mass immigration of predominantly religious elements from oriental countries. The transition of these children from the traditional Jewish atmosphere of the home to a purely secular one at school would be too sudden and would meet with opposition unless it could be bridged. "Jewish consciousness" was intended to provide that bridge without making it imperative for these children to go to religious schools. Moreover, there is a broader political motive: the State of Israel is interested in maintaining a link with the past because this link adds greatly to Israel's prestige and stature. It is in the interest of the state to appear not as a newly fledged political entity but as the heir to an old and great civilization, thus enhancing its status among the family of nations.

Furthermore, the education authorities deemed it necessary to counteract the tendency of Israeli youth to become estranged from Jewish tradition and the history of the Diaspora. The education authorities, no less than the individual educators, regard the "Young Hebrews," or "Canaanites" as they are sometimes called, as a warning example as to what might happen if the "normalization" of Israel youth was allowed to proceed unchecked. This group of young people wish to sever all links with the Jewish history of the last two thousand years, regard themselves as Hebrews as distinct from Jews, claiming, as it were, direct spiritual descent from the indigenous population of the land of Canaan. True enough, this movement represents only a small minority of Israel's youth, but many educators feel (the Hebrew poet Abraham Shlonsky has added his voice in support of this opinion) that Israeli youth as a whole is really Canaanite rather than Jewish in make-up and spirit.

This striving for "normality" has its roots in Zionism, whose chief aim was to bring about this very normalization of the Jewish people. The paradox of Zionist ideology is that, while it was born of a revolt against Jewish tradition and Orthodoxy, it was nevertheless deeply rooted in Jewish history, purporting merely to restore nationhood and normality to the Jewish people. Normality and nationhood have indeed been realized, but at a price: the younger generation has been estranged from the history and tradition of the Exile out of which Zionism was born.

Here is where the danger lies. In the Diaspora the difference between Jew and gentile is mainly religious. The *Sabra,* having no religion, has nothing in common with the Jews of the Diaspora; and the Jewish people, once united, are thus in danger of becoming divided.

It will now be our task to find the right historical setting for the introduction of "Jewish consciousness" into Israeli schools. How does "Jewish consciousness" link up with modern Jewish national thought which inspired the creation of the first all-Hebrew schools in Palestine, as well as in the Diaspora? What is the philosophical background to the introduction of this subject into the school syllabus?

It is our opinion that the modern Jewish nationalist movement has not produced an educational theoretician of note whose thought can be said to embody completely the resurgent Jewish spirit of the nineteenth century. Had such an educational writer existed our analysis would have been confined to educational literature only. We must reiterate what we have already said in our section on the revival of Hebrew (Chapter 6)—that the creation of the all-Hebrew type of school was the outcome of the combined effort of the Zionist movement as a whole rather than that of one outstanding personality.

In order to trace back the question of Jewish consciousness in its wider implications (the relation between modern Jewish nationalism and Jewish tradition) to the spiritual source of these schools, we have to enter the field of modern Hebrew literature, in which the spirit which has sustained these schools crystallized. We must therefore now make an attempt to analyze the spiritual undercurrents of modern Hebrew literature.

III

There is in modern Hebrew literature a certain strain which, because of its opposition to traditional Judaism, may be regarded as anti-Jewish. This trend started with Yehuda Leib Gordon, the greatest of the *Haskalah* writers (not to be confused with Aharon David Gordon), whose poetry on Biblical themes shows a clearly antitraditional tendency. He attacks the Hebrew prophets for weakening the political and military power of the Hebrew kings, trying to subdue them to a law which was not compatible with normal statehood and the wielding of wordly power. Altogether, he represents the prophets as men who tried to impose their own will upon the Hebrew kings for ulterior motives. According to Y. L. Gordon, prophetic teaching was detrimental to normal statehood, since it transformed the people into good-for-nothing idlers and caused them to despise work and neglect the security of the state. The following is a quotation from his poem "Zedekiah in the House of Confinement":

. . . I shall neither plough nor thresh,
For I am the son of a priestly house and a holy people.
No voice of the artisan shall be heard,
Only of those who sing the praises of the Lord,
And pronounce blessings and prayers of thanksgiving.
The land will be filled with bands of prophets,
Sly beggars and idle daydreamers given to hallucinations and
    vain fancies.

Can such a nation exist under the Heavens?
Who will plough a furrow, who will earn his bread,
And who will fight in time of trouble and tribulation?
Such a people will never set up a government.
They will be destroyed and go under. . . .

According to Y. L. Gordon, the teaching of the prophets is not of this world, and it leads the ordinary man away from worldly pursuits. In other words, it undermines normal life and eventually destroys the nation. Zionism strove for normality, and the obvious trend of Gordon's writing is to show that as long as Jews adhere to their religious tradition (in the above-mentioned poem, *prophetic* tradition) they will never become a normal people. The views he expresses reflect the climate of opinion prevailing then among many of the young Zionists of Eastern Europe.

Y. L. Gordon is not the only representative of this antireligious trend. The same attitude is descernible in Brenner (as mentioned in our essay on "Brenner in London," Chapter 6). Brenner fought against the Bible's taking a central place in Jewish schools and Jewish thought in general. He freed himself from the undue influence—what he terms "hypnosis"—of Holy Writ, and finds secular literature of recent times far deeper and more satisfying. "If the Hebrew Bible is of some importance because it contains the remnants of our recollections of ancient times and is the embodiment of the spirit and human character of our people through many generations and epochs, then the same importance attaches to the books of the New Testament, which is our book, bone of our bone, and flesh of our flesh. . . ." [1] He finds the same spirit of humility and self-surrender to the Will of God permeating both books. The world outlook and way of life of Jeremiah is the same as that of the Nazarene. Besides, Brenner felt that his Zionist consciousness had nothing whatsoever to do with his attitude to the Bible or his religious or antireligious feelings. He saw Zionism as completely divorced from religion. The Zionist may be even antitheist or atheist without his national consciousness being affected one way or another. We have already noted in our essay on Brenner that he viewed Hebrew culture as being characterized by a purely formal criterion, the Hebrew language. The content and general character of Jewish culture is irrelevant. Culture is "Hebrew" if its medium of expression is Hebrew.

The cycle of poems by Zalman Schneour, which the poet rather characteristically calls *Luchot Gnuzim* (*Hidden Tablets*), referring to the books mentioned in the Bible which were either lost or condemned to oblivion, such as the Book of the Just, The Wars of the Lord, etc., constitutes an attempt to reconstruct poetically fragments of the book The Wars of the Lord, which, in the poet's opinion,

[1] J. C. Brenner, *Ketavim*, III, *Am Oved*, (Tel Aviv: 1951) 34-36.

was made up of war songs composed during the conquest of Canaan by the Hebrews. Schneour is strongly attracted by the pagan civilization of the ancient Hebrew before they became Israelites. He glorifies their ancient heathen customs, fertility rites, and primitive orgies. He describes with enthusiasm the processions of priests marching arm in arm with harlots, worshipping the fertility goddess Astarte. His poetry reflects a violent reproach to Jewish tradition, which consigned these pagan elements to oblivion, and he objects to the criteria which guided our Hebrew sages in deciding which of the Holy Books were to be included in the Biblical Canon. He finds the content of the present Bible, with the sensual and pagan elements largely expurgated, far too meager and unsatisfying.

. . . How poor and austere, how scanty are the verses
We recited in our childhood.
They only arouse our burning thirst,
Only the Prophets and Holy writings have remained.
They are like the broken shards of a costly vase
That we have rescued from destruction;
We have cemented them together, but the original shape is
      destroyed,
And no sign remains of the precious oil [it once contained]. . . .

Schneour himself endeavors to supply some of that "precious oil" which was expurgated by our Sages; he means the ancient voluptuous Canaanite poetry.

      . . . On the right and left of the priest
      The temple harlots dance along,
      With naked breasts and thighs
      They approach the pilgrims. . . .

Elsewhere he bewails the disappearance of unbridled freedom and the substitution of restraint and conformity to the laws of the prophets.

. . . Then we knew not the meaning of restraint,
No gnawing desires, only abundance of joy and gladness.
In the absence of restraining laws, man cannot sin. . . .
The heart that is satisfied and fulfilled does not steal forbidden
    pleasures.

Then came the prophets of Judah,
And turned our laughter to mourning:
Fasting, torment of the soul, and prayer,
And groveling in ashes until morning;
It is a day of Atonement, the tenth day,
An atoning for sins we have not committed. . . .

The prophets had imposed on the nation an austere ethical code; substituted mourning for rejoicing; drained the sap and lifeblood of the nation.

Similarly the poet Saul Tschernichovsky regrets Judaism's rejection of the Hellenic spirit and voices his admiration for ancient Greek culture in many of his poems, notably "Before the Statue of Apollo," in which he glorifies the sensual culture of the ancient Hellenes.

Micah Joseph Berdichevski, the poet and philosopher, wrote many essays on the question of Jewish culture and tradition. Many of his articles are polemics against Achad Ha'am, who viewed Jewish culture as one continuous stream. Achad Ha'am's conception of Judaism may be called "biological," because he likens Judaism to a tree with roots in the past: if these roots are cut, the tree will wither. From this attitude to Jewish tradition, despite his secular outlook, stems his conviction that a Jew imbued with national feeling cannot but identify himself with that tradition. Berdichevski attacks Achad Ha'am's biological conception of Judaism. He maintains that Judaism contains many separate "strands" or trends that are opposed to one another. It embraces, on one hand, an ascetic trend, manifested in *Halachah* with its many laws and ordinances, which, in his view, constrain man's freedom and kill his soul. On the other hand, we have the Song of Songs and the wonderful nature poetry embodied in the Book of Psalms, presenting an entirely different outlook on life. Moreover, there isn't just one Jewish culture common to all generations, but many. The Lord God of Hosts is not identical with the God who dons the phylacteries. There is the pre-Sinaitic culture, that of the prophets, the Hellenistic Alexandrine culture with which the name of Philo is linked; there is the culture of the Talmud, of medieval Jewish philosophy, *Kabbalah*, and *Chassidism*. Why, asks Berdichevski, should not the Zionists too be permitted to make a new start and create a new trend within the Jewish civilization? "Let us also go our own way. Give us a little fresh air to breathe. . . . The tablets of stone upon which the Ten Commandments were engraved should be renewed, replaced by others. Let us sing the song of life in our own way. . . ." [2] Elsewhere he says: "Our blood boils within us at the attempt [of Achad Ha'am] to unify and combine the sum total of the Jewish past into one uniform spiritual edifice which is turned against us and our very basis of existence. . . ." [3] In his view, the Zionist movement should sever this bond which links the Jewish people to Diaspora life and culture.

[2] Berdichevski, *Baderech* (Tel Aviv: Stiebel, 1936), p. 48.
[3] *Ibid.*, p. 49.

Furthermore, Berdichevski thinks that secular and religious culture cannot exist side by side; in other words, he saw no possibility for even the existence of a religious trend within Zionism. Hence his violent polemics against the religious Zionist movement founded by Rabbi Reines, a movement whose legitimacy within the Zionist fold Berdichevski questioned precisely because it endeavored to preserve traditional Jewish values. There can be no doubt that Berdichevski was the most extreme and intolerant exponent of Zionist thought.

The contemporary Hebrew writer Hazaz may be regarded as the spiritual descendent of Y. L. Gordon, Brenner, and Berdichevski, if we assume that he identifies himself with the rebellious characters in his novels and stories. (Recent pronouncements by Hazaz have tended to negate this assumption, or may possibly indicate a change in his outlook.) He makes some of these characters state categorically that Zionism and Judaism can never exist side by side. Zionism is not a continuation of traditional Judaism: it arises out of the disintegration of traditional Judaism and supersedes it. The main theme of his story *"HaDrashah"* is the rejection of the Jewish past by the younger Palestinian generation. The hero, Yudka, finds the teaching of the history of the Diaspora useless and boring, and would much rather send the children out to play football. "What is in this history," he asks; "only an ever-recurring cycle of persecution, suffering, and martyrdom, persecution, suffering, and martyrdom!" Hazaz would reject all the Jewish past and make history begin again with the nation restored in Israel. Another of Hazaz's heroes is made to say that "Zionism spells the end of Judaism." In other words, in Israel, Zionism is not a continuation or natural result of Judaism but the basis and beginning of a new life, a new history built upon the ruins of one that has ceased to be. It is not enough merely to modify the character of the Judaism born of the exile; it has to be completely uprooted and rejected; redemption has to be brought about on the ruins of the exile. On one side stand the Torah, Judaism, and the Rabbi; on the other, redemption and the pioneers.

This kind of literature, with its complete rejection of the Jewish exilic past and its assertion that history must be made to begin again with the nation restored in Israel, reflects the feeling of a considerable part of Israeli youth and forms the basis of the ideology of the Canaanites, who profess to be Hebrews and not Jews.

IV

Although we have given a full description of this anti-religious trend in modern Hebrew literature, we do not wish to create the impression that this is the only one in evidence, or even the predominant one. Jewish thought reflected in modern Hebrew literature is extremely complex, entailing a multiplicity of views on Jewish history and tradition. In our attempt to expose and clarify various trends within the "modern Jewish-national thought" we may be guided by Professor Nathan Rottenstreich, who discerns four distinct schools of thought.

In his essay *"HaMachshava HaLeumit HaChadasha"* ("New National Thought")[4] Professor Rottenstreich men-

---

[4] This essay is printed in *Erkei Ha-Yahadut* (*The Values of Judaism*) (Tel Aviv: Hotza-at Machbarot Le-Sifrut, 1953).

tions Berdichevski as representative of merely *one* trend, which we have called the antireligious one. *The second stream* is represented by A. D. Gordon. Since we have already devoted a whole essay to Gordon's philosophy of education (Chapter 5), it will be sufficient to sum up briefly his views concerning the relation of Zionism to Judaism.

It is true enough that Gordon loved traditional Judaism, and his Zionist consciousness in no way detracted from that love. To the end of his days he regarded himself as a traditional *Chumash Rashi* Jew, one who studies a prescribed portion of Holy Writ every Sabbath. But this feeling was based on a romantic delusion. We have already noted the latent revolutionary character of his teaching and his tendency to reduce the 613 precepts of Judaism to one supreme command, namely, "Man shall live by his toil." It cannot be denied that the problem of religion remains essentially unsolved in his writings. He, as it were, postpones its solution, expecting it to be found with the Jewish people's return to the soil and their renewed contact with nature. Professor Rottenstreich rightly observes that a problem is not solved by merely expressing faith in its eventual solution. He puts it rather succinctly in his essay: "He [Gordon] turns from history to nature, in the hope that nature will solve a problem which, to some extent at least, is historical." In view of the problematic character of such a solution, we should not be surprised that Gordon was unable to make a solid contribution to the problem of the relationship between secular nationalism and Jewish tradition.

On the other hand, we have already noted in our chapter on A. D. Gordon that he was essentially a moderate.

He opposed the radical break with Jewish tradition propounded by men such as Brenner and Berdichevski, whose
"free national consciousness" he characterized as "assimilation in a Hebrew garment." "These men wish to preserve the wine while breaking the keg. They certainly do
not wish the Jewish people to perish. In fact, they regard
their ideology as the means to save the Jewish people from
spiritual destruction. In reality, however, their ideology
can only lead to disaster." [5]

The third trend within Zionist thought is represented
by Achad Ha'am. As we have already pointed out, he too
was one of the moderate thinkers among the Zionist leaders, his moderation stemming from his "biological" conception of Judaism. Nevertheless, this conception itself
and his Jewish philosophy in general were markedly secular. He repudiated the revelational character of Judaism
and regarded Holy Writ as merely the product of the
Jewish genius. He believed profoundly in the Jewish
people's powers of endurance and their Will to Live, and
it was to these qualities, and not to Divine Providence,
that he attributed their survival as a people. There is
some justification in Brenner's discernment of a streak
of hypocrisy or at least inconsistency in Achad Ha'am's
thought. Brenner failed to understand Achad Ha'am's
violent opposition to him, seeing that Achad Ha'am himself was essentially a secular thinker whose Judaism was
devoid of metaphysical roots. Moreover, Achad Ha'am
left unsolved the problem of how to bridge the gulf between the essentially religious Jewish culture of the past

[5] *Ha-arachat atzmenu* in *Gordon's Collected Works*, II, 221 f. (See also
S. H. Bergmann, *Faith and Reason* (A Little Hillel Book, 1951), pp.
119-20.

and modern Jewish culture, which is nationalistic and essentially secular. How does the metaphor of the tree in his biological conception of Judaism fit in with reality? Surely, secular Zionism means a break with the past rather than symbolizing continuous development and growth. Achad Ha'am would have replied that the continuity was symbolized by the ethical content of Judaism, which is pervasive and lasting and which has not been repudiated by modern Jewry. However, is religion merely ethics? Furthermore, are ethics specifically "Jewish"?

The fourth trend is represented by Rabbi Kook, late Chief Rabbi of Palestine, who was the greatest exponent of what may be termed "religious Zionism." The adherents of this movement, which has deep roots in the Jewish spiritual heritage, had supreme faith in the redemption of the Jewish people and in the restoration of Zion and Jerusalem. They form a long unbroken chain of settlers. Their love of the Holy Land is rooted in the literature of the Talmud, continued by the great Jewish Commentators such as Nachmanides (died 1270), who fulfilled the religious precept enjoining the Jews to settle and live in Israel; Joseph Caro, the compiler of the *Shulchan Aruch;* religious Spanish Jews who settled in Palestine after the expulsion; and the various groups of *Chassidim,* disciples of the Ba'al Shem Tov, who came to settle in Palestine during the eighteenth century. The stream of religious Jews who came to settle in the country (mainly in the four towns of Jerusalem, Tiberias, Safad, and Hebron), though their number was not large, continued this chain unbroken right down to the *Chovevei Zion* movement and Moses Hess. Rabbi Isaac Jacob Reines (1894-1915) actually founded the *Mizrachi* movement, whose motto is: "The

Land of Israel for the People of Israel, according to the Law of Israel"; and, in spite of Berdichevski's protests, this movement became integrated into the Zionist Organization.

All these movements were inspired by purely religious motives. To them, Zionism and settling in the land of Israel meant fulfillment of Judaism.

Rabbi Kook fully realized that the Zionist movement and the *Yishuv* of his time were completely secularized. For him, however, there was no conflict between Zionism and Judaism, for he viewed Zionism as a movement which heralded the first beginning of Israel's redemption. Though he felt the sharp contrast between traditional Judaism, on the one hand, and secular Zionism, on the other, this contrast is obliterated and the most divergent views become harmonized in his all-embracing system of thought.

Following the traditions of *Chassidism,* and in particular the renowned Rabbi Levy Yitzhak of Berdichev,[6] who was famous for his love and defense of the Jewish people, Rabbi Kook, too, endeavored to justify the way of life of even the most free-thinking Zionists. He likened them to the workers building the holy Temple, who, according to tradition, were free from many of the restrictive commandments of Jewish Law. He thought of them as righteous and godly. He believed that their lack of religious

---

[6] It is told of Rabbi Levy Yitzhak of Berdichev that he once approached a Jew whom he saw smoking a cigarette on the Sabbath, and asked him if he was aware that it was the Sabbath. "Yes," answered the Jew, "of course I know it is the Sabbath today." "Then perhaps you don't know that one shouldn't smoke on the Sabbath?" asked the Rabbi. "Certainly I know that one is forbidden to smoke on Sabbath," replied the man. "What an admirable character that man has!" said Rabbi Levy Yitzhak; "he only speaks the truth, and hides nothing."

observance did not spring from any opposition to spirituality and godliness. Their estrangement from Judaism was, in his opinion, accompanied by noble ideals, and, viewed psychologically, a result of the fact that their parents, who were religious, took no part either in the Zionist or in the Socialist revolutionary movement. Religion therefore came to be associated in their minds with an unprogressive way of life. As Dr. Isidore Epstein puts it, "The Messianic fervor with which the national movement was charged and the universal ideals of justice and righteousness which animated it, could only be accounted for by the spirit of the heritage of the nation which informed the Jewish masses. This made the national movement one of redemption, notwithstanding the fact that the religious conduct of the individuals was not much in evidence." [7]

Rabbi Kook's philosophy furnished the superstructure to this attitude. In his philosophy—which has been described by Professor S. H. Bergmann as "panentheism" (*pan en theo* — everything is in God)[8]—there is no fundamental distinction between the holy and the profane. There are only degrees of holiness since all reality is in God. Besides, the land of Palestine is distinguished from other countries by its unique and holy character. "In the Diaspora, Jews may have become alienated from the flow of holiness. But Kook was deeply convinced that the return to the Holy Land would renew and reactivate Israel's holiness. Palestine was designated by God for the flow of His divine grace. Like Yehuda Halevi before him, Kook

[7] Isidore Epstein, *Judaism* (Pelican Book, 1959), p. 311.

[8] S. H. Bergmann, *Faith and Reason*, (Washington: A Little Hillel Book, 1961), p. 124.

felt and taught that a Jew could reach the highest level of piety only in Israel where he could absorb the wisdom of the past, the knowledge and certainty that the divine harmony and unity of the world would ultimately be restored and that the separation of the world from its divine source would be overcome." [9]

In Rabbi Kook's opinion, the measure of Israel's attachment to the Holy Land is the measure of their holiness; the deeper rooted we are in the Holy Land the greater our degree of holiness. Holiness is enhanced, as it were, by strengthening the material, earthly ties of the Jewish people, which is precisely what the pioneers were endeavoring to do.

It follows from this teaching that those who are engaged in securing the material basis of the Jewish people in its homeland are virtually engaged in a sacred task. This constitutes a most daring attempt to eliminate the fundamental conflict between the spirit of Jewish tradition, on one hand, and secular nationalism, on the other.

However, it must be borne in mind that, in view of the existing dichotomy in Israeli education, the philosophy of Rabbi Kook did not penetrate the secular schools, which, at that time, more than ever, regarded themselves outside the orbit of all influence emanating from religious circles.

V

We have made a rather lengthy analysis of the spiritual undercurrents in modern Hebrew literature and have tried to show its various trends, associating them with

[9] *Op. cit.*, p. 137.

the names of outstanding individuals and bearing in mind the generally accepted view of Hegel that the great men of an age give expression to the people's latent will and thus make possible the fulfillment of that will.

We have mentioned a number of great men whose writings expressed the views of an important section of the Jewish people, notably of those who identified themselves with the resurgent Jewish spirit which inspired the first Hebrew schools.

If we disregard Rabbi Kook's philosophy for a moment, seeing that its influence never penetrated the general schools, we discern that *the common denominator of the various trends was a totally secular conception of Judaism. This is true despite the important differences that distinguish the trend represented by Y. L. Gordon, Brenner, and Berdichevski, on one hand, and by Achad Ha'am, Bialik, and A. D. Gordon on the other.* The Hebrew schools founded in Palestine, as well as the *Tarbut* schools of Eastern Europe, are the fruit of the impact of modern nationalism on Jewish history; their philosophical background was that of the men who laid the foundations of modern Hebrew literature, that most eloquent mouthpiece of modern Jewish nationalism.

The new secular spirit made itself strongly felt in the first Hebrew schools founded in Palestine. It may be mentioned here how shocked Achad Ha'am was when he visited Bible lessons in the *Herzlia Gymnasium* in Jaffa, the first school of its kind in Palestine. He condemned the use in class of all the paraphernalia of higher criticism, such as the checking of sources, the correction of "mistakes," and interpolations in the Biblical text, all of which were laboriously noted down by the pupils in special note-books.

Achad Ha'am strongly disapproved of this method of Bible instruction. "This is what the children do," he writes; "they keep a special notebook for each Book of the Bible. On one side they keep a record of all the cor-rections to be made in the accepted version [of the Bible] and on the other they write the whole Book again in the new version. And should the pupil lose this notebook, then he has lost the whole Book of the Prophets, and can-not find another among the many thousands of Bibles there are in the world. . . ." As against this "modern" approach to the Bible, Achad Ha'am states categorically: "The basis of our national education can only be the Bible as it stands, as it was created more than two thousand years ago in the depths of our national life, and whose basis it constituted throughout the generations." [10]

Viewed historically, the introduction of "Jewish con-sciousness" as a subject of study in Israel's general schools *reflects the victory of the moderate trend of Jewish na-tional thought represented by Achad Ha'am, Bialik, and A. D. Gordon.* During the *Knesseth* debate on *Toda-ah Yehudit,* Education Minister Aranne said that "it would constitute a gross injustice if there were any compulsion, either religious or antireligious, however idealistic the motives from which that compulsion may spring. . . . We respect religion, because religious faith in its pure form elevates man. We adopt the Jewish tradition which embodies both national and religious elements, because it epitomizes the glory of former times and ancient glory never wanes. . . . Therefore love and respect for tradi-

[10] *Kol Kitvei Achad Ha'am,* (Tel Aviv: Dvir, 1950), p. 418.

tion must permeate our national schools; not in order to educate for religion but in order to uphold the national character of our educational system."

This weighty pronouncement constitutes a clear repudiation of the ideas propounded by Brenner, Y. L. Gordon, and Berdichevski, and an affirmation of the ideas of A. D. Gordon, Bialik, and Achad Ha'am.

In conclusion we wish to add a few remarks in order to amplify our explanation of the meaning of "Jewish consciousness" as a subject of school instruction.

We have pointed out that "Jewish consciousness" includes three elements, of which only one is concerned with Jewish tradition. The previously quoted paragraph from Mr. Aranne's speech in the *Knesseth* makes it abundantly clear that "Jewish consciousness" does not imply education toward religion and the observance of religious commandments. What he meant was that *information* about Jewish tradition is to be imparted, i.e., pupils are merely to be instructed about the various facets of Jewish life and custom. Similarly, the reading of the prayer book at school is intended to make children acquainted with Jewish prayers, but does not imply that teachers have to encourage children to pray or attend synagogue services (although many headmasters and parents would in actual fact raise no objection if individual teachers attempted to do this). The main aim is to impart knowledge about the Hebrew prayer book, its structure and history. The official program introducing the study of "Jewish consciousness" into Jewish schools was meant primarily to eradicate ignorance of things Jewish—and does not go beyond this.

On the other hand, it must be borne in mind that throughout Jewish history Jewish education always made the teaching of religious knowledge subservient to religious observance. We say in our daily prayers, "O put it into our hearts to understand and to discern, to mark, learn, and teach, to heed, to do, and to fulfill in love all the words of instruction in Thy Law." This prayer expresses succinctly the spirit of Jewish education, which regarded learning and teaching as a means to "fulfilling in love" the Divine Commandments. Consequently, Jewish education always demanded the complete identification of the teacher with his subject. Even Liberal Judaism identifies itself with Jewish law, although it accepts only a part and not the whole of Judaic law; and Liberal Jewish schools, while using a reformed prayer book, definitely teach prayers as a means to educating children for corporate religious service. Similarly Franz Rosenzweig, who is outside both the Orthodox and Liberal Jewish tradition, interprets *Religionsunterricht* as implying identification with Jewish law and Jewish religious observance. According to Rosenzweig, Jewish law, though it cannot be equated with Judaism, is an essential feature of it. Judaism is not identical with law, but it creates law.

It is quite clear that the teaching of "Jewish consciousness," precisely because it does not imply religious observance, cannot be called religious instruction in the historic meaning of this term. Indeed, it must be admitted that, owing to the spirit of religious neutrality in which "Jewish consciousness" is imparted, it is alien to the spirit of Jewish education in its historic connotation. Nevertheless its introduction into general schools must be welcomed, for it is better that Israeli children be given some knowledge of matters Jewish—even divorced from religious observance—than be kept in complete ignorance of them. "Great is learning, for it leads to doing," is the saying of a Rabbinic sage. In other words, knowledge of Judaism may eventually lead to its practice.

An entirely new type of religious education—reaching beyond the mere introduction of "Jewish consciousness" —has been advocated by educators such as Professor S. H. Bergmann, Professor Ernst Simon, and Mr. Joseph Bentwich, whose views on Jewish education converge with those of M. Buber. These educators are within the Zionist tradition, yet they repudiate the secular conception of Judaism inherent in it. Nor do they identify themselves with Orthodoxy. They represent an interesting historical phenomenon, a new educational trend within Israeli philosophy, a trend which asserts the revelational character of the Jewish religion and upholds the holiness of the Jewish people without accepting fundamentalism. This school of thought exercises a certain religious influence within the general trend of Israeli education. It is natural that these men should feel very close to the philosophy of Franz Rosenzweig, despite the individual differences in outlook among themselves.

It must, however, be admitted that for the time being their influence is not very marked. They are respected as an élite rather than followed as leaders. They are often invited by the education authorities to address teachers' meetings on various occasions. The readers' or listeners' response to their teaching is, poetically expressed, somewhat like that of Faust: *"Die Botschaft höre ich wohl, allein mir fehlt der Glaube."* ("I hear the call, but I lack faith.") These men are opposed to the present dual character of Jewish education, and the clear-cut division of schools into "religious" and "secular" ones. In their view,

Jewish education which is secular in character is almost a contradiction in terms. Only the future can tell whether their influence will grow and strengthen the specifically Jewish character of Israeli general schools.

13

Postscript

In his Hebrew essay on Franz Rosenzweig (published in 1956 by the Magnes Press, The Hebrew University, Jerusalem), Professor A. E. Simon draws attention to the peculiar fact that Jewish tradition does not give prominence to those teachers who have left their mark on Jewish education. Jewish tradition views education objectively, detached from the names of those persons who contributed most to its development. Nevertheless, a number of educators have gained prominence, and, of the post-emancipation period, Simon mentions Mendelssohn, Rabbis Hirsch, Salanter, and Kook, A. D. Gordon, and Franz Rosenzweig. This list is rather short and could undoubtedly be expanded.

I have confined myself in this book to educators who have contributed to the enrichment of Jewish educational thought but who were not necessarily instrumental in the establishment of new educational institutions. For example, I have included essays on A. D. Gordon, Korczak, Salanter, Buber, and Franz Rosenzweig, who cannot be called founders of new types of schools. I have preferred to include an essay on Weisel rather than one on Mendels-

sohn, because it was Weisel who wrote the first system-
matic book on Jewish pedagogy, a book which exercised
a decisive influence on the subsequent course of Jewish
education. On the other hand, Mendelssohn, apart from
preparing a *Reader* for Jewish schools, did not actually
establish himself as an educational writer, although he
was undoubtedly the inspirer—here I agree with Simon
—of the modern post-Emancipation type of Jewish school,
whose assimilationist tendencies, however, went far beyond
his original intentions.

I have also included an essay on Buber, although I am
quite aware of the fact that Buber's contribution to educational thought is not specifically Jewish. However, his
ideas should be applicable to Jewish education, if only
because they stem from Jewish sources.

No apology is required for the inclusion of essays on
Korczak and Sarah Schenirer. The latter was mainly responsible for the establishment of a network of schools
bearing the imprint of her ideas and personality. These
schools have not lost their vitality to the present day. As
for Korczak, I have included him, firstly, because of the
characteristically Jewish socio-pedagogical tendency of his
work and, secondly, because he sacrificed his life in the
holocaust for the sake of the children in his care. Thus his
educational activities are forever linked with that tragic
period in Jewish history.

However, some justification may be necessary for my
including a piece on Brenner. His place is undoubtedly
in Hebrew literature rather than in education, though
he was a practicing schoolmaster for some time. I have
included him on account of his devout espousal of the
cause of modern Hebrew; yet I do not deny that I was, to

some extent at least, moved by a personal consideration, as his way of life and activities in London hold a peculiar fascination for me.

As regards the *kibbutz* and *Tarbut* schools, it has to be borne in mind that these have grown out of the collective effort of many people who belonged to the Zionist and pioneering movements; hence it is difficult to link the educational tradition established by these schools with the name of particular individuals.

Since the posthumous appearance of two volumes of S. Golan's work on collective education there is little doubt that he will be regarded as the outstanding theoretician of *kibbutz* education, though representing the extreme left-wing element only. It cannot, however, be claimed that Golan contributed more than other teachers to the practical development of *kibbutz* education and the establishment of *kibbutz* schools.

I hope the reader, glancing at the essays included in this volume, will not judge me harshly for any possible sin of omission. This is, after all, a collection of essays on Jewish education and does not claim to be an exhaustive survey. On the other hand, I do not think that I have omitted any Jewish pedagogue who has made an outstanding contribution to the Jewish educational thought of the last two centuries.

Judged from a purely historical point of view, the Yiddishists would undoubtedly deserve more detailed treatment than they have received in this volume, particularly in view of their many achievements in the field of practical education. Yet no one will deny that that movement has lost much of its former vitality and is now on the wane. In the language controversy Hebrew emerged victorious (as was to be expected) and Yiddish today is merely fighting a last desperate rear-guard action.

The essays included in this volume will no doubt convey to the reader some impression of the rich and variegated character of Jewish education. Indeed, if the reader is unfamiliar with Jewish history he may even feel somewhat confused by the multiplicity of educational currents described here. However this may be, it will be helpful to refer to some principle of classification and reduce the various currents to a number of basic categories.

In attempting to evolve some kind of typology applicable to the personalities described in this volume, it may be convenient to divide them into *traditionalists* and *rebels*. However, this division is not quite satisfactory, because of the many cases where the distinction between rebel and traditionalist is very blurred indeed. Weisel, who considered himself a staunch supporter of tradition, gave rise to a movement in Jewish education that revolted against traditional Judaism. A. D. Gordon, in spite of the latent revolutionary character of his ideas, never consciously detached himself from religion and Jewish tradition. Brenner, who was most definitely a rebel, was moved to tears when he heard the *Yom Kippur* prayers resounding from a synagogue in the East End of London. Even an unimpeachable traditionalist such as Rabbi Kook was bitterly attacked by certain circles of Orthodox Jewry who thought his ideas on education too liberal and even revolutionary. Again, Franz Rosenzweig can be called neither a rebel nor a traditionalist. His background was assimilationist but his way in Jewish education was one of return to Judaism, although he stopped short of embracing traditional Judaism, taking objection to some of its doctrinal presuppositions. The same applies, at least to some extent, to Korczak.

Another principle of classification that may be applied here would be one based on Sir Isaiah Berlin's characterization of the Russian and Western European intellectual. "In Russia," says Sir Isaiah, "there was among the educated classes a moral and intellectual vacuum due to the absence of a Renaissance tradition of secular education and maintained by the rigid censorship exercised by the government, by widespread illiteracy, by the suspicion and disfavor with which all ideas as such were regarded, by the acts of a nervous and often massively stupid bureaucracy. In this situation, ideas which in the West competed with a large number of other doctrines and attitudes so that to become dominant they had to emerge victorious from a fierce struggle of survival, in Russia came to lodge in the minds of gifted individuals and, indeed obsessed them, often enough simply for lack of other ideas to satisfy their intellectual needs." [1] The outstanding characteristic of this type of intelligentsia is, according to Sir Isaiah, its integrity and total commitment to the ideal they advocate. "What this ideal is, is comparatively unimportant. The essential thing is to offer oneself without calculation, to give all one has for the sake of the light within (whatever it may illuminate) from pure motives. For only motives count." [2]

I have already mentioned that this characterization fits Brenner admirably. The same "romantic" attitude characterizes A. D. Gordon, J. Korczak, and, in a way, also Sarah Schenirer. All these educators were dedicated per-

---

[1] Isaiah Berlin, "A Marvellous Decade," *Encounter*, June, 1955.
[2] *Ibid.*

sons, committed to one ideal and characterized by outstanding integrity. The Western European Jewish educators—men such as Weisel, Hirsch, Rosenzweig, and Buber—are, on the whole, characterized by a broader range of ideas; they were not committed to any single idea but endeavored to reconcile the various and sometimes conflicting trends that were a part of their intellectual world. Such a typology (apart from raising controversial points) leaves out of account those educational thinkers who were more or less exclusively rooted in Judaism and remained uninfluenced by European thought (Rabbis Salanter and Kook). These may be regarded as forming a separate category.

Finally, we may view the Jewish educators of the post-Emancipation period in the light of the main forces impinging upon Jewish history of that epoch. In that case they appear as the exponents of these forces in the field of Jewish education.

These forces were emancipation and assimilation, on the one hand, modern Jewish nationalism and the pioneering spirit, on the other. Weisel may be regarded as the modern exponent of the post-Emancipation trend in Jewish education leading to assimilation—his personal convictions on Jewish tradition do not matter—while A. D. Gordon, the Hebraists, Buber and Rabbi Kook, can be linked with the resurgent national and pioneering movement. But this classification would leave out of account educators such as Hirsch, Salanter, Rosenzweig, and Sarah Schenirer, who belong to neither of these categories.

It may be said that these last-mentioned educators emerged in order to answer certain specific needs of the Jewish people; in any case it would be true to say that this is the way they themselves interpreted their missions. They saw themselves and their activities as an antidote to the tendency of religious disintegration which came in the wake of "enlightenment," emancipation, and assimilation. It must be emphasized that this group of educators *fulfilled this historic function without linking themselves to the tradition of the Zionist movement,* which in turn was created to no small a measure as an antidote to anti-Semitism then rampant in Eastern Europe. Jewish nationalism was not the cause of anti-Semitism, as Julien Benda and Herbert Read seem to assume,[3] but most decidedly its effect. It is a known fact that Herzl became a Zionist after hearing the cry *"À bas les Juifs"* in the streets of Paris at the time of the Dreyfus affair. The point I am trying to make is that the group of Jewish educators I refer to was not impelled to act in the way they did by any "extraneous" influence such as anti-Semitism but by an inner urge and sense of mission born of a "holy spark" within their souls. Of their activities it may be said that they conformed to the organic law that an ailing body spontaneously produces its own remedy. The historic function of their activities was in many ways similar to the role played by the educators who acted within the Zionist tradition. Both worked for the preservation of the Jewish people. Those who believe in the prophecy of Isaiah, "For as the new heavens and the new earth which I will make, shall remain before me, saith the Lord, so shall your seed and your name remain," cannot help seeing in the emergence of these educators the wondrous working of Divine Providence.

[3] See Julien Benda, *The Betrayal of the Intellectuals* (Beacon Press, 1955), p. XX.

Viewed in this light, Rabbi S. R. Hirsch deserves more appreciation than he is accorded by some modern historians, notably the writers of Hebrew textbooks for use in Israeli schools. (One of them actually rates Hirsch as a "negative factor" in Jewish history merely because of the fact that he stresses the universal mission of Judaism and does not identify himself with the secular nationalist movement.)

I have mentioned that traditionalists and rebels have both contributed to the preservation of the Jewish people —the first by strengthening the religious ties of the Jews and laying open the treasures of the Jewish heritage; the second by upholding the national consciousness of the Jewish people and laying the foundations for its re-establishment as a nation in its historic homeland. From a pragmatic point of view it may not be entirely wrong to view their activities as complementary. I am inclined to accept Rabbi Kook's view that, consciously or unconsciously, both were instrumental in the fulfillment of the Divine purpose.

Index

313